WORKSHOP MANUAL
FOR
TRIUMPH TWINS

COVERING

T140 E/S ELECTRO BONNEVILLE
T140 E   BONNEVILLE
T140 E/2 BONNEVILLE
TR7   TIGER
TR7T   TIGER TRAIL
TR65   THUNDERBIRD 650

PUBLICATION PART No. 99-7059

2nd Publication March 1984
Printed by ABBOT LITHO PRESS LTD.

INTRODUCTION

Welcome to the world of digital publishing ~ the book you now hold in your hand was printed using the latest state of the art digital technology. The advent of print-on-demand has forever changed the publishing process, never has information been so accessible and it is our hope that this book serves your informational needs for years to come. If this is your first exposure to digital publishing, we hope that you are pleased with the results. Many more titles of interest to the classic automobile and motorcycle enthusiast, collector and restorer are available via our website at www.VelocePress.com. We hope that you find this title as interesting as we do.

NOTE FROM THE PUBLISHER

The information presented is true and complete to the best of our knowledge. All recommendations are made without any guarantees on the part of the author or the publisher, who also disclaim all liability incurred with the use of this information.

TRADEMARKS

We recognize that some words, model names and designations, for example, mentioned herein are the property of the trademark holder. We use them for identification purposes only. This is not an official publication.

INFORMATION ON THE USE OF THIS PUBLICATION

This manual is an invaluable resource for those interested in performing their own maintenance. However, in today's information age we are constantly subject to changes in common practice, new technology, availability of improved materials and increased awareness of chemical toxicity. As such, it is advised that the user consult with an experienced professional prior to undertaking any procedure described herein. While every care has been taken to ensure correctness of information, it is obviously not possible to guarantee complete freedom from errors or omissions or to accept liability arising from such errors or omissions. Therefore, any individual that uses the information contained within, or elects to perform or participate in do-it-yourself repairs or modifications acknowledges that there is a risk factor involved and that the publisher or its associates cannot be held responsible for personal injury or property damage resulting from the use of the information or the outcome of such procedures.

WARNING!

One final word of advice, this publication is intended to be used as a reference guide, and when in doubt the reader should consult with a qualified technician.

INTRODUCTION

This manual is intended for use by both workshop personnel and enthusiastic owners. It provides full descriptions and comprehensive step by step dismantling and reassembly procedures. Use of this manual should enable the operator to carry out maintenance and overhaul work on the Triumph Twin Cylinder Models.

The manual is divided into sections dealing with major assemblies throughout the machine, each section sub-divided into sequence order corresponding to normal operations of strip down, examination and rebuilding procedure.

Note: All references to the L.H. or R.H. side of the machine relate to a rider sitting astride the machine and facing forwards.

ENGINE AND FRAME NUMBERS

The engine number is located on the left side of the engine, immediately below the cylinder barrel flange. The number is stamped onto a raised pad on the crankcase.

The frame number is stamped into the L.H. frame down tube near the steering head tube.

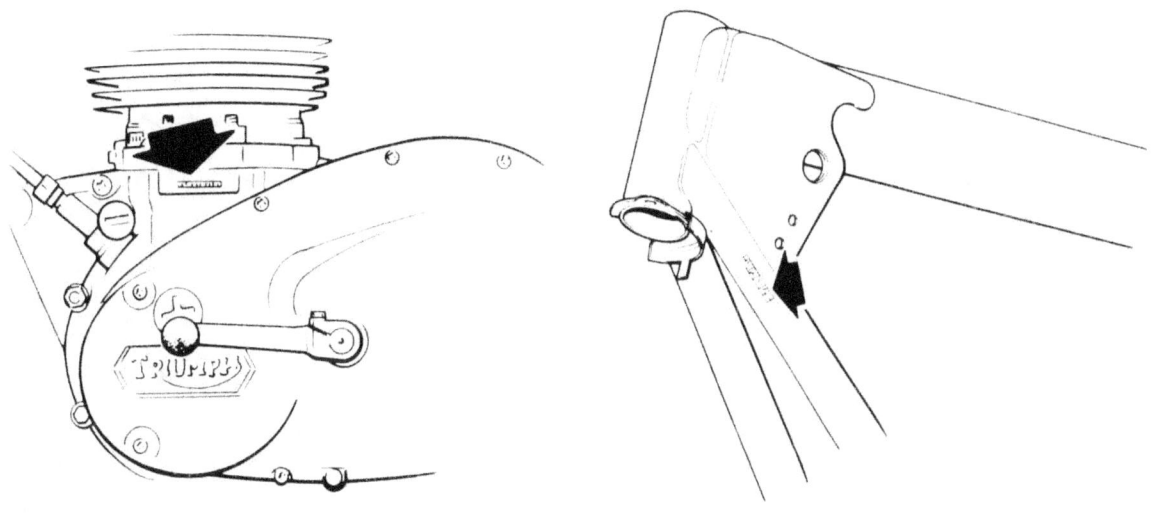

Illustration (A)
Engine No.

Illustration (B)
Frame No.

IMPORTANT NOTE

Any modifications to any Triumph Motorcycle made by you in the future shall be held by our Company to have been modified at your own risk and responsibility and without either the explicit or implied consent of Triumph Motorcycles Ltd or Triumph Motorcycles America inc. we will assume no liability, obligation or responsibility for any defective or modified parts or for the modified motorcycle itself, or for any claims, demands or legal action for property damage or personal injuries which may result from the modification of any Triumph motorcycle.

CONTENTS

	Section
TECHNICAL DATA...	TD
LUBRICATION SYSTEM..	A
ENGINE..	B
TRANSMISSION...	C
FIVE SPEED GEARBOX..	D
FRAME AND ATTACHMENT DETAILS.....................................	E
BRAKES, WHEELS AND TYRES..	F
TELESCOPIC FORKS..	G
ELECTRICAL SYSTEM..	H
WORKSHOP SERVICE TOOLS..	J
CONVERSION TABLES...	CT

SECTION TD
TECHNICAL DATA

TECHNICAL DATA

ENGINE
Read for T140 unless otherwise stated

		TR65	TR7T	T140	TR7
Bore	mm	76	76	76	76
	in	2.992"	2.992"	2.992"	2.992"
Stroke	mm	71	82	82	82
	in	2.795"	3.228"	3.228"	3.228"
Capacity	cc	649	747	747	747
	in	39.6	45.	45.	45.
Compression Ratio		8·6:1	7·4:1	7·9:1	7·9:1

VALVE TIMING - CHECKED WITH NIL TAPPET CLEARANCE AT T.D.C.

		TR65	TR7T	T140	TR7
Inlet	in	0.151"	0.109"	0.190"	0.190"
	mm	3.83	2.77	4.83	4.83
Exhaust	in	0.088"	0.130"	0.130"	0.130"
	mm	2.23	3.27	3.27	3.27

TAPPET CLEARANCE-COLD

	TR65	TR7T	T140	TR7
Inlet	0.008"(0.208mm)	0.006"(0.015)	0.008"(0.203mm)	0.008(0.208mm)
Exhaust	0.006"(0.150mm)	0.006"(0.015)	0.006"(0.150mm)	0.006(0.150mm)

CRANKSHAFT

Big End Journal Diameter	1.6235"/1.6240"	(41.237/41.25mm)
Main Bearing Journal Diameter		
Drive Side	1.1247"/1.1250"	(28.576/28/575mm)
Timing Side	1.1812"/1.1808"	(30.00/29.99mm)
Crankshaft End Float	0.003"/0.017"	(0.0762/0.432mm
Crankshaft Oil Feed Dia	0.622"/0.623"	(15.798/15.810mm)
Balance Factor	74%	
Maximum Advised Regrind	−·020"	(0.5080)

MAIN BEARINGS

	PRE EDA 30,000	POST EDA 30,000
Drive Side	SINGLE LIPPED ROLLER 2 ¹³⁄₁₆ " x 1 ⅛ " x ¹³⁄₁₆ "	SINGLE LIPPED ROLLER 2 ¹³⁄₁₆ " x 1 ⅛ " x ¹³⁄₁₆ "
Timing Side	SINGLE ROW BALL 72mm x 30mm x 19mm	TWIN LIPPED ROLLER 72mm x 30mm x 19mm

CONNECTING RODS

Length Between Centres	6.001"/5.999" (152.4254/152.3746mm
Small End Diameter	0.7510"/0.7507" (19.085/19.077mm.)
Big End Diameter	1.7700"/1.7695" (273.568/273.553mm)
Big End Bearing Type	STEEL BACKED WHITE METAL SHELLS
Bearing Diametrical Clearance	0.0005"/0.0002" (0.0127/0.508mm)
Bearing Side Clearance	0.012"/0.016" (0.305/0.406mm)

CYLINDER BLOCK

Material		CAST IRON	
		Low (L) Grade	High (H) Grade
Bore Size	ins	2.9918"/2.9913"	2.9924"/2.9919
	mm	75.992/75.979	76.007/75.994

TD3

TECHNICAL DATA

CYLINDER HEAD.

Material	Aluminium Alloy
Valve Guide Bore	0.4985"/0.4980" (12.66/12.64mm)
Valve Seat Interference	0.004" (0.1016mm)
Exhaust Port Thread	1 5/8 " x 16 T.P.I. U.N.
Valve Seat Angle	45°

VALVES

Stem Diameter	Inlet	0.3100"/0.3095" (7.874/7.861mm)
	Exhaust	0.3095"/0.3090" (7.861/7.849mm)
Head Diameter	Inlet	1.596"/1.592" (40.538/40.437mm)
	Exhaust	1.440"/1.434" (36.576/36.388mm)

VALVE GUIDES

Bore Diameter	0.3130"/0.3120"
Outside Diameter	0.5010"/0.5005" (12.725/12.713)
Length Inlet	1 31/32 " (50mm)
Length Exhaust	2 11/64 " (55.2mm)

VALVE SPRING

	OUTER	INNER
Free Length	1 5/8 " (41.3mm)	1 17/32 " (38.9mm)
Total No. Of Coils	5½	7½

PUSH ROD

	650	750
Overall Length	5.674"/5.646" (144.11/143.40mm)	5.905"/5.877" (149.98/149.27mm)

ROCKERS

Bore Diameter	0.5012"/0.5002 (12.731/12.705mm)
Spindle Diameter	0.4995"/0.4990 (12.687/12.675mm)

CAMSHAFTS

Journal Diameter	Left	0.8105"/0.8100 (20.577/20.564mm)
	Right	0.8735"/0.8730 (22.187/22.174mm)
Diameter Clearance	Left	0.0025"/0.001" (0.0635/0.0254mm)
	Right	0.0020"/0.0005" (0.508/0.127mm)
End Float		0.020"/0.013" (0.508/0.331mm)

TAPPETS

Material	STELLITE TIPPED STEEL
Tip Radius	0.750" (19.1mm)
Body Diameter	0.3115"/0.3110" (7.913/7.90mm)
Clearance In Guide Block	0.0015"/0.0005" (0.267/0.127mm)

TAPPET GUIDE BLOCK

Diameter of Bores	0.3125"/0.3120" (7.938/7.925mm)
Outside Diameter	1.000"/0.0005" (25.4/25.387mm)
Interference Fit In Cylinder Block	0.0015"/0,0005" (0.267/0.127mm)

TECHNICAL DATA

CAMSHAFT BEARING

Bore Diameter Left	0.8135"/0.8125"	(20.663/20.648mm)
Right	0.875"/0.874"	(22.225/22.199mm)
Outside Diameter Left	1.9015"/1.0010"	(25.638/25.425mm)
Right	1.127"/1.126"	(28.628/28.601mm)
Length -Left Inlet	1.114"/1.104"	(28.296/28.042mm)
Left Exhaust	0.942"/0.932"	(23.927/23.637mm)
Right Inlet & Exhaust	1.020"/1.010"	(25.508/25.025mm)
Interference In C/Case	0.002"/0.001"	(0.051/0.025mm)

STARTER GEARS/SHAFTS

Clutch Hub		
Outside Diameter	1.2503"/1.2498"	(31.657/31.644mm)
Bore Diameter	0.7505/0.7498	(19.187/19.054mm)
Clutch Hub Bush		
Outside Diameter	0.7520"/0.7515"	(19.110/19.098mm)
Bore Diameter	0.5008"/0.5003"	(12.720/12.7076mm)
Length	0.680"	(17.272mm)
Spindle Shaft-Gear No. 4 & 6		
Diameter	0.5023"/0.6016"	(12.758/12.740mm)
Gear No. 4 & 6		
Bore Diameter	0.5040"/0.5034"	(12.801/12.786mm)

OIL PUMP

Bore Dia: Feed	0.40675"/0.40625	(10.330/10.317mm)
Scavenge	0.4877"/0.4872"	(12.388/12.375mm)
Plunger Dia: Feed	0.4615"/0.40585"	(10.315/10.307mm)
Scavenge	0.4872"/0.4869"	(12.375/12.377mm)
Valve Spring Length	0.500"/0.520"	(1.270/1.778mm)
Valve Ball Diameter	$7/32$ "	(5.556mm)
Cross Head Drive Width	0.498"/0.497"	(12.649/12.624mm)
Clearance In Plunger Head	0.0045/0-0015"	(0.124/0.038mm)

TD TECHNICAL DATA

TIMING GEARS	ELECTRIC START	KICKSTART
Camshaft Pinions		
No. Of Teeth	50	50
Interference Fit On Camshaft	0.001"/0.000 0.254/0.000mm.	0.001"/0.000 0.254/0.000mm
Intermediate Pinion		
No. Of Teeth	47	47
Bore Dia At Spindle	0.5625"/0.5618" 14.280/14.269mm	0.5625"/0.5618" 14.280/14.269mm
Bore Dia At Clutch	1.9065"/1.9055" 48.425/48.399mm	—
Intermediate Pinion Bush		
Outside Dia	—	0.5640"/0.5635" 14.326/14.313mm
Bore Dia	—	0.4995"/0.4990 12.687"/12.675mm
Length	—	0.6825"/0.6775" 17.366/17.209mm
Working Clearance On Spindle	—	0.0015"/0.0005" 0.267/0.0127mm
Intermediate Pinion Spindle		
Diameter	0.4988"/0.4981" 12.669/12.651	0.4985"/0.4980" 12.662/12.649mm
Interference In Crankcase	—	0.0015"/0.0005" 0.267/0.0127
Bush-Intermediate Pinion Spindle	Pre Eng No. 33065	
Outside Diameter	0.6270"/0.6265 15.925/15.913mm	—
Bore Diameter	0.5005/0.5000 12.827/12.70mm	—
Length	0.6825"/0.6775" 17.335/17.208mm	—
Interference Fit In C/Case	0.0015" 0.040mm	—
Bush Intermediate Pinion Spindle	Post Eng No. 33065	
Outside Diameter	0.8288"/0.8283" 21.051/21.038mm	—
Bore Diameter	0.5005"/0.5000 12.827/12.70mm	—
Length	0.6825/0.6775" 17.335/17.208mm	—
Interference Fit In C/Case	0.004 0.1016mm	—
Crankshaft Pinion		
No. Of Teeth	25	25
Fit On Crankshaft	+ 0.003"-0.0005" + 0.0076-0.0127mm	+ 0.003-0.0005" + 0.0076-0.0127mm

TECHNICAL DATA

OIL PRESSURE RELEASE VALVE

Piston Diameter	0.5610"/0.4605"	(14.249/14.237mm)
Body Bore Diameter	0.5625/0.5620	
Pressure Release Operates	60lb/sq.in	(4.22kg/sq.cm.)
Spring Length	1 3/8 "	(263.52)
No. Of Coils	13	

OIL PRESSURE

Normal Running	60/65 lb/sq in	(4.22/4.570kg/sq cm)
Idling	20/25lb/sq in	(1.406/1.76kg/sq cm)

OIL PRESSURE SWITCH

Operating pressure	3/5lb sq in	(.20/.35kg/sq cm)

IGNITION TIMING

Crankshaft Position	38° Fully Advanced	
Piston Position - Fully Advanced	0.415"	(10.4mm)
Advance Range - Centrifugal	24°	
Advance Range - Electronic	38°	
Engine RPM When Full Advance Occurs - Centrifugal 2500		
Engine RPM When Full Advance Occurs - Electronic 3500		

CONTACT BREAKER

Gap Setting	0.015"	(0.38m)

SPARK PLUG

Type-Champion N5		
Gap Setting	0.025"	(0.635mm)
Thread Size	14mm	
Reach	3/4 "	(19.06)

PISTONS

	Low (L) Grade	High (H) Grade	
Diameter	2.9876"/2.9871"	2.9882"/2.9877"	
	75.885/75.872mm	75.900/75.999mm	
Gudgeon Pin Bore Dia		0.7504"/0.7502"	(19.162/19.065mm)
Gudgeon Pin Dia		0.7502"/0.7500	(19.065/19.060mm)

PISTON RINGS

Compression Rings		
Width	0.121"/0.113"	(3.073/2.896mm)
Thickness	0.0625"/0,0615	(1.589/1.563mm)
Fitted Gap	0.013"/0.008"	(0.330/0.203mm)
Clearance In Groove	0.0035"/0.0015"	(0.089/0.038mm)

OIL CONTROL RING

Width	0.121"	(3.073mm)
Thickness	0.125"	(3.18mm)
Fitted Gap	0.010"/0.008"	(0.254/0.203mm)
Clearance In Groove	0.0025"/0.0015"	(0.0635/0.038mm)

TD TECHNICAL DATA

CARBURETTOR

MODEL	T140E	T140ES/2	TR7	TR7T	TR65	TR65T
MAKE	AMAL MKII	BING C.D.	AMAL MKI	AMAL MKI	AMAL MKI	AMAL MKI
TYPE No.	2930/1-2930/2	64 C.D.	930/94	930/108	930/108	930/108
BORE SIZE	30mm	-	30mm	30mm	30mm	30mm
MAIN JET	200	145	270	240	240	220
NEEDLE JET	106	2 66	106	106	106	106
NEEDLE TYPE	2C3	STD	STD	STD	STD	STD
NEEDLE POSITION	2	3	1	1	1	1
THROTTLE VALVE	3	-	3	3	3	3
PISTON	-	5	-	-	-	-
PILOT JET	20	45	STD	STD	-	-
STARTER JET	35	-	-	-	-	-

TRANSMISSION

CLUTCH DETAILS

Type	Multiplate with integral shock absorber
No. of Plates: Driving (bonded)	6
Drive (plain)	7
Bonded Insert Thickness	0.035"/0.045" (0.853/1.153mm)
Pressure springs:	
Number	3
Free Length	1 13/16 "
No. Of Working coils	9 1/2
Spring Rate	113 lb.in.
Approximate fitted load	62lbs
Bearing Rollers:	
Number	20
Diameter	2495/.2500in. (6.337/6.35mm)
Length	231/.236in. (5.831/5.958mm)
Clutch Hub Bearing Diameter	1.3733/1.3743in. (33.882/34.907mm)
Clutch Sprocket Bore Diameter	1.8745/1.8755in. (47.612/47.638mm)
Thrust Washer Thickness	052/.054in. (1.312/1.372mm)

CLUTCH OPERATING MECHANISM

Conical Spring:		
Number Of Working Coils	2	
Free Length	13/16 in	(10.3mm)
Diameter Of Balls	3/8 in	(9.525mm)
Clutch Operating Rod:		
Diameter Of Rod	7/32 in.	(5.6mm)
Length Of Rod	11.722/11.712"	(297.74/297.49mm)

KICKSTART OPERATING MECHANISM

Bush Bore Diameter	751/.752"	(19.085/19.11mm)
Spindle Working Clearance In Bush	003/.005"	(.076/.127mm)
Ratchet Spring Free Length	1/2 ".	(12.7mm)

TECHNICAL DATA

GEARCHANGE MECHANISM

Plungers:
   Outer Diameter   4315/.4320"   (10.92/10.937mm)
   Working Clearance In Bore   005/.0015"   (.0127/.038mm)
Plunger Springs:
   No. Of Working Coils   12
   Free length   1 ¼ "   (31.75mm)

GEAR CHANGE SHAFT BUSHES

R.H. Side Outer   0.6260"/0.6255"   (15.90/15.887mm)
R.H. Side Inner   0.7510"/0.7505"   (19.075/19.063mm)
L.H. Side Inner   0.7510/0.7505"   (19.075/19.063mm)
L.H. Side Outer   0.753"/0.752"   (19.136/19.110mm)

GEARCHANGE SHAFT DIAM.

R.H. Side Outer   0.6238"/0.6218"   (15.84/15.79mm)
R.H. Side Inner   0.749"/0.747"   (19.03/18.98mm)
L.H. Side Inner   0.747"/0.746"   (18.98/18.95mm)
L.H. Side Outer   0.749"/0.747"   (19.03/18.98mm)

QUADRANT RETURN SPRINGS

Total No. Of Coils   12
Free Length   1 ¾ "   (44.5mm)
Rate   22-24lbs in.   (9.079/10.886kg cm)

CAMPLATE PLUNGER

Plunger Dia   0.4365"/0.4355"   (11.05/11.02mm)
Plunger Length   1 $^{23}/_{32}$ (45.243mm)
Plunger Spring Length   2.14   (54.356mm)
No. Of Coils   19
Rate   9.6lb/in   (4.35kg/cm)

GEARBOX

RATIOS - ALL MODELS

INTERNAL RATIOS

5th Top	1·00:1
4th	1·19:1
3rd	1·40:1
2nd	1·837:1
1st Bottom	2·585:1

OVERALL RATIO'S - PRE EDA 30,000

	T140	TR7
5th	4.70	4.70
4th	5.59	5.59
3rd	6.58	6.58
2nd	8.63	8.63
1st	12.14	12.14
Engine RPM AT 10MPH in 5th Gear	669	669

TD — TECHNICAL DATA

OVERALL RATIOS POST EDA 30,000

	T140	TR7	TR7T	TR65	TR65T
5th	4·5:1	4·5:1	5.22:1	4.95:1	5.22:1
4th	5·36:1	5·36:1	6.21:1	5.89:1	6.21:1
3rd	6·30:1	6·30:1	7.31:1	6.93:1	7.31:1
2nd	8·27:1	8·27:1	9.59:1	9.09:1	9.59:1
1st	11·63:1	11·63:1	13.49:1	12.79:1	13.49:1
Engine RPM at 10 MPH in 5th Gear	640	640	680	660	680

SPROCKET DETAILS PRE EDA 30,000

	T140	TR7
Engine	29	29
Gearbox	20	20
Clutch	58	58
Rear Wheel	47	47

SPROCKET DETAILS POST EDA 30,000

	T140	TR7	TR7T	TR65	TR65T
Engine	29	29	29	29	29
Gearbox	20	20	18	19	18
Clutch	58	58	58	58	58
Rear Wheel	45	45	47	47	47

GEAR DETAILS

Mainshaft High Gear:
  Bearing, type   Needle roller (torrington B1314)
  Bearing length   ·875/·865in. (22.23/21.97mm.).

GEARBOX SHAFTS

Mainshaft:
  Left End Diameter   0·8120"/0·8115" (20·625/20·612mm)
  Right End Diameter   ·7494/·7498in. (19.044/19.054mm.)
  Length   11.27in. (286.25mm.)
Layshaft:
  Left end diameter   ·6875/·6870in. (17·46/17·404mm.)
  Right End Diameter   ·6875/·6870in. (17.46/17.404mm.)
  Length   6.47in. (164.33mm.)
  Min End Float   0.0025" (0.0632mm)
  Max End Float   0.0475" (1.2065mm)

BEARINGS

Mainshaft bearing (left) $1\frac{1}{2}$ x $2\frac{1}{2}$ x $\frac{5}{8}$ in. roller bearing (38.1x63.5x15.9mm.)
Mainshaft bearing (right) $\frac{3}{4}$ x $1\frac{7}{8}$ x $\frac{9}{16}$ in. Ball Journal (19x47.5x14.3mm.)
Layshaft bearing (left) $1\frac{1}{16}$ x $\frac{7}{8}$ x $\frac{3}{4}$ in. Needle roller (17.5x22.23x19mm.)
Layshaft bearing (right) $1\frac{1}{16}$ x $\frac{7}{8}$ x $\frac{3}{4}$ in. Needle roller (17.5x22.23x19mm)
Layshaft 1st gear bush:
  Bore diameter   ·800/·795in.(20·32/20·203mm.)
  Shaft diameter   ·8075/·8070in. (20·511/20·498mm.)
Layshaft 2nd gear bush:
  Bore diameter   ·800/·795in. (20.32/20.203mm.)
  Shaft diameter   ·8075/·8070in. (20·511/20·498mm.)

No. Of Teeth On G/Box Pinions

Layshaft			Mainshaft		
	5th	15		5th	21
	4th	17		4th	20
	3rd	18		3rd	18
	2nd	21		2nd	16
	1st	24		1st	13

TECHNICAL DATA   TD

CHAIN DETAILS

Primary — Triplex Endless 3/8" Pitch x 84 Links

Secondary — Single 3/8" x 5/8" x 107 Links (Pre EDA 30,000)
Single 3/8" x 5/8" x 106 Links (Post EDA 30,000)

FRAME ETC.

HEAD BEARINGS

TYPE	TIMKEN TAPER ROLLER
Bore Size	0.7508"/0.7500" (19.08/19.06mm)
Outer Diameter	1.7820/1.7810 (45.27/45.24mm)

SWINGING FORK BEARINGS

TYPE	PHOSPOR BRONZE BUSH
Bush Outer Dia	1.1255"/1.1245" (28.58/28,56mm)
Bush Bore Dia	1.0015"/1.000 (25.43/25.40mm)
Bush Length	0.755/0.750 (19.07/19.06mm)
Sleeve O/D	0.9984"/0.9972" (25.35/25.32mm)
Sleeve Length	2.200"/2.195" (51.31/51.29mm)

REAR SUSPENSION UNITS

Type	Girling Gas Filled	
Length Extended	12.4"	(314.96mm)
Spring Wire Diameter	0.268"	(6.80mm)
Spring Free Length	9.0"	(228.6mm)

REAR SUSPENSION UNITS

Type	Marzocci	
Length Extended	12.32"	(313mm)
Spring Wire Diameter	0.283"	(7.2mm)
Spring Free Length	8.27"	(210mm)

REAR SUSPENSION UNITS TR7T/TR65T

Type	Marzocci	
Length Extended	13.18"	(335mm)
Spring Wire Diameter	0.299"	(7.59mm)
Spring Free Length	9.00"	(228.6mm)

WHEELS, BRAKES, & TYRES

WHEEL FRONT-TR7-T140-TR65

Rim Size			WM2 x 19"	
Spokes-Inner RH & LH	20 Off	10SWG	7.75" (196.86mm)	96° Head Angle
Spokes-Outer RH & LH	20 Off	10SWG	7.85" (199.39mm)	80° Head Angle

TR7T-TR65T

RIM SIZE			WMI X 21"	
Spokes-Inner RH & LH	20 Off	10SWG	8.85" (224.79mm)	96° Head Angle
Spokes-Outer RH & LH	20 Off	10SWG	8.80" (223.52mm)	80° Head Angle

Wheel Bearing RH	14 x 20 x 47mm
Wheel Bearing LH	15 x 25 x 52mm

TD TECHNICAL DATA

WHEEL FRONT - CAST ALLOY

	LESTER	MORRIS
Rim Size	19x2.15	19x2.15
Bearing RH	14x20x47mm	14x20x47mm
Bearing L.H.	14 x 20 x 47mm	15 x 25 x 52mm

WHEEL REAR-ALL MODELS-SPOKE

Rim Size			WM 3 x 18	
Spokes Inner LH	10 Off	9SWG	5.7" (144.79mm)	102° Head Angle
Spokes Outer LH	10 Off	9SWG	5.8" (147.32mm)	100° Head Angle
Spokes Inner/Outer RH	20 Off	9SWG	7.2" (182.80mm)	135° Head Angle
Bearing LH & RH			15 x 25 x 52mm	

WHEEL REAR - CAST ALLOY

	LESTER	MORRIS
Rim Size	18 x 2.50	18 x 2.50
Bearing LH	15 x 25 x 52mm	15 x 25 x 52mm
Bearing RH	14 x 20 x 47mm	15 x 25 x 52mm

BRAKES - FRONT

Type	Disc Hydraulically Operated
Disc Dia.	9.800"(248.92mm)
Brake Pads-Pre EDA 30,000	Don 230
Brake Pads-Post EDA 30,000	Dunlop Sintered
Minimum Permissable Lining Thickness	0.078" (1.984mm)

BRAKES - REAR

Type	Disc Hydraulically Operated
Disc Dia	9.800 (248.92mm)
Brake Pads -Pre EDA 30,000	Don 230
Brake Pads -Post EDA 30,000	Dunlop Sintered
Minimum Permissable Lining Thickness	0.078" (1.984mm)

BRAKE - REAR

Type	Drum Mechanically Operated
Drum Dia	7.000 (177.80mm)
Minimum Permissable Lining Thickness	0.040" (1.016mm)

SPEEDO DRIVE

Drive Gearbox Ratio	1·25:1
Drive Cable Length Outer	71.250"
Drive Cable Length Inner	72.750"

TECHNICAL DATA

TYRES

MODEL	FRONT	REAR	PRESSURES FRONT	PRESSURES REAR	TYPE
T140	4.10x19	4.10x18	28 P.S.I. 1.90kg	32 P.S.I. 2.25kg	Avon R/R Dunlop T T100
TR7	4.10x19	4.10 x 18	28 P.S.I. 1.90kg	32 P.S.I. 2.25kg	Avon R/R Dunlop TT 100
TR7T/TR65T	2. x 21	4.00 x 18	22 P.S.I. 1.54kg	24 P.S.I. 1.68kg	Avon Mudplugger
TR65	3.25 x 19	4.00 x 18	24 P.S.I. 1.68kg	24 P.S.I. 1.68kg	Dunlop K70
T140D	4.10 x 19	4.25 x 18	28 P.S.I. 1.90kg	22 P.S.I. 2.25kg	Avon R/R Dunlop TT 100
T140 US	4.10 x 19	4.25 x 18	28 P.S.I. 1.90kg	32 P.S.I. 2.25kg	Avon R/R Dunlop TT 100

TELESCOPIC FRONT FORKS

FRONT FORK

Total Travel	6.750"	(171.46mm)
Stanchion Dia	1.3610"/1.3605"	(33.04/33.03mm)
Bottom Member Bore Dia	1.365"/1.363"	(33.15/33.1mm)

Spring Details
Free Length   19.1in   (485mm)
No. Of Coils   68

ELECTRICAL DETAILS

BULBS

Headlight	12 volt 60/45W Sealed Beam L.H. Dip
Headlight	12 Volt 60/50W Sealed Beam R.H. Dip U.S.A
Headlight	12 Volt 45/40W R.H. Dip
Pilot Light	12 Volt 6W Lucas 233
Stop/Tail Light	12 Volt 5/21W Lucas 380 Offset Pin
Speedo/Tacho	12 Volt 3W Lucas 504
Warning Lights	12 Volt 2W Lucas 281
Direction Indicator	12 Volt 21W Lucas 382
Fuse Rating	35 Amperes

TR7T/TR65T
Stop	12 Volt 21W Lucas 382
Tail	12 Volt 5W
Headlight	12 Volt 45/40W Lucas 410 L.H. Dip

TD TECHNICAL DATA

ELECTRICAL SYSTEMS

	T140/TR7-1979/80 K/S	T140/TR7/TR7T 1980/81 E/S 1981 K/S	TR65-1981
VOLTAGE	12	12	12
POLARITY	NEGATIVE EARTH	NEGATIVE EARTH	NEGATIVE EARTH
BATTERY	9 AMP/HR	14 AMP/HR E/S 9 AMP/HR K/S	9 AMP/HR
RECTIFIER	LUCAS 3DS	LUCAS 3DS	LUCAS 3DS
ZENER DIODE	ZD 715 SINGLE	XD 715A TRIPLE PACK	ZD 715 TWIN PACK
ALTERNATOR	RM 24	RM 24	RM 21
IGNITION COIL	6 VOLT	6 VOLT	12 VOLT
IGNITION SENSOR	LUCAS 5PU	LUCAS 5PU	
IGNITION AMPLIFIER	LUCAS AB11	LUCAS AB11	
AUTO ADVANCE UNIT			LUCAS 10CA
CONTACT POINTS			LUCAS 10CA
ADVANCE RANGE	9°-38° (ENGINE)	9°-38° (ENGINE)	14°-38° (ENGINE)
FLASHER UNIT	LUCAS 8FL	LUCAS 8FL	LUCAS 8FL
IGNITION SWITCH	LUCAS 149SA	LUCAS 149SA	LUCAS 149SA
HORN	LUCAS 6H	LUCAS 6H	LUCAS 6H

GENERAL

CAPACITIES

Fuel Tank	Small	2.8 Imp Gall 3.4 US Gall 12.72 Litres
	Large	4.0 Imp Gall 5.0 US Gall 18.184 Litres
Oil Tank		4.0 Pints 4.8 Pints US 2.27 Litres
Gear Box		500cc
Primary Chaincase (Initial Fill Only)		150cc
Telescopic Fork Legs (Each)		190cc
Front Brake Hydraulic System		189cc Approx
Rear Brake Hydraulic System		205cc Approx

DIMENSIONS

Wheel Base	56in (165cm)
Overall Length	87in (222cm)
Overall Width	32in (84cm)
Seat Height	31in (79cm)

TECHNICAL DATA TD

WEIGHT

Unladen-Dry	K/S Model	395lbs (179kg)
	E/S Model	429lbs (195kg)

TORQUE WRENCH SETTINGS (DRY)

ENGINE

Flywheel Bolts	33 lb ft	(4.6kg m)
Con Rod Bolts	22 lb ft	(3.9kg m)
Crankcase Junction Bolts	13 lb ft	(1.8kg m)
Crankcase Junction Studs	20 lb ft	(2.8kg m)
Cylinder Head Bolts 3/8Dia	18 lb ft	(2.49kg m)
Cylinder Head Bolts 5/16 Dia	16 lb ft	(2.07kg m)
Rocker Box Bolts Inner	10 lb ft	(1.38kg m)
Rocker Box Bolts Outer 1/4 Dia	5 lb ft	(0.7kg m)
Rocker Box Nuts	5 lb ft	(0.7kg m)
Rocker Spindle Dome Nuts	22 lb ft	(3.0kg m)
Oil Pump Fixing Screws	5 lb ft	(0.7kg m)
Crankshaft Pinion Nut	80 lb ft	(5.6kg m)
Crankshaft Pinion Nut	80 lb ft	(5.6kg m)
Cylinder Barrel Base Nuts	20 lb ft	(2.8kg m)
Oil Release Valve	20 lb ft	(2.8kg m)

GEARBOX & TRANSMISSION

Kickstart Ratchet Nut	35 lb ft	(2.5kg m)
Clutch Centre Nut	70 lb ft	(9.6kg m)
Gearbox Final Drive Sprocket Nut	80 lb ft	(5.6kg m)
Engine Sprocket/Rotor Nut	50 lb ft	(3.5kg m)
Stator Fixing Nuts	20 lb ft	(2.8kg m)
Primary Cover Dome Nuts	10 lb ft	(1.38kg m)

FRAME & FORKS

S/Arm Spindle Retaining Nut	60 lb ft	(8.29kg m)
Stanchion Pinch Bolts	25 lb ft	(3.45kg m)
Stanchion Top Nut	30 lb ft	(4.14kg m)
Stanchion Bottom Nut	30 lb ft	(4.14kg m)
Fork Damper Fixing Screw	18 lb ft	(2.49kg m)
Front Wheel Spindle Cap Nuts	15 lb ft	(2.07kg m)
Rear Wheel Spindle Nut	60 lb ft	(8.29kg m)

WHEELS

Disc Retaining Bolt Nuts	27 lb ft	(3.73kg m)

ELECTRICAL

Zener Diode Fixing Bolt	1.5 lb ft	(0.207kg m)
Rectifier Fixing Nut		

General Torque Settings Where Not Specifically Stated

1/4 " Nuts/Bolts 10-12lb ft	5/16 " Nuts/Bolts	15-17lb ft
3/8 " Nuts/Bolts 18-20lb ft	7/16 " Nuts/Bolts	18-20lb ft

SECTION A
LUBRICATION SYSTEM
INDEX

Description	Section
RECOMMENDED LUBRICANTS & MAINTENANCE CHART	A1
ENGINE LUBRICATION SYSTEM	A2
CHANGING THE ENGINE OIL AND CLEANING THE OIL FILTERS	A3
OIL PRESSURE	A4
STRIPPING AND REASSEMBLING THE OIL PRESSURE RELEASE VALVE	A5
STRIPPING AND REASSEMBLING THE OIL PUMP	A6
REMOVING AND REPLACING THE OIL PIPE JUNCTION BLOCK	A7
REMOVING AND REPLACING THE ROCKER OIL FEED PIPE	A8
CONTACT BREAKER LUBRICATION TR65 ONLY	A9
GEARBOX LUBRICATION	A10
PRIMARY CHAINCASE LUBRICATION	A11
REAR CHAIN LUBRICATION AND MAINTENANCE	A12
GREASING THE STEERING HEAD RACES	A13
WHEEL BEARING LUBRICATION	A14
TELESCOPIC FORK LUBRICATION	A15
LUBRICATION NIPPLES	A16
LUBRICATING THE CONTROL CABLES	A17
SPEEDOMETER AND TACHOMETER CABLE LUBRICATION	A18
BRAKE PEDAL SPINDLE LUBRICATION	A19
CHECK PROCEDURE FOR WET SUMPING	A20

SECTION A1
RECOMMENDED LUBRICANTS

RECOMMENDED LUBRICANTS (All Markets) THE PRODUCTS RECOMMENDED ARE NOT LISTED IN ORDER OF PREFERENCE.

	Engine and Primary Chaincase	Gearbox	Telescopic Fork	Wheel Bearings, Swinging Fork Steering Races
MOBIL	Mobiloil Super	Mobilube GX90	Mobil ATF 210	Mobilgrease MP or Mobilgrease Super
DUCKHAM'S	Duckham's 4 Stroke M/Cycle Oil	Duckham's Hypoid 90	Duckham's Q-Matic	Duckham's LB10 Grease
CASTROL	Castrol GTX or Castrol Grand Prix	Castrol Hypoy EP 90	Castrol Fork Oil	Castrol LM Grease
B.P.	B.P. Super Visco-Static	B.P. Gear Oil SAE 90 EP	B.P. 'B' Autron	B.P. Energrease L2
ESSO	Uniflo	Esso Gear Oil GX90/140	Esso Glide	Esso Multipurpose Grease H
SHELL	Shell Super Motor Oil	Shell Spirax 90 EP	Shell Donax T.7	Shell Retinax A
TEXACO	Havoline Motor Oil 20W/50	Multigear Lubricant EP 90	Texomatic 'F'	Marfak All Purpose

LUBRICATION SYSTEM

MAINTENANCE CHART

RECOMMENDED ROUTINE MAINTENANCE CHART	Daily	Weekly	First 500 Mile Service	1500 ML	3000 ML	4500 ML	6000 ML	7500 ML	9000 ML	10500 ML	12000 ML	13500 ML	15000 ML	16500 ML	18000 ML	19500 ML	21000 ML	22500 ML	24000 ML	25500 ML	27000 ML	28500 ML	30000 ML
Engine																							
Check oil level & return	■																						
Change oil/clean filter			■		■		■		■		■		■		■		■		■		■		■
Re torque cylinder head			■				■				■				■				■				■
Check cylinder base nuts			■				■				■				■				■				■
Adjust tappets			■		■		■		■		■		■		■		■		■		■		■
Check ignition timing			■				■				■				■				■				■
Clean and adjust spark plugs			■		■		■		■		■		■		■		■		■		■		■
Replace spark plugs							■				■				■				■				■
Gearbox																							
Check oil level					■		■		■		■		■		■		■		■		■		■
Change oil			■				■				■				■				■				■
Clutch																							
Check push rod adjustment			■		■		■		■		■		■		■		■		■		■		■
Primary case																							
Drain & refill			■				■				■				■				■				■
Front forks																							
Drain & refill							■				■				■				■				■
Check & adjust head race											■								■				
Re pack races with grease																			■				
Rear swinging fork pivot																							
Grease							■				■				■				■				■
Wheels																							
Check spoke tension		■			■		■		■		■		■		■		■		■		■		■
Check wheel bearing											■								■				
Check tyres for wear		■			■		■		■		■		■		■		■		■		■		■
Check tyre pressures		■			■		■		■		■		■		■		■		■		■		■
Transmission																							
Check & adjust rear chain		■			■		■		■		■		■		■		■		■		■		■
Check & adjust primary chain							■				■				■				■				■
Lubricate rear chain		■			■		■		■		■		■		■		■		■		■		■
Brakes																							
Lubricate brake pedal spindle					■		■		■		■		■		■		■		■		■		■
Check operation		■			■		■		■		■		■		■		■		■		■		■
Check pads for wear					■		■		■		■		■		■		■		■		■		■
Check fluid levels		■			■		■		■		■		■		■		■		■		■		■
Control cables																							
Adjust & lubricate					■		■		■		■		■		■		■		■		■		■
Tacho/Speedo/Horn/Lights																							
Check working	■																						
Battery																							
Check level of acid		■			■		■		■		■		■		■		■		■		■		■
Filters																							
Clean elements							■				■				■				■				■
Nuts & bolts																							
Check all fasteners for tightness			■		■		■		■		■		■		■		■		■		■		■
Change headlamp bulb																							

LUBRICATION SYSTEM

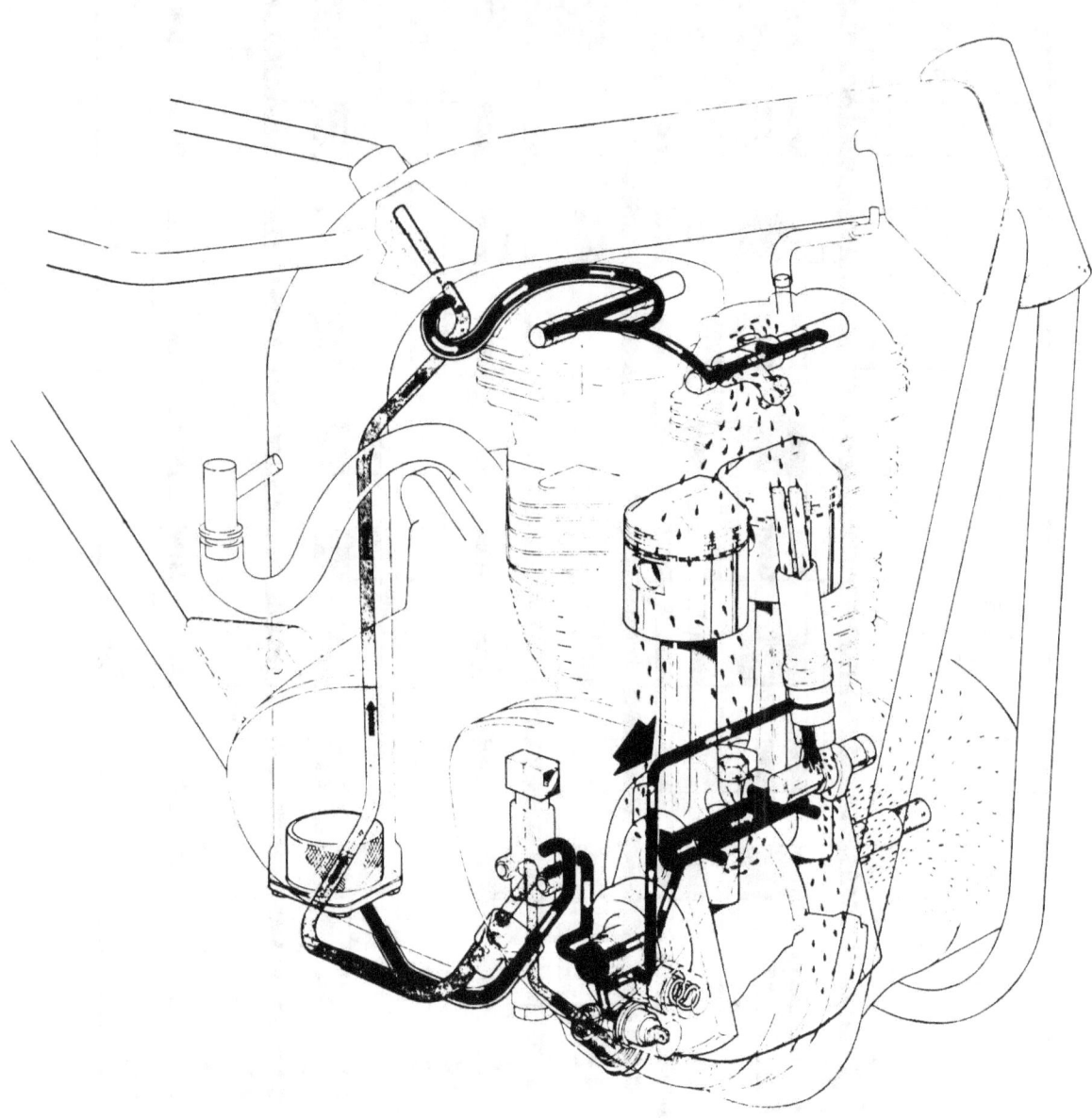

➤ Not used from engine No. EDA 30,000

Fig. A1. Engine lubrication diagram

LUBRICATION SYSTEM   A

SECTION A2

ENGINE LUBRICATION SYSTEM

The engine lubrication system is of the dry sump type. The oil is fed by gravity from the oil reservoir tank to the oil pump; the oil, under pressure from the oil pump, is forced through drillings to the crankshaft big ends, where it escapes, and lubricates the cylinder walls, ball journal main bearings and the other internal engine parts.

The oil pressure between the oil pump and crankshaft is controlled by the oil pressure release valve. After lubricating the engine, oil falls to the sump where it is scavenged through the sump filter, and returned to the oil reservoir by the action of the oil pump scavenge plunger. The oil pump has been designed so that the scavenge plunger has a greater capacity than the feed plunger; thus ensuring that the sump does not become flooded.

Oil is fed to the valve operating mechanism by means of the rocker oil feed pipe which is connected to the scavenge return pipe just below the oil reservoir. After travelling through the rokker spindles, the oil is fed into the rocker boxes after which it falls by gravity down the push rod cover tubes. The oil then passes through holes drilled in the tappet guide blocks and into the sump, where it is subsequently scavenged.

Engines Pre EDA 30,000

A positive oil feed is provided for the exhaust tappets. The lubricant is ported through drillways from the timing cover, and on through the crankcase and cylinder block base flange to an annular groove machined in the tappet guide block. Two oil holes are provided in the groove to mate with the oil holes in the tappets which provide a channel for the lubricant to the tappet and camshaft working faces. See Fig. A3 and Fig. A4.

SECTION A3

CHANGING THE ENGINE OIL AND CLEANING THE OIL FILTERS

It is advisable to drain the oil when the engine is warm as the oil will flow more readily. When changing the oil it is essential that the oil filters are thoroughly cleaned in paraffin (kerosene).

The hexagon-headed sump drain plug, which also houses the sump filter, is situated underneath the engine adjacent to the engine bottom mounting lug, as shown in Fig. A2, reference No. 4. Remove the plug and allow the oil to drain for approximately ten minutes. Clean the filter in paraffin (kerosene) and refit the plug but do not forget the joint washer.

The oil reservoir filter is contained in the bottom of the reservoir by means of a rectangular plate secured by four nuts. Remove the reservoir filler cap, place a drip tray underneath the base of the reservoir and remove the drain plug from the centre of the base plate. Allow the oil to drain for approx. 10 mins. Remove the four nuts and withdraw the cover plate from its studs. Note that there are two gaskets, one above the filter base flange and the other below. Clean the filter thoroughly in kerosene (paraffin).

It is advisable to flush out the oil reservoir with a flushing oil, or, if this is not available, paraffin (kerosene) will do. However, if this is used ensure that all traces are removed from the inside of the oil reservoir prior to re-filling with oil. (For the correct grade of oil see Section a1).

When refitting the filter do not forget to replace the gaskets. Refit the drain plug.

The capacity of the reservoir is 4 imperial pints (4.8 U.S. pints, 2.27 litres). The level can be checked with the combined dipstick and filler cap.

Check that the oil is returning from the engine sump by starting the engine and removing the reservoir filler cap. Oil should be seen to be flowing from the pipe which protrudes into the filler neck tube.

LUBRICATION SYSTEM

1. Primary Drain Plug
2. Primary Chain Adjuster
3. Gearbox Drain And Level Plug
4. Engine Filter

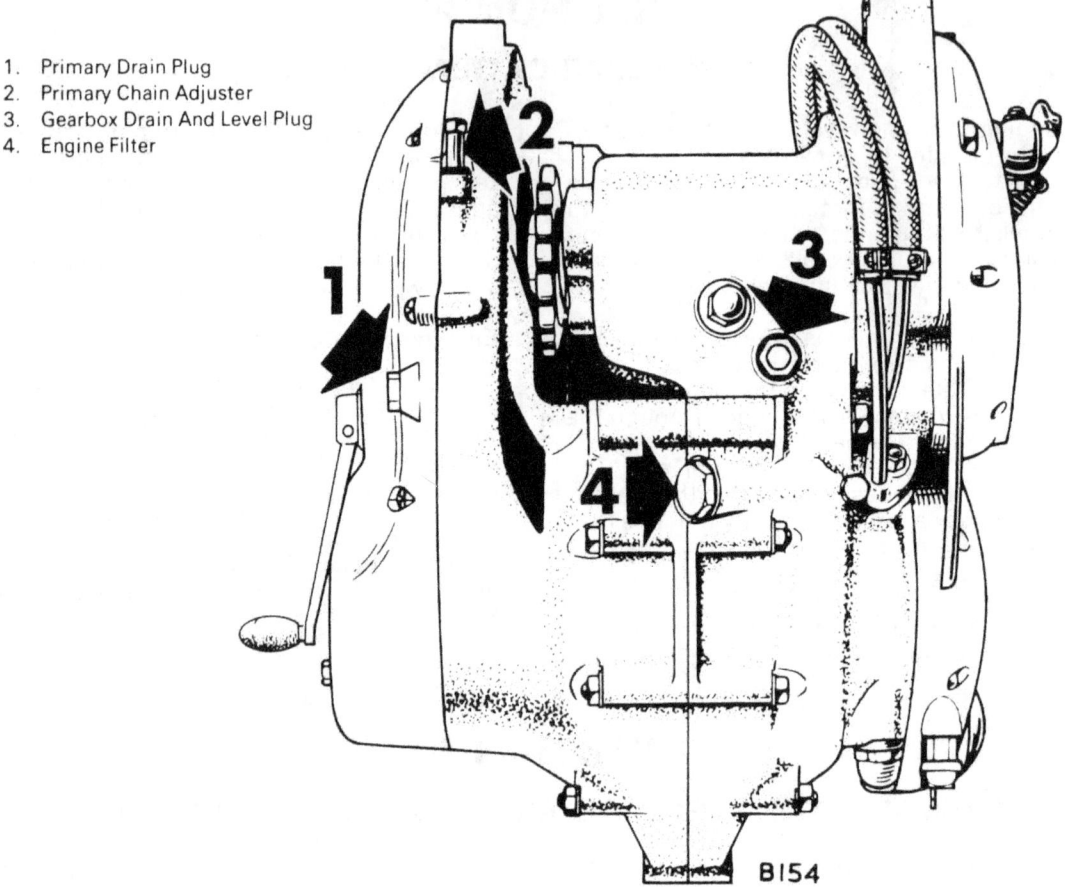

Fig. A2. Underside view of engine/gearbox unit

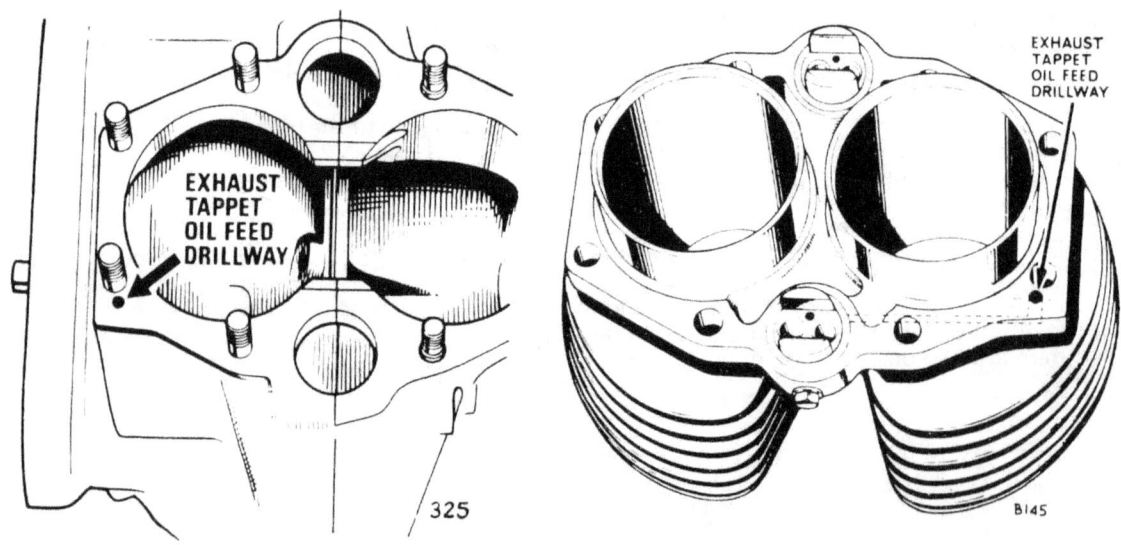

Fig. A3. Tappet oil feed drillway

Fig. A4. Tappet oil feed arrangement

Pre Eng No. EDA 30,000

LUBRICATION SYSTEM

SECTION A4

OIL PRESSURE

The oil pressure is controlled by means of the release valve situated at the front of the engine at the right side adjacement to the timing cover.

When the engine is stationary there will be nil oil pressure. When the engine is started from cold pressure may be as high as 80lb./sq. in. reducing when hot to a normal running figure of 60/lb/sq. in. At a fast idle when hot pressure should be 20/25lb./sq.in.

Pressure can only be checked with an oil gauge connected to an adaptor replacing the oil pressure switch on the front of the timing cover.

If satisfactory readings are not obtained, check the following:-

(1) That the oil pressure release valve is clean and that the piston has the correct working clearance in the valve body as detailed in "Technical Data".

(2) That the oil reservoir level is not below minimum and that the oil is being returned to the reservoir.

(3) That the sump filter and oil reservoir filter are clean and not blocked.

(4) That the oil pump is functioning properly and that there is a supply of oil to the pump.

Refer to Sections A6 and A8 for checking the oil pump and oil pipes with junction block respectively.

(5) That the drillings in the timing cover are clean and that the drillings in the crankcase connecting the oil pipe junction block to the oil pump are clear.

(6) That the oil seal in the timing cover which fits over the crankshaft is not badly worn, thus resulting in the oil escaping to the sump.

(7) That the big ends are not badly worn. Should the big end bearings not have the correct working clearance, the oil will escape more readily, particularly when the oil is warm and is more fluid, thus giving a drop in pressure.

Extensive periods of slow running (such as in heavy traffic), or unnecessary use of the air control, can cause dilution in the oil reservoir, and an overall drop in lubricating pressure due to the lower viscosity of the diluted oil.

Most lubrication and oil pressure troubles can be avoided by regular attention to the recommended oil changes.

SECTION A5

STRIPPING AND REASSEMBLING THE OIL PRESSURE RELEASE VALVE

Oil pressure is governed by the single spring situated within the release valve body. When the spring is removed it can be checked for compressive strength by measuring the length. Compare this figure with that given in TECHNICAL DATA".

To remove the complete oil pressure release unit from the crankcase, unscrew the hexagonal nut adjacent to the crankcase surface. When removed the cap can then be unscrewed from the body thus releasing the piston which should be withdrawn.

Thoroughly clean all parts in paraffin (kerosene) and inspect for wear. The piston should be checked for possible scoring and the valve body filter for possible blockage or damage. To reassemble the release valve unit offer the piston into the valve body and screw on the valve cap using a suitable loctite thread sealant and a new fibre washer. Similarly, when screwing the release valve unit into the crankcase, fit a new fibre washer between the release valve body and the crankcase. See Fig. A5.

LUBRICATION SYSTEM

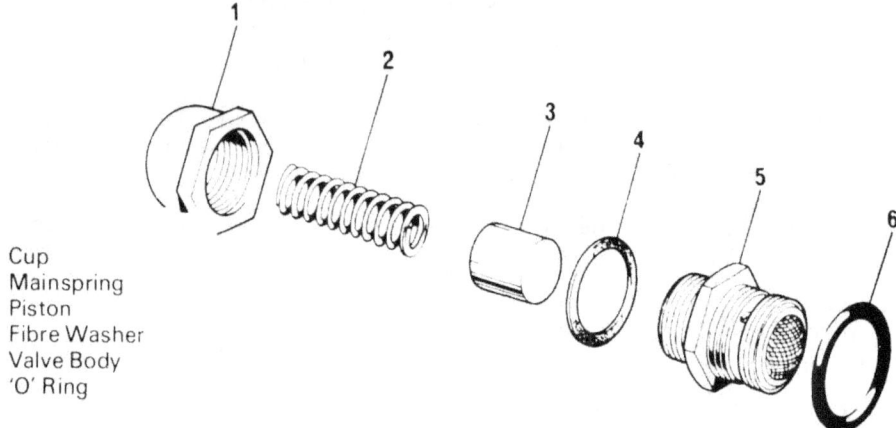

1. Cup
2. Mainspring
3. Piston
4. Fibre Washer
5. Valve Body
6. 'O' Ring

Fig. A5 Oil pressure release valve

To dismantle, remove the complete valve and cap and seperate the cap from the valve body. The spring and piston can then be removed for cleaning and examination.

One reassembly, note that the open end of the piston faces towards the spring and cap.

SECTION A6

STRIPPING AND REASSEMBLING THE OIL PUMP

The oil pump is situated inside the timing cover and is driven by an eccentric peg on the nut fitted to the end of the inlet camshaft. The only part likely to show wear after considerable mileage is the oil pump drive block slider, which should be replaced to maintain full oil pumping efficiency. The plungers and pump body being constantly immersed in oil, wear is negligible.

For removal of the timing cover see Section B30. The oil pump is held in its position by two conical nuts. When these are removed the oil pump can then be withdrawn from the mounting studs. The scavenge and feed plungers should be removed and the caps from the end of the oil pump unscrewed. This will release the springs and balls.

All parts should be thoroughly cleaned in paraffin (kerosene).

The plungers should be inspected for scoring, and for wear by measuring their diameters and comparing them with those given in "TECHNICAL DATA". The springs should be checked for compressive strength by measuring their lengths. Compare the actual lengths with those given in "TECHNICAL DATA".

When reassembling the oil pump all parts should be well lubricated and the oil pump finally checked for efficiency by the following means:-

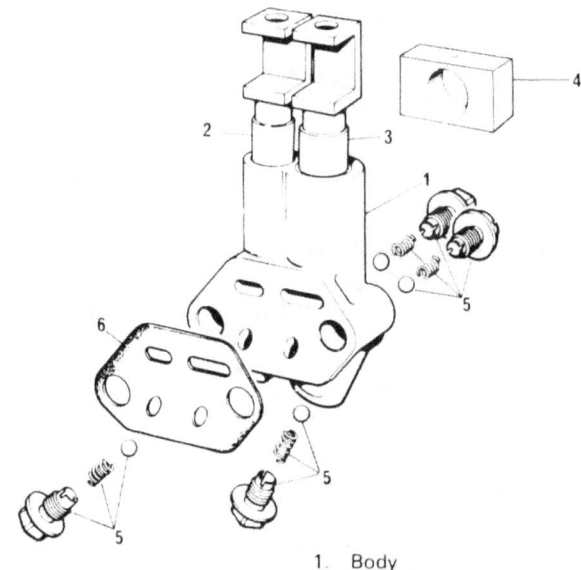

1. Body
2. Feed Piston
3. Scavenge
4. Drive Block
5. Valves Springs & Caps
6. Gasket

Fig. A6. Exploded view of oil pump

LUBRICATION SYSTEM

Place a small amount of oil in both bores (approximately 1c.c.) and press the plungers until oil is forced through both outlet ports (these are the two holes nearest the square caps (See Fig. A6). Place the thumb over the intake ports (the holes nearest the plunger tops) and withdraw the plungers slightly. If the oil level falls in either outlet port then the ball valve is not seating properly and the square caps should be removed and the cleaning process repeated. The ball valve can be tapped lightly, but sharply to ensure an efficient and adequate seal.

The aluminium drive block slider which fits over the eccentric peg on the inlet camshaft nut should be checked for wear on both the bore and in the plunger cross-head.

When refitting the oil pump a new gasket should be used and always remember that the cones of the conical nut and washers fit into the countersunk holes in the oil pump body.

When replacing the timing cover care should be taken that the junction surfaces are cleaned prior to application of the fresh coat of jointing compound.

SECTION A7

REMOVING AND REPLACING THE OIL PIPE JUNCTION BLOCK

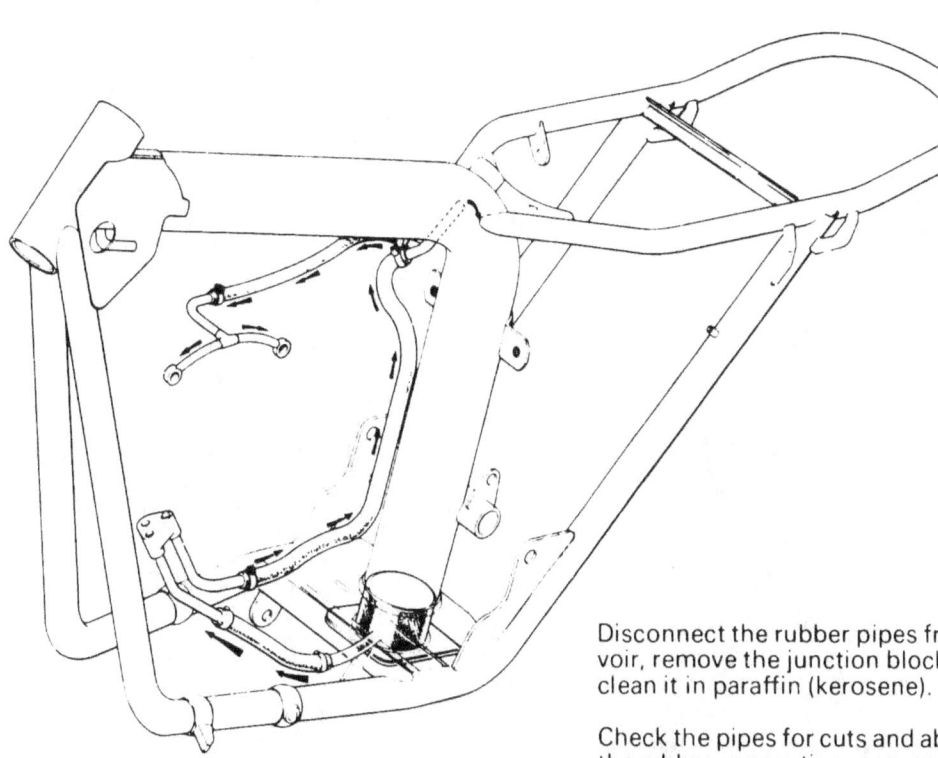

Fig. A7 Oil pipe securing clips

Drain the oil from the gearbox by removing the oil drain plug situated underneath the gearbox as shown in Fig. A2, reference No.3.

Remove the right-hand exhaust pipe, and the right footrest, then remove the gearbox outer cover as shown in Section D2.

Place a drip tray underneath the engine and remove the drain plug where fitted, or, alternatively, remove the nut securing the oil pipe junction block to the crankcase and allow the oil reservoir to drain for approximately ten minutes.

Disconnect the rubber pipes from the oil reservoir, remove the junction block and thoroughly clean it in paraffin (kerosene).

Check the pipes for cuts and abrasions and that the rubber connections are a good tight fit on the junction block pipes. If there is any doubt about the reliability of the rubber connectors, they should be renewed.

Reassembly is the reversal of the above instructions but remember to fit a new gasket between the junction block and the crankcase.

When replacing the rubber connection tubes, care mut be exercised to prevent chaffing the inside of the rubber connections. Failure to observe this may result in fragments of rubber entering the oil system and causing blockage.

Replace the screwed clips and firmly clamp them in position.

LUBRICATION SYSTEM

SECTION A8

REMOVING AND REPLACING THE ROCKER OIL FEED PIPE

To disconnect the rocker oil feed pipe for removal, the two domed nuts should be removed from the ends of the rocker spindle, and the banjos withdrawn.

Disconnnect the rocker oil feed pipe from the oil reservoir.

When removed, the rocker oil feed pipe should be thoroughly cleaned in paraffin (kerosene) and checked for blockage by sealing the first banjo with the thumb and first finger, whilst blowing through the other. Repeat this procedure for the other banjo.

When refitting the rocker oil feed pipe it is advisable to use new copper washers, but if the old ones are annealed they should give an effective oil seal. Annealing is achieved by heating to cherry red heat and quenching in water. Any scale that is formed on the washers should be removed prior to re-fitting them.

SECTION A9

CONTACT BREAKER LUBRICATION TR65 ONLY

The contact breaker is situated in the timing cover and it is imperative that no oil from the engine lubrication system gets into the contact breaker chamber. For this purpose there is an oil seal at the back of the contact breaker unit pressed into the timing cover. However slight lubrication of the auto advance unit spindles is necessary.

To lubricate the auto advance mechanism it is necessary to withdraw the mounting plate. Mark the C.B. plate and housing so that it can be subsequently replaced in exactly the same location, then unscrew the two hexagonal pillar bolts. When the mounting plate is removed, the mechanism should be lightly oiled (see arrows shown in Fig. A8) at the same interval that is given above for the cam wick. Do not allow more than one drop onto each pivot point, and wipe off any surplus.

Two drops of oil should be applied to the spindle which supports the cam to prevent corrosion and possible seizure.

Finally, replace the mounting plate and re-set the ignition timing. If the setting has been disturbed, the correct procedure for accurate ignition timing is given in Section B27, B28 and B29.

The lubricating wicks adjacent to the contact breaker nylon heels are treated intially with Shell Retinax A grease and thereafter, 3 drops of clean engine oil should be added to the wicks at 3,000 mile intervals.

Fig. A8 Contact breaker mechanism lubrication points 10CA TR65 only.

SECTION A10

GEARBOX LUBRICATION

1. Clutch Cable Nipple
2. Drain Plug
3. Level Plug

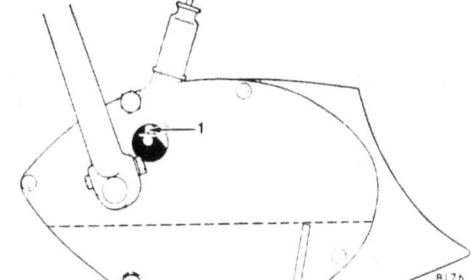

Fig. A9. Gearbox drain and level plugs

The gearbox is lubricated by means of an oil bath. Oil is splash fed to all gearbox components including the enclosed gearchange and kick-starter mechanisms. The oil in the gearbox should be drained and the gearbox flushed out after the initial 500-mile (800km) running-in period. Thereafter, the oil should be changed as stated in "Routine Maintenance".

The oil can be drained from the gearbox by means of the oil drain plug located underneath the gearbox (see Fig. A2, reference No. 3. It is best to drain the oil whilst the engine is warm as the oil will flow more readily.

The gearbox oil filler plug is situated on the outer cover. When replenishing the oil, the oil drain plug A.3 should be replaced omitting the smaller oil level plug which screws into it. Oil should be poured into the gearbox until it is seen to drip out through the oil level plug hole. (See Fig. A9). The correct level has then been obtained (see Section A1 for recommended oil).

SECTION A11

PRIMARY CHAINCASE LUBRICATION

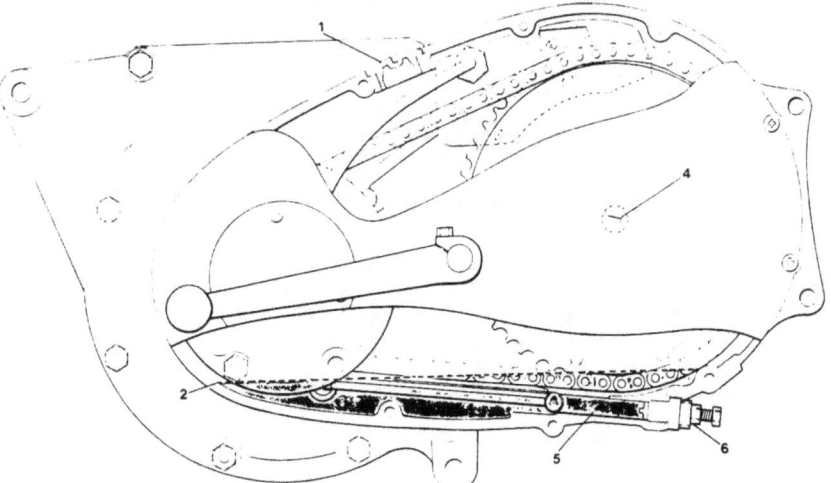

Fig. A10. Section through the primary chaincase

The level of the oil in the primary chaincase is automatically maintained by the engine breathing system which operates through the drive side roller bearing. Three small holes drilled in the crankcase provide an inlet back into the crankcase when the oil reaches a predetermined level.

Oil should be added to the chaincase when the oil has been drained, by removal of drain plug Fig A2 Ref 2. When 'priming' the chaincase with fresh oil use approximately 1/4 pint of engine oil. (See Section A1). Added through filler plug Fig A10 Ref 1.

LUBRICATION SYSTEM

SECTION A12

REAR CHAIN LUBRICATION AND MAINTENANCE

The rear chain should be periodically lubricated with a proprietary chain lube aerosol whenever signs of dryness occur. But as recommended in "Routin Maintenance" the chain should be removed and thoroughly cleaned and greased.

Disconnect the connecting link and remove the chain. If available, connect an old chain to the end of the chain being removed and draw it onto the gearbox sprocket until the chain to be cleaned is clear of the machine and can be diconnected.

Remove all deposits of road dust etc. by means of a wire brush. Clean thoroughly in paraffin or kerosene and allow to drain.

Inspect the chain for excessive wear of the rollers and pivot pins and check that the elongation does not exceed 1 1/2%. To do this first scribe two marks on a flat table exactly 12 1/2 inches (31.75cm.) apart, place the chain opposite the two marks. When the chain is compressed to its minimum free length the marks should coincide with two pivot pins 20 links apart. When the chain is stretched to its maximum free length, the extension should not exceed 1/4in. (6.25mm.). If it is required to remove a faulty link, or shorten the chain, reference should be made to Section C12.

To lubricate use a proprietary chain lubricant. Grease.

To chain is now ready for refitting to the machine.

For chain adjustment refer to Section F.

NOTE: The connecting link retaining clip must be fitted with the nose-end facing in the direction of motion of the chain.

SECTION A13

GREASING THE STEERING HEAD RACES

The steering head bearings are packed with grease on assembly and require re-packing with the correct grade of grease at the interval stated in "Routin Maintenance". Removal and replacement of the bearings is comprehensively covered in the front fork section.

When the bearings are removed they should be cleaned in paraffin (kerosene), also, the races fitted to the frame head lug should be cleaned thoroughly by means of a paraffin (kerosene) soaked rag, then inspected for wear, cracking or pocketing.

SECTION A14

WHEEL BEARING LUBRICATION

All models are fitted with sealed bearings which do not require external lubrication. These can be recognised by the plastic covers fitted on each side of the ball races. (To inspect first remove the wheel and bearing retainers, see Section F).

Removing and replacing the bearings for the front and rear wheels is comprehensively covered in Section F11 and F14.

Note: It is essential that only sealed type bearing are used when replacement is necessary.

SECTION A15

TELESCOPIC FORK LUBRICATION

The oil contained in the front fork has the dual purpose of lubricating the stanchion bearing surface and also acting as the suspension damping medium. Therefore it is imperative that the fork legs have an equal amount of oil in them and that it is the type as stated in Section A1.

Oil leakage at the junction between the stanchion and bottom fork leg is prevented by means of an oil seal. If there is excessive oil leakage at this junction it may be necessary to renew the oil seal (see Section G3), but before undertaking this work, the fork should be chekked to ensure that there is the correct amount of oil in each of the fork legs.

The correct amount is 190c.c.

Particular attention should be given to the oil change period.

To drain the oil from the fork legs remove the two small drain plugs adjacement to the left and right ends of the frond wheel spindle.

Oil can be expelled at a greater rate by compressing the fork two or three times.

To refill the fork legs, the fork screw caps and the stanchion top nuts must be unscrewed and withdrawn, and the correct amount of oil poured into each fork leg. This will necessitate removal of the handlebar.

On reassembly use a suitable jointing compound on the stanchion top nut threads. To obviate leakage.

SECTION A16

LUBRICATION NIPPLES

Both the rear brake operating camshaft and the swinging fork pivot bearings should be lubricated by means of the lubrication nipples.

TR65 ONLY

The rear brake camshaft has an integral lubrication nipple. Care should be taken that the surface of the nipple is not damaged. Slight distortion may be removed with a fine grade file.

The rear wheel brake cam and spindle bearing surfaces should be sparingly lubricated with correct grade of grease (Section A1). This can be done by giving the lubrication nipple on the end of the camshaft one stroke from a grease gun. However, if the grease does not penetrate the brake cam should be removed and cleaned thoroughly in paraffin (kerosene). The can bearing surfaces should then be greased on reassembly.

SWINGING FORK PIVOT

The two nipples are situated at each end of the fork pivot. Give each nipple several strokes with a high pressure grease gun until grease is visible at the dirt excluders.

If the grease does not penetrate then the pivot must be removed to ensure adequate lubrication.

Removal of the swinging fork is detailed in section E20. When the fork is removed all parts should be thoroughly cleaned out in paraffin (kerosene) and allowed to drain.

Reassembly is a reversal of the above instructions. The space surrounding the distance tube should be carefully packed with the correct grade of grease, and the sleeves should be well greased on their bearing surfaces.

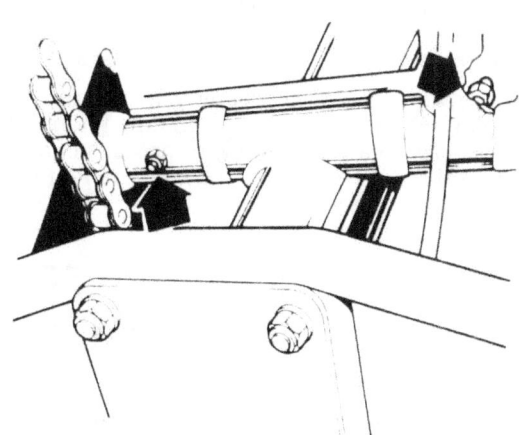

Fig. A11. Swinging fork pivot lubrication nipples

LUBRICATION SYSTEM

SECTION A17

LUBRICATING THE CONTROL CABLES

The control cables can be periodically lubricated at the exposed joints with a thin grade oil (see Section A1).

A more thorough method of lubrication is that of feeding oil into one end of the cable by means of a reservoir. For this the cable can be either disconnected at the handlebar end only, or completely removed.

The disconnected end of the cable should be threaded through a thin rubber stopper and the stopper pressed into a suitable narrow-necked can with a hole in its base. If the can is then inverted and the lubricated oil poured into it through the hole, the oil will trickle down between the outer and inner cables. It is best to leave the cable in this position overnight to ensure adequate lubrication.

SECTION A18

SPEEDOMETER AND TACHOMETER CABLE LUBRICATION

The speedometer and tachometer cables should be lubricated by means of grease (see Section A1 for correct grade).

It is not necessary completely to remove the cable, but only to disconnect if from the speedometer or tachometer and withdraw the inner cable. Unscrew the union nut at the base of the instrument, withdraw the inner cable and clean it in paraffin (kerosene). Smear the surface with grease, except for 6in. (15cm.) nearest to the instrument head.

The cable is now ready to be offered into the outer casing and excess grease wiped off. Care should be taken that both "squared" ends of the inner cables are located in their respective "square" drive housings before the union nut is tightened.

SECTION A19

BRAKE PEDAL SPINDLE LUBRICATION

No external grease nipple is provided, therefore the spindle must be removed and greased at the intervals state in "Routine Maintenance".

See Section E6 for removing and servicing the brake pedal spindle on disc brake models.

TR65-TR7T

The brake pedal spindle is bolted to the right rear engine mounting plate. The spindle should be covered with a fresh supply of grease occasionally otherwise corrosion and inefficient operation may result.

To gain access to the spindle, slacken off the rear brake rod adjustment, unscrew the brake pedal spindle retaining nut and withdraw the pedal complete with spindle.

Remove any rust from the spindle with fine emery. Clean the bore of the pedal and smear the spindle with grease (see Section A1) prior to refitting.

SECTION A20

CHECK PROCEDURE FOR WET SUMPING

'Wet sumping' or a lack of scavenge is a condition which can occur due to a number of causes. The symptoms of this condition are:-

(1) Excessive oil emitting from crankcase breather tube and resulting high oil consumption.
(2) Smoking exhaust.

To verify that a wet-sumping condition exists, run the engine until it is thoroughly warm. Within five minutes after engin shutoff drain the sump. Measure the amount of oil that drains out. An amount of oil over 200c.c. indicates a wet-sumping condition and corrective measures should be taken.

LUBRICATION SYSTEM   A

POSSIBLE CAUSES OF WET-SUMPING ARE

(1) Foreign material preventing ball valve from seating in the scavenge side of oil pump (most common cause).
(2) Poor check valve ball seat.
(3) Air leak in crankcase oil scavenge pipe.
(4) Air leak in oil pump to crankcase joint.
(5) Porous crankcase casting.
(6) Air leak at E9336 plug bottom of engine.
(7) Oil pressure release valve piston in full bypass position due to a stuck piston or broken or missing spring.
(8) Restriction in oil reservoir return pipe.

SCAVENGE SUCTION TEST (for checking above causes numbers 1 to 6)

Obtain a vacuum gauge calibrated in inches of mercury. Attach a length of standard Triumph oil pipe to it and proceed as follows:

(1) Run engine until it is thoroughly warn.
(2) Remove the oil sump cap and screen.
(3) Connect hose from vacuum gauge to oil scavenge pipe.
(4) Run engine at a fast idle-gauge should read a vacuum of 18-26 inches of mercury.
(5) Stop engine and observe gauge. The needle should gradually-not immediately-drop to zero.

IF THE SCAVENGE SUCTION TEST IS SATISFACTORY

(1) Check oil pressure relief valve assembly and also check oil pressure.
(2) Check the return system from the pump to the oil reservoir and also the reservoir vent.

IF THE ABOVE TEST IS NOT SATISFACTORY

(1) Remove oil pump-clean thoroughly and see that ball seats are concentric and free from pits or grooves. Re-assemble pump, tighten check valve caps securely and re-install pump with a new gasket.

To check for crankcase scavenge tube leakage or case porosity, fill a **good** "pumper" type oil can with light oil and squirt through a folded rag into pickup tube. Back pressure could prevent pumping oil out of the can in a few pumps. If the oil can still be pumped with no evidence of substantial back pressure, obviously there is a leak in the crankcase tube or crankcase scavenge oil passageways.

To be sure that the oil can is satisfactory for this test, fill it with light oil and block the outlet tube. After one or two pumps the can should "liquid lock". If the can can still be pumped, the pump mechanism is suffering from excessive blow-by and the can will not suffice for this test.

SECTION B

ENGINE

INDEX

DESCRIPTION	Section
REMOVING AND REPLACING THE ENGINE UNIT	B1
REMOVING AND REPLACING THE ROCKER BOXES	B2
INSPECTING THE PUSH RODS	B3
STRIPPING AND REASSEMBLING THE ROCKER BOXES	B4
ADJUSTING THE VALVE ROCKER CLEARANCES	B5
REMOVING AND REPLACING THE AIR CLEANER	B6
CONCENTRIC CARBURETTER-DESCRIPTION	B7
REMOVING AND REPLACING THE CARBURETTER	B8
STRIPPING AND REASSEMBLING THE CARBURETTER	B9
INSPECTING THE CARBURETTER COMPONENETS	B10
CARBURETTER ADJUSTMENTS	B11
TWIN CARBURETTER ARRANGEMENT	B12
REMOVING AND REPLACING THE EXHAUST SYSTEM	B13
REMOVING AND REFITTING THE CYLINDER HEAD ASSEMBLY	B14
REMOVING AND REPLACING THE VALVES	B15
RENEWING THE VALVE GUIDES	B16
DECARBONISING	B17
RE-SEATING THE VALVES	B18
REMOVING AND REPLACING THE CYLINDER BLOCK AND TAPPETS	B19
INPECTING THE TAPPETS AND GUIDE BLOCKS	B20
RENEWING THE TAPPET GUIDE BLOCKS	B21
REMOVING AND REFITTING THE PISTONS	B22
REMOVING AND REPLACING THE PISTON RINGS	B23
INSPECTING THE PISTONS AND CYLINDER BORES	B24
TABLE OF SUITABLE REBORE SIZES	B25

ENGINE

INDEX - CONTINUED

	Section
REMOVING AND REPLACING THE CONTACT BREAKER	B26
IGNITION TIMING - INITIAL PROCEDURE	B27
IGNITION TIMING WHERE A STROBOSCOPE IS NOT AVAILABLE	B28
IGNITION TIMING BY STROBOSCOPE	B29
REMOVING AND REPLACING THE TIMING COVER	B30
REMOVING AND REPLACING THE OIL PUMP	B31
VALVE TIMING	B33
DISMANTLING AND REASSEMBLING THE CRANKCASE ASSEMBLY	B34
SERVICING THE CRANKSHAFT ASSEMBLY	B35
REFITTING THE CONNECTING RODS	B36
INSPECTING THE CRANKCASE COMPONENTS	B37
RENEWING THE MAIN BEARINGS	B38
RENEWING THE CAMSHAFT BUSHES	B39
REMOVING AND REFITTING TACHOMETER DRIVE	B40
SUPPLEMENT FOR T140-TSS	—

ENGINE

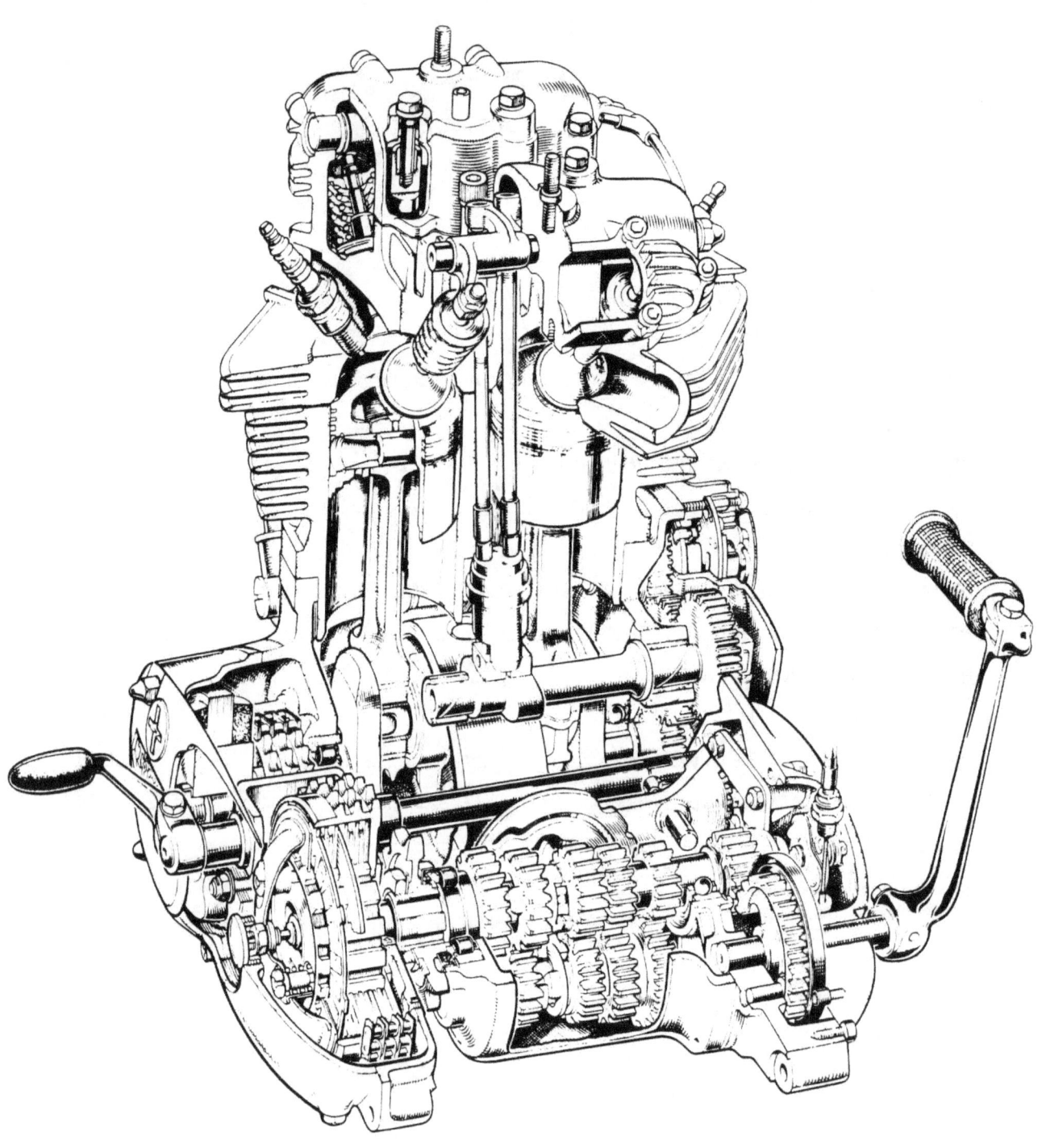

Fig. B1. Cutaway view of 750c.c. engine gearbox unit

ENGINE B

DESCRIPTION

The engine is of unit construction having two aluminium alloy mating crankcase halves, to gearbox housing being an integral part of the right half crankcase and the primary chain case an integral part of the left half-crankcase.

The aluminium alloy cylinder head has shrunk in Austenitic valve seat inserts, and houses the over-head valves, which are operated by rocker arms housed in detachable alloy rocker boxes. Four aluminium alloy push rods operate the rocker arms, which are each fitted with adjusters, accessible when the rocker box inspection covers are removed.

The aluminium alloy die cast pistons each have two compression rings and one oil scraper ring. The connecting rods are of H Section in RR56 Hiduminium alloy, with detachable caps, and incorporate steel-backed renewable "shell" bearings. Each of the connecting rod caps is machined from a steel stamping and held in position by means of two high tensile steel bolts, which are tightened to a predetermined torque figure to give the correct working clearance of the bearings on the crankshaft journals.

The inlet and exhaust camshafts operate in sintered bronze bushes which are housed transversely in the upper part of the crankcase. The inlet and exhaust camshafts are driven by a train of timing gears from the right end of the crankshaft. The inlet camshaft also operates the oil pump whilst the exhaust camshaft drives the reluctor which rotates within a magnetic sensor unit and so forming an electronic advance and retard, and the tachometer gearbox (when fitted).

The two-throw crankshaft has a detachable shrunk-on cast-iron flywheel which is held in position by three high tensile steel bolts, locked by the use of "270 LOCTITE" sealant and tightened to a pre-determined torque figure.

The big end bearings are lubricated at pressure with oil which travels along drillings in the crankcase and crankshaft from the double plunger oil pump: oil pressure in the lubrication system is governed by means of the oil pressure release valve situated at the front of the engine, adjacent to the timing cover.

The cylinder barrel is made from a high-grade cast-iron and houses the press-fit tappet guide blocks.

Power from the engine is transmitted through the engine sprocket and primary chain to the shock absorbing clutch unit and five speed gearbox. Primary chain tension is governed by an adjustable rubber-pad chain tensioner which is in the primary chain oil bath.

The electrical generator set consists of a rotor, which is fitted to the left end of the crankshaft, and an encapsulated coil stator which is mounted on three pillar bolts inside the primary chain housing.

Carburation is by twin or single carburetters with integral float chamber.

SECTION B1

REMOVING AND REPLACING THE ENGINE UNIT

Disconnect the leads from the battery terminals Ensure that the fuel taps are in the "OFF" position and disconnect the feed pipes. Remove petrol tank, see section E1.

Remove Exhaust system as described in Section B17.

Disconnect the oil pressure switch at the timing cover, the contact breaker pulse sensor leads and the alternator leads.

Detach the engine torque stay by removing the securing nut at each rocker box and removing the nut and bolt at the frame.

Disconnect the tachometer cable (where fitted) by unscrewing the union nut at the drive gearbox on the left side crankcase.

Detach the carburetter(s) see Section B8.

Drain the oil from the reservoir by removing the drain plug situated at the base of the main frame tube behind the gearbox. Allow to drain into a suitable receptacle for approximately 10 minutes. The oil feed pipe and return pipe should then be disconnected from the base of the reservoir and from below the oil filter neck respectively.

Detach rocker feed pipe by undoing the two dome nuts at the rocker spindles.

At this stage it is advisable to drain the oil from the gearbox and primary chaincase by removing the respective drain plugs. (See Section A2). The sump should also be drained; this is done by unscrewing the hexagon headed filter drain plug situated underneath the engine adjacent to the bottom engine mounting-lug. (See Fig. A2, No.4).

Slacken off the clutch adjustment at the handlebar, withdraw the rubber sleeve from the clutch abutment at the gearbox and unscrew the abutment. Unscrew and remove the plug on the gearbox outer cover. Slip the bottom nipple of the clutch cable free of the operating arm and withdraw the cable. (Fig B2, 1)

Disconnect the engine breather tubes at the rear left crankcase by loosening the clips.

Remove the chainguard by removing the front retaining bolt and loosening the left side bottom rear suspension unit bolt. Withdraw the guard from the rear of the machine.

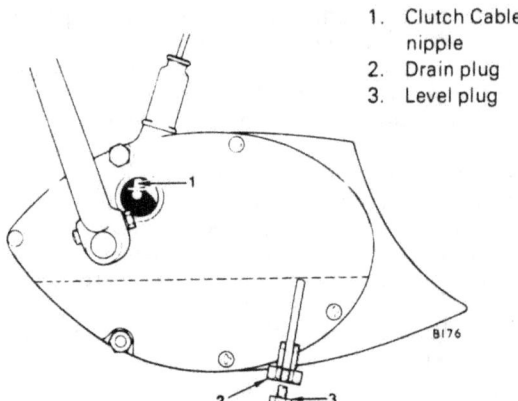

1. Clutch Cable nipple
2. Drain plug
3. Level plug

Fig. B2. Clutch cable adjustment and gearbox drain

Remove the connecting link from the rear chain and withdraw the chain from the gearbox sprocket.

Remove the left and right side footrests. These are retained by bolts that screw into the engine plates

Detach the two rear engine plates by removing the ten nuts and bolts.

Remove the bottom and front engine mounting studs. Note assembly of distance pieces on both these studs. The wider distance pieces fit on the right side of the machine in each case and the narrow ones on the opposite side.

It is now possible to remove the engine unit from the left side, but as the unit weighs approximately 135lbs. (61kg.) the use of a second operator or a small hoist is advised.

Replacement is the reversal of the above instructions. To ensure that the wiring harness is reconnected correctly refer to the appropriate wiring diagram in Section H19.

Do not forget to fit the distance pieces on the engine mounting studs.

For correct grade and quantity of lubricant for the engine, gearbox and chaincase, see Section A1.

SECTION B2

REMOVING AND REPLACING THE ROCKER BOXES

Disconnect the leads from the battery terminals and remove the fuel tank as detailed in Section E1.

Remove the torque stay by removing the nut at each rocker box and the bolt and nut at the frame.

Unscrew the two domed nuts from the rocker spindles and disconnect the rocker oil feed pipe. Care should be taken not to bend the pipe excessively as this may ultimately result in a fracture.

Remove the rocker inspection covers.

Unscrew three nuts from the studs fitted to the underside of the exhaust rocker box. Remove the outer exhaust rocker box securing bolts and unscrew the central hexagon retaining bolts. (Note that, at this stage the rocker box may rise slightly, due to a valve spring being compressed). The exhaust rocker box is now free to be removed. The procedure is the same for the inlet rocker box.

Care should be taken to collect the six plain washers which are fitted (one beneath each of the underside securing nuts), as they sometimes adhere to the cylinder head flanges and may be subsequently lost.

After completion of the rocker box removal operation, the push rods should be withdrawn and stored in the order of their removal so that they can be replaced in their original positions.

The junction surfaces of the rocker boxes and cylinder head should be cleaned for reassembly, by means of a soft metal scraper.

Replacement is a reversal of the above instructions.

When replacing the push rods place a small amount of grease into the bottom cup of each of the push rods, then locate the push rods, one at a time, by means of feeling the engagement of the tappet ball end and the push rod cup, and then testing the resistance to lifting caused by suction between the dome of the tappet and push rod cup. When the push rods are correctly located, remove the sparking plugs and turn the engine over until the INLET push rods are level and at the bottom of their stroke. The inlet rocker box should then be assembled. Repeat this procedure for the exhaust rocker box.

Before finally clamping the rocker boxes in position, check that the valves are being operated by turning the engine over slowly.

NOTE: It is important that the four central rocker box bolts are tightened to the correct torque setting. (See GENERAL DATA). The setting must be less than that of the cylinder head bolts which the rokker box bolts screw into.

Before fitting the rocker oil feed pipe the four copper washers which fit over the rocker spindle should be annealed by quenching in water from cherry red heat. Finally, remove any scale that may have formed. Annealing softens the copper thus restoring its original sealing qualities.

SECTION B3

INSPECTING THE PUSHRODS

When the pushrods have been removed, examine them for worn, chipped or loose endcups; also check that the push rod is true by rolling it slowly on a truly flat surface (such as piece of plate glass).

Bent pushrods are found to be the cause of excessive mechanical noise and loss of power and should be straightened if possible, or, preferably, renewed.

SECTION B4

STRIPPING AND REASSEMBLING THE ROCKER BOXES

Removal of the rocker spindles from the rocker boxes is best achieved by driving them out, using a soft metal drift. When the spindles are removed the rocker arms and washers can be withdrawn. All parts should be thoroughly cleaned in paraffin (kerosene) and the oil drillings in the spindles and rocker arms should be cleaned with a jet of compressed air.

Remove the oil seals from the rocker spindles and renew them.

If it is required to renew the rocker ball pins, the old ones should be removed by means of a suitable drift.

To ensure an oil-tight seal between the rocker box and cylinder head, in cases where an oil leak cannot be cured by fitting new gaskets, the joint surface of the rocker box should be linished to remove any irregularities.

An effective finish can be achieved by first extracting the rocker box studs (two nuts locked together on the stud should facilitate an easy removal) then lightly rubbing the junction surface on a sheet of emery cloth mounted on a truly flat surface (such as a piece of plate glass).

Assembly of the rocker spindles into the rocker boxes is assisted by the use of the oil seal compressor 61-7019. Fig B4.

The following method of assembly incorporates the use of a home made alignment bar, which can be made from a $7/16$ in. dia. bolt x 6in. long by grinding a taper at one end.

Before reassembly note that the four plain washers on each rocker spindle are of differing size. The inside ones have a $1/2$ in. dia. hole and the outside ones have a $3/8$ in. dia. hole.

Smear two plain washers with grease and place them one either side of the centre bearing boss. Place the left rocker arm in position, bringing it into line with the alignment tool and slide a plain washer and a spring washer (in the order shown in Fig. B3) into position. Carefully repeat this procedure for the other rocker arm and spring washer and slide the last plain washer into position. Finally bring each rocker arm in turn into line with the alignment bar.

Lubricate the spindle with oil and slide it (complete with oil seal) through the compressor (61-7019) and has far as possible into the rocker box, finally tapping it home with a hammer and soft metal drift (see Fig. B4).

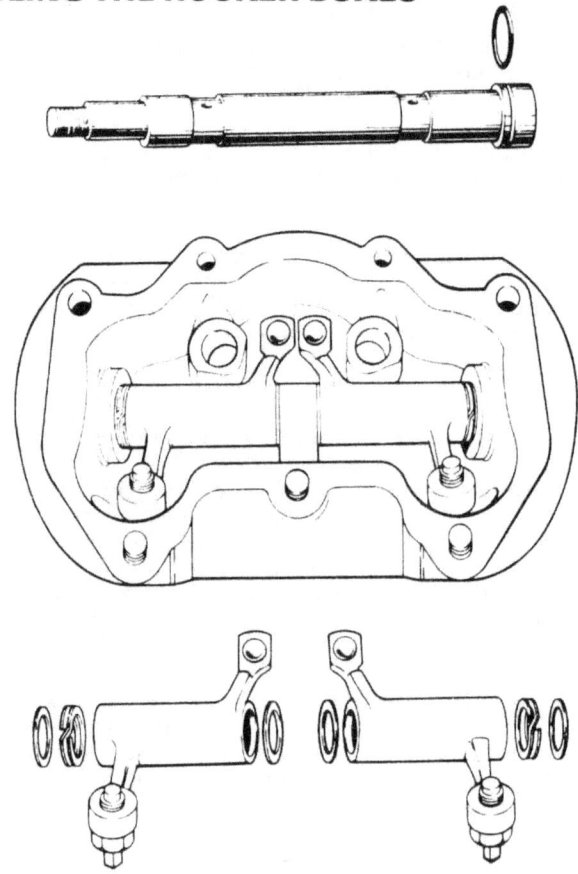

Fig. B3. Rocker box assembly

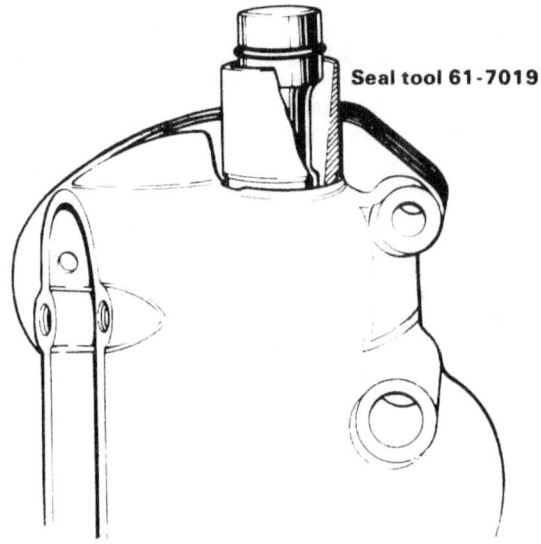

Seal tool 61-7019

Fig. B4. Refitting the rocker spindle

SECTION B5

ADJUSTING THE VALVE ROCKER CLEARANCES

The valve rocker clearance should be checked and adjusted if necessary every 3,000 miles (4,800Km.). The correct clearance, for the type of camshaft employed, ensures that a high valve operating efficiency is maintained and that the valves attain their maximum useful lives. The correct clearances are given in "Technical Data".

NOTE: Adjustments should only be made when the engine is COLD.

There are four adjusters on the rockers which are accessible after removing the inspection covers from the rocker boxes. A feeler gauge of the correct thickness can then be inserted. (See Fig. B5). The clearance must always be checked when the engine is cold. It will be easiest to find the correct point of the stroke to adjust the valve clearance if the machine is placed on the centre stand, top gear engaged and the sparking plugs removed. By revolving the rear wheel slowly the crankshaft will be turned and the valves can be positioned.

Inlet valves (towards the rear of the engine)

Turn the rear wheel until one of the inlet rockers moves downwards, thus opening the valve. When this valve is fully open the operating mechanism of the other inlet valve will be seated on the base of the cam and clearance can now be checked and adjusted if necessary. The clearance is correct when a feeler gauge of the correct thickness is a tight sliding fit between the

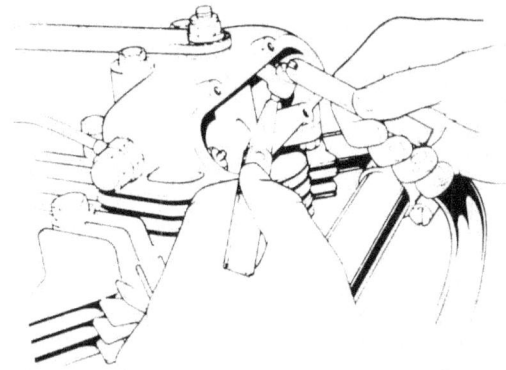

Fig. B5. Adjusting the valve rocker clearance

valve tip and the adjuster. Tighten the locknut and re-check the clearance. Having adjusted one inlet valve, turn the rear wheel until the valve which you have adjusted is now fully open and repeat the procedure for the other inlet valve.

Exhaust valves

Having adjusted the inlet valves proceed to the exhaust valves which are situated at the front of the engine. Proceed in the same way as for the inlet valves and position one valve fully open whilst you check the clearance on the other. See technical data for settings.

Check that the inspection cover gaskets are in good condition and replace the covers making sure that they are tight.

SECTION B6

REMOVING AND REPLACING THE AIR CLEANERS

The TR7 models have a similar air filter assembly to the T140 range except that it only has one aperture in the housing. Access is easily gained to the filter element by first removing the outer trim panels (disconnect the retaining springs) then removing the central fixing bolt and pulling the side cover away. The element can then be withdrawn.

On certain models the outer trim panels are retained by a centre fixing nut. Access to the filter is gained by first removing the blanking plug, then using an Allen Key undoing the centre fixing sleeve nut. The panel can then be lifted clear.

The element is constructed from surgical gauze bound with metal gauze. They may be washed in paraffin (kerosene) and finally cleaned with a jet of compressed air.

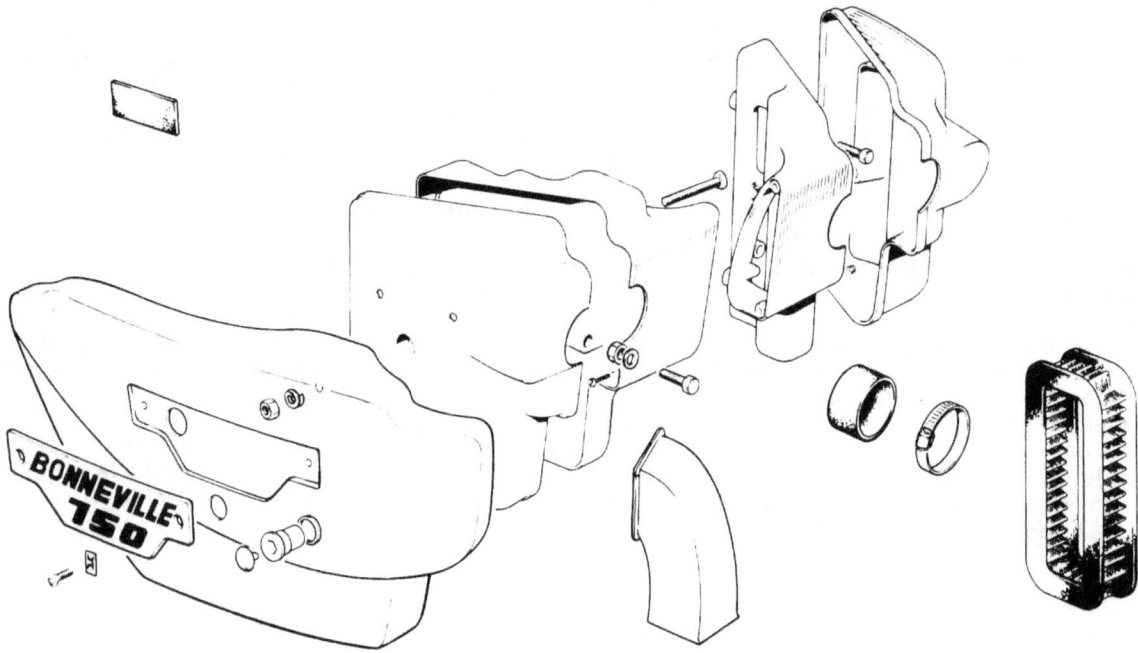

Fig. B6. Air cleaners (T140V shown)

ENGINE   B

AMAL MKI
CONCENTRIC CARBURETTOR TYPE 900
TR7/TR7T and TR65

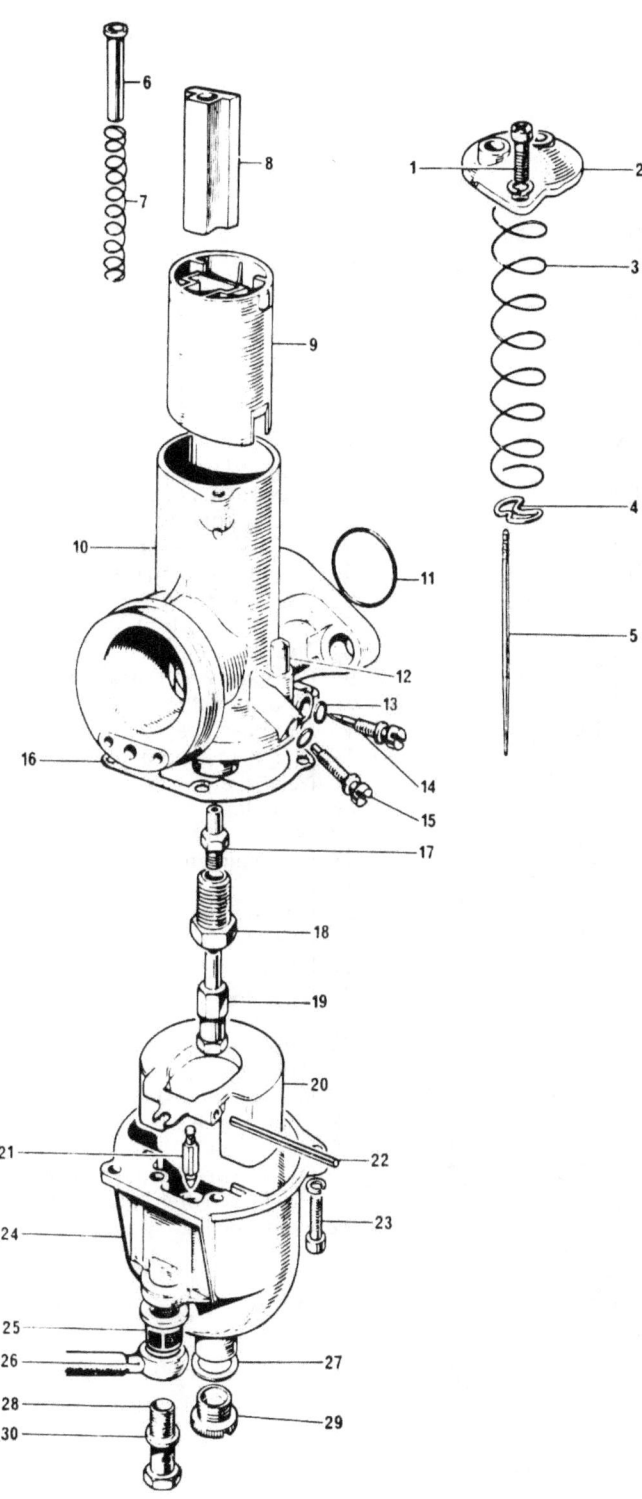

1. Carburettor complete
2. Mixing chamber
3. Chamber top
4. Screw
5. Throttle valve
6. Spring
7. Needle clip
8. Needle
9. Air slide
10. Spring
11. Guide sleeve
12. Stop screw
13. Air screw
14. 'O' ring
15. Needle jet
16. Jet holder
17. Main jet
18. Float bowl
19. Hinge pin
20. Float chamber
21. Joint gasket
22. Needle
23. Filter
24. Banjo bolt
25. Sealing washer
26. Drain plug
27. Sealing washer
26. Drainplug
27. Sealing washer
28. Banjo
29. 'O' ring

B11

AMAL MKII
CONCENTRIC CARBURETTER TYPE 2900 SERIES
T140E ONLY

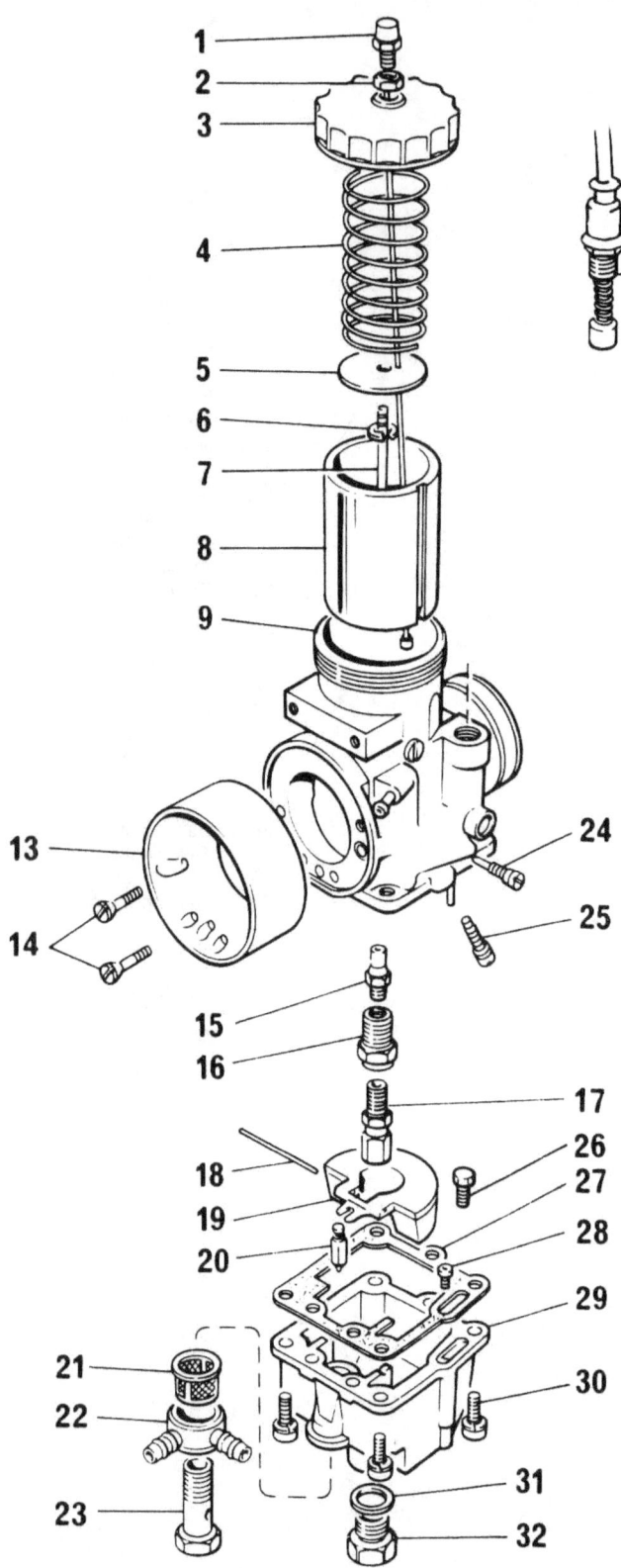

1 Cable adjuster
2 Cable-adjuster locknut
3 Mixing-chamber top
4 Throttle-slide spring
5 Needle retaining disc
6 Needle clip
7. Throttle needle
8 Throttle slide
9 Carburetor body assembly
10 Cold start plunger assembly
13 Air intake adaptor
14 Air intake adaptor securing screws
15 Needle jet
16 Jet holder
17 Main jet
18 Float spindle
19 Float
20 Float needle
21 Filter
22 Banjo
23 Banjo bolt
24 Pilot-air adjusting screw
25 Throttle-stop adjusting screw
26 Pilot jet
27 Float bowl washer
28 Cold start jet
29 Float bowl
30 Float bowl securing screws
31 Float-bowl drain-plug washer
32 Float-bowl drain-plug

ENGINE B

SECTION B7

AMAL CONCENTRIC CARBURETTER

DESCRIPTION

Amal concentric carburetters where fitted are fully adjustable. Briefly, they operate in the following way:

When the engine is idling, mixture is supplied from the pilot jet system, then as the throttle slide is raised, via the pilot by-pass. With the throttle just opening the mixture is controlled by the tapered needle working in the needle jet and finally by the size of the main jet. The pilot system is supplied by a pilot jet, fitted into the carburetter body. The main jet does not feed direct into the mixing chamber but discharges through the needle jet into the primary air chamber and the fuel goes from there as a rich petrol-air mixture through the primary air choke into the main air choke.

This primary air choke has a compensating action in conjunction with bleed holes in the needle jet, which serves the double purpose of air-compensating the mixture from the needle jet, and allowing the fuel to provide a well, outside and around the needle jet, which is available for snap acceleration. The idling mixture is controlled by the pilot air screw which governs the amount of air that is allowed to mix with the fuel at tick-over speeds. The throttle stop screw is used to adjust the slide so that the throttle is kept open sufficiently to keep the engine running at a slow tick-over, when the twist-grip is closed.

On T140 machines the carburetters are left and right handed to allow for easy adjustment of the pilot air and throttle stop screws.

The carburetter(s) have a drain plug provided in the base of the float bowl. This plug is hollow and collects foreign matter that may be present in the carburetter.

SECTION B8

REMOVING AND REPLACING THE CARBURETTER-AMAL

SINGLE CARBURETTOR MODELS ONLY AMAL MKI

Due to the carburetter top securing screws being inaccessible with the petrol tank fitted it will be necessary to dismount the carburetter before removing the top for any reason.

Ensure both taps are in the "Off" position and disconnect the fuel pipes at the taps beneath the rear of the tank. Unscrew the two carburetter flange securing nuts (self-locking) then carefully withdraw the carburetter from over its mounting studs at the same time disconnecting the rubber connector from the air box. Slacken the clip securing the single rubber connector lift off the cups and "O" ring.

As the carburetter is lowered, the top can be removed by taking out the two Phillips headed screws. Unless the top, slides etc. are to be removed from the cables they can be wrapped carefully in a piece of cloth until the carburetter is to be refitted.

When replacing the carburetter, great care should be taken to ensure that the slide does not become damaged as it is lowered into the mixture chamber. The peg at the top right of the slide locates in the corresponding groove in the carburetter body. Care must be taken when replacing the slide as the needle must be located in the needle jet, before the slide can be positioned in the mixing chamber. When the slide has been assembled satisfactorily, refit the mixing chamber top, two screws and lock washers.

Refit the 'O' ring to the carburettor flange.

Refit the carburetter over the locating studs followed by the rubber washers and cups.

Care should be taken not to overtighten the two carburetter securing nuts. Refitting continues as a reversal of the previous instructions.

T140 MODELS
AMAL MKII

Remove the petrol tank, see Section E I.

Remove both side cover trim panels, see Section B6, then remove the L.H. and R.H. air filter covers by removing central securing nut. Completely Remove the L.H. cross brace securing bolt. Remove both choke plunger assemblies by unscrewing main seating nut, and withdrawing plungers.

Disconnect the fuel feed pipe from the L.H. carburetter. Withdraw the retaining clip from the R.H. choke linkage and disconnect the linkage where fitted.

Slacken off the carburetter to cylinder head jubilee clips (4 off).

Withdraw the R.H. carburetter out to the R.H. side, disconnecting the cross brace for the L.H. carburetter at the same time where fitted.

Withdraw the L.H. carburetter then unscrew the top caps and withdraw the throttle slides.

Refitment is the reverse of the above instructions.

SECTION B9

STRIPPING AND REASSEMBLING THE CARBURETTER-AMAL MK.I & MK.II

When the carburetter is removed, disconnect the slide assembly from the throttle cable. To do this pull back the return spring and remove the needle and needle clip. With the spring still retracted, push the cable through the slide and when the nipple is clear, across the figure of eight slot. The slide and return spring (and needle retaining disc - T140E) can now be removed.

TR7T-TR65 AMAL MKI
To remove the air valve, push the valve guide tube and spring along the air cable until the cable nipple protrudes sufficiently out of its counterbore to be pushed out of the slot. The cable spring and guide can now be pulled clear of the valve.

T140 AMAL MKII
To remove the cold start enrichment device unscrew the plunger assembly and remove the lever and bracket assemblies or cable assemblies.

ALL MODELS
Unscrew the petrol pipe banjo connection and remove the banjo and nylon filter.

Unscrew four Phillips screws and remove the float bowl. The nylon float, spindle and triangular needle can now be withdrawn.

Unscrew the jet holder which will allow the main jet to be removed.

Unscrew the air adjusting screw and throttle stop screw.

Thoroughly clean all parts in paraffin (kerosene) several times and dry with compressed air, or a hand pump, to remove any particles of dirt. Any external deposits are best removed with the use of a light wire brush.

Reassemble in the reverse order, referring to Figs. B8 and B9 for guidance.

When refitting the float and needle valve, make certain that the recess on the valve is properly located in the "U" shaped slot in the float. Replace the float bowl sealing gasket, and if necessary, the two rubber "O" rings fitted to the adjusting screws.

When refitting the needle retaining disc on T140E carburetters only ensure the 'ear' on the disc faces downwards and locates against the lug inside the throttle valve casting. This prevents the throttle cable becoming twisted. See Fig. B9.

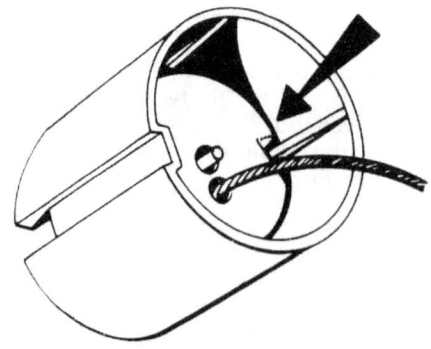

Fig. B9. T140E Needle retaining disc location

SECTION B10

INSPECTING THE CARBURETTER COMPONENTS - AMAL

The only parts liable to show wear after considerable mileage are the throttle valve slide and mixing chamber and the air slide.

(1) Inspect the throttle valve slide for excessive scoring to the front area and check the extent of wear on the rear slide face. If wear is apparent the slide should be renewed. In this case, be sure to replace the slide with the correct degree of cutaway (see "Technical Data").

(2) Examine the air valve for excessive wear and check that it is not actually worn through at any part. Check the fit of the air valve in the body. Ensure that the air valve spring is serviceable by inspecting the coils for wear.

(3) Inspect the throttle return spring for efficiency and check that it has not lost compressive strength.

(4) Check the needle jet for wear or possible scoring and carefully examine the tapered end of the needle for similar signs. Check the correct needle is in use.

(5) Check the float bowl joint surface for flatness and flatten if necessary on emery paper on a perfectly flat surface.

(6) Ensure that the float does not leak by shaking it to see if it contains any fuel. Do not attempt to repair a damaged float. A new one can be purchased for a small cost.

(7) Check the petrol filter, which fits into the petrol pipe banjo, for any possible damage to the mesh. Ensure that the filter has not parted from its supporting structure, thus enabling the petrol to by-pass it un-filtered.

(8) Concentric MKI carburetters have a pressed-in pilot jet which is not removable If the jet becomes blocked the machine will be hard to start and will not run at low speeds. This can be cleared by blocking the low speed air passage at the bell end of the carburettor removing the pilot air screw and using a jet of air at this point.

Concentric Mk II carburettors have a removeable jet, see page B12, which can be removed to clean.

(9) T140E carburetter only: Check the cold start enrichment plunger for cleanliness and correct seating - incorrect seating will cause rich running below 2500 RPM.

SECTION B11

CARBURETTER ADJUSTMENTS - AMAL

Throttle Stop Screw. This screw, which is situated on the right side of the carburetter (L.H. in case of the T140 left hand carburetter) sloping upwards and is fitted with a friction ring, should be set to open the throttle sufficiently to keep the engine running at a slow tick-over, when the twist-grip is closed.

Pilot Air Screw. To set the idling mixture, this screw, which is situated on the right side, is also fitted with a friction ring and should be screwed in to enrichen the tick-over mixture or outwards to weaken it. As a guide to its approximate required position, screw it in fully, then unscrew it approximately 2 ½ turns.

The screw controls the suction on the pilot jet by metering the amount of air which mixes with the petrol.

Needle and Needle Jet. Carburation is governed by the cut-away and needle jet in varying degrees from when the throttle is just open to when it is approximately ¾ full throttle. The needle jet orifice is governed by the position of the needle. The needle position should not be altered from its specified setting without specialist advice.

Throttle Valve Cutaway. The amount of cutaway to the bottom of the throttle valve slide is indicated by a number marked on the slide, e.g. 930 3½ means throttle type 930 with number 3 ½ cutaway; a larger number such as 4 means that the throttle valve slide has a slightly larger cutaway and consequently gives a weaker mixture during the period of throttle opening through which a cutaway is effective, i.e. from just open to approximately quarter throttle. Similarly, 3 indicates a slightly smaller cutaway and a slightly stronger mixture.

Jet Sizes. The recommended jet sizes are given in "General Data". The main jet is operative from approximately three quarter to full throttle, this is when the needle jet or orifice ceases to have any reduction effect on the petrol flow.

Float Level. The float level is correct when the light pressure being applied to the float at the seating position the float rests in the horizontal position in the float bowl. Adjustment can be made by tapping the needle seating up or down accordingly.

NOTE. Only the slightest deviation will be required due to the leverage ratio.

SECTION B12

TWIN CARBURETTER ARRANGEMENT - AMAL

DESCRIPTION

Twin AMAL carburetters are fitted to T140 machines. There is a balance pipe fitted between the inlet manifolds to improve tickover.

THROTTLE CABLE

The single throttle cable from the twistgrip enters a junction box where it is fitted into a slide. The twin shorter carburetter cables are fitted to the other side of the junction box slide. Both the slide and junction box being made of plastic require no maintenance.

A similar cable arrangement is used for choke operation on T140 models.

SETTING TWIN CARBURETTERS

The twin carburetters fitted to the T140 may require synchronisation and a simple method is as follows:

Start the motor and take off one plug lead and then adjust the pilot air screw and throttle stop screw in the OPPOSITE carburetter until the motor runs regularly. Replace the plug lead and repeat and process similarly for the other carburetter. With both plug leads replaced the tickover will be too fast and the stop screws should be lowered simultaneously until correct. It is most important the throttle slides lift simultaneously or the motor will run roughly, particularly when accelerating. Therefore adjust the cables from the junction box so that both have the same free play of 1mm.

SECTION B13

BING CONSTANT DEPRESSION CARBURETTER TYPE 64

DESCRIPTION

Bing Constant Depression Carburettors comprise a cross-draught, butterfly-valve carburettor with variable choke tube, double-float arranged centrally below the carburettor venturi and a rotary-valve type starting carburettor. They feature a throttle slide which is suspended from a roller diaphragm and projects into the venturi. It changes the smallest cross-section ("choke tube") of the venturi as a function of the vacuum at this point.

Fuel intake control

The float (40) of the carburettor consists of two plastic float elements joined by a metal hinge. The float is arranged centrally below the carburettor choke tube so that the carburettor can be tilted very far in all directions without impairing operation. The object of the float is to maintain the fuel level in the float chamber (44) constant. When the fuel has reached a specified level in the float chamber, then the float (40) mounted on pin (41) is lifted until the float needle valve, thus preventing any further supply of fuel. When the engine draws in fuel from the carburettor, the level in the float chamber (44) drops and so does the float. The float needle then opens the valve again and allows fuel to flow in from th tank.

The float needle valve regulates the fuel supply in conjunction with the float but it does not act as a stop valve when the engine is at a standstill. Minute foreign bodies may be deposited between the valve seat and the needle tip, thus preventing complete closure of the valve. When stopping the engine, therefore, the fuel cock on the tank should always be closed. In addition the fuel should be filtered before it reaches the carburettor. The filter should be selected so that foreign bodies greater than 0.1mm are filtered out and the fuel supply is not impeded to too great an extent.

The float needle (42) contains a spring-loaded plunger which contacts the float hinge.

ENGINE B

This absorbs vibrations of the float (40). In addition the float needle (42) is connected to the float hinge by the retaining spring (43) to prevent it from moving between float and valve seat and thus reducing the fuel supply. Spring and retaining guide make a considerable contribution towards keeping the fuel level in the float chamber constant.

When fitting a new float, the fuel level must be adjusted. When doing this care must be taken to ensure that the fuel needle spring is not compressed by the float weight. It is therefore advisable to put the carburettor in a horizontal position until the float just contacts the float needle. In this position the pointer on the float hinge is set in such a way that the float top edges are parallel to the top edge of the float chamber.

The float chamber (44) is secured to the carburettor housing by a spring yoke (45). A seal (46) is provided between float chamber and carburettor housing. the space above th fuel level is connected to atmosphere by two ducts. When these ducts are blocked, an air cushion forms above the fuel level. The fuel will not lift the float sufficiently to close the needle valve and the carburettor overflows.

The float chamber (44) incorporates an overflow pipe to allow fuel to drain off if the specified level in the float chamber is exceeded substantially due to a faulty needle valve.

Main regulating system with pressure regulator

The amount of mixture drawn in by the engine and thus its performance is determined by the cross-sectional area in the choke tube which is opened up by the throttle valve (23). The throttle valve is secured to the valve shaft (24) and two screws (25). The end projecting for the carburettor housing carries the throttle levers (27) and (28) which are secured by the nut (30) and washer (29) to which the Bowden cable is attached which is used to operate the throttle shaft. The sealing ring (26) provides the seal between valve shaft and housing. The retaining arm (31) attached to the carburettor housing by means of screws (32) and washers (33) engages the notch in the valve shaft and thus prevents it from moving in axial direction. The return spring (35) whose action opposes the Bowden cable is attached between a bent-over tab at the lower end of the retaining arm and the throttle lever (28).

If the throttle valve (23) is opened while the engine is running, the increased air flow in the choke tube results in a vacuum building up at the outlet of the needle jet (3) which draws fuel from the float chamber through the jet system. At low speeds and in particular in the case of four-stroke engines, this vacuum is not sufficient for an adequate fuel supply; it must therefore be increased artificially by using a pressure regulator. For this purpose BING constant depression carburettors are provided with a plunger (13) operating in conjunction with a diaphragm (16); which reduces the cross-sectional area of the needle jet outlet by virtue of its own weight, and thus increases air velocity and vacuum at this point.

The plunger (13) is located centrally in the cover (20) which is secured to the carburettor housing by screws (21). The diaphragm (16) is connected to the plunger (13) by a retaining ring (17) and four screws (18) and washers (19) each. The vacuum in the choke tube acts on the top of the diaphragm and the plunger via a bore (U) in the plunger (13) and attempts to lift the plunger against its own weight. The considerably lower vacuum between air filter anc arburettor is applied to the underside of the diaphragm via duct (V) as a reference pressure.

If the throttle valve (23) is opened when the plunger (13) is closed, then a vacummn will build up in the small cross-section at the bottom of the plunger (13) which is sufficient to provide a supply of fuel. the eight of the plunger (13) is matched in such a way that this vacuum will be maintained with increasing speed until the plunger has fully opened the carburettor cross-section. From this point onwards the carburettor acts as a throttle valve carburettor with fixed choke tube. The vacuum increases with increasing speed.

The space in the cover (20) above the plunger guide is vented through bore (D). Its diameter is designed in such a way that it acts as a restrictor for air flowing in and out therefore acts as a vibration damper for the plunger.

On its way from the float chamber to the choke tube the fuel passes through the main jet (1), the jet stock (10) and the needle jet (3); as it leaves the needle jet it is pre-mixed with air which is brought in from the air filter via an air duct (Z) and the atomizer (2) in an annular flow around the needle jet. This air flow assists the atomizing process to form minute fuel droplets and thus favourably affects the fuel distribution in the intake manifold and combustion in the engine.

The conical section of the jet needle (4) which is secured to the plunger (13) with the retaining spring (14) and the serrated washer (15) engages into the needle jet (3). Depending on the dimension of the flat cone at the end of the jet needle, the annular gap between jet needle and needle jet is enlarged or decreased and thus the fuel supply is throttled to a lesser or greater extent. The jet needle (4) can be located in the plunger (13) in four different positions which, similarly to the jet needle cone, affect the amount of fuel drawn in. For example "needle position 3" means that the jet needle has been suspended from the retaining spring (14) with the third notch from the top. To achieve the height adjustment the jet needle is turned through 90 and pushed up or down, the retaining spring engaging the next notch in the jet needle. If the needle is suspended higher up,

ENGINE

this will result in a richer mixture and vice versa.

In short the main regulating system is set using main jets and needle jets of various diameters and also jet needles, plungers and pistons of various types.

Between main jet (1) and nozzle stock (10) a washer (12) is provided which, together with the float chamber, forms an annular gap. In particularly severe operating conditions this ensures that the fuel is not spun away from the main jet.

A rubber ring (11) seals the nozzle stock (10) off from the carburettor housing to avoid any fuel being drawn in via the thread and thus bypassing the main jet.

Idling System
During idling and low-load running the throttle valve (23) is closed to such an extent that the air flow underneath plunger (13) no longer forms a sufficient vacuum. The fuel is then supplied via an auxiliary system, the idling system, which consists of the ilding jet (5), the idling air jet (LLD) - no spare part - and the mixture control screw (7) which is sealed off against the carburettor housing by the rubber ring (9) and secured by spring (8) to prevent it from becoming slack. The fuel passes through the idling jet (5) whose bore will determine the amount of fuel. Behind the jet bore the fuel mixes with air which is supplied via cross ducts in the jet throat from the idling air channel, the amount of air admitted being determined by the size of the idling air jet at the inlet of this duct. This initial mixture then flows through the idling outlet bore (LA), the cross-sectional area of which can be adjusted by the mixture control screw (7); it then reaches the choke tube via bypass or transition passages (BP) where it is mixed further with pure air.

Starting Carburettor
BING constant depression carburettors are provided with a rotary valve starting carburettor as an aid for starting a cold engine using a Bowden cable. A disc (47) resting against the carburettor housing is turned via a shaft in the starting carburettor housing (48) so that the starting carburettor chamber into which air enters from the air filter side of the carburettor is connected to the engine side of the main carburettor via a duct. The airport in the disc (47) is shaped in such a way that depending on the disc position, more or less air is drawn in. At the same time the disc opens the fuel system of the starting carburettor via bores matched to the disc position. The fuel flows from the float chamber through the starting jet into the vented starting chamber also contained in the float chamber (44) and from their through a riser where it is pre-mixed with air via transverse bores, into the starting carburettor. There it forms a particularly rich mixture with the air drawn in, and this mixture bypasses the main caburettor to flow into the intake manifold of the engine direct. During starting the throttle valve has to be closed to make sufficient vacuum available for the starting carburettor. Whent the engine is at a standstill and also during normal operation the fuel level in the float chamber compartment incorporating the riser will be the same as in the rest of the float chamber. When starting with opened-up starting carburettor, the fuel will initially be drawn in from this compartment which forms a very rich mixture. The fuel supplied subsequently will only be the amount allowed through by the starting jet. This ensures that, once the engine has started, it is not supplied with an exfessively rich mixture and stalled. The starting carburettor is therefore matched to any given engine by modifying the starting jet and matching the space behind it.

The starting carburettor is secured to the carburettor housing by four screws (51) and protected against ingress of dirt and water by the seal (50) between the two. The starting shaft is also sealed against the starting carburettor housing by a rubber ring (49).

ENGINE

BING

CONSTANT DEPRESSION CARBURETTOR
TYPE 64

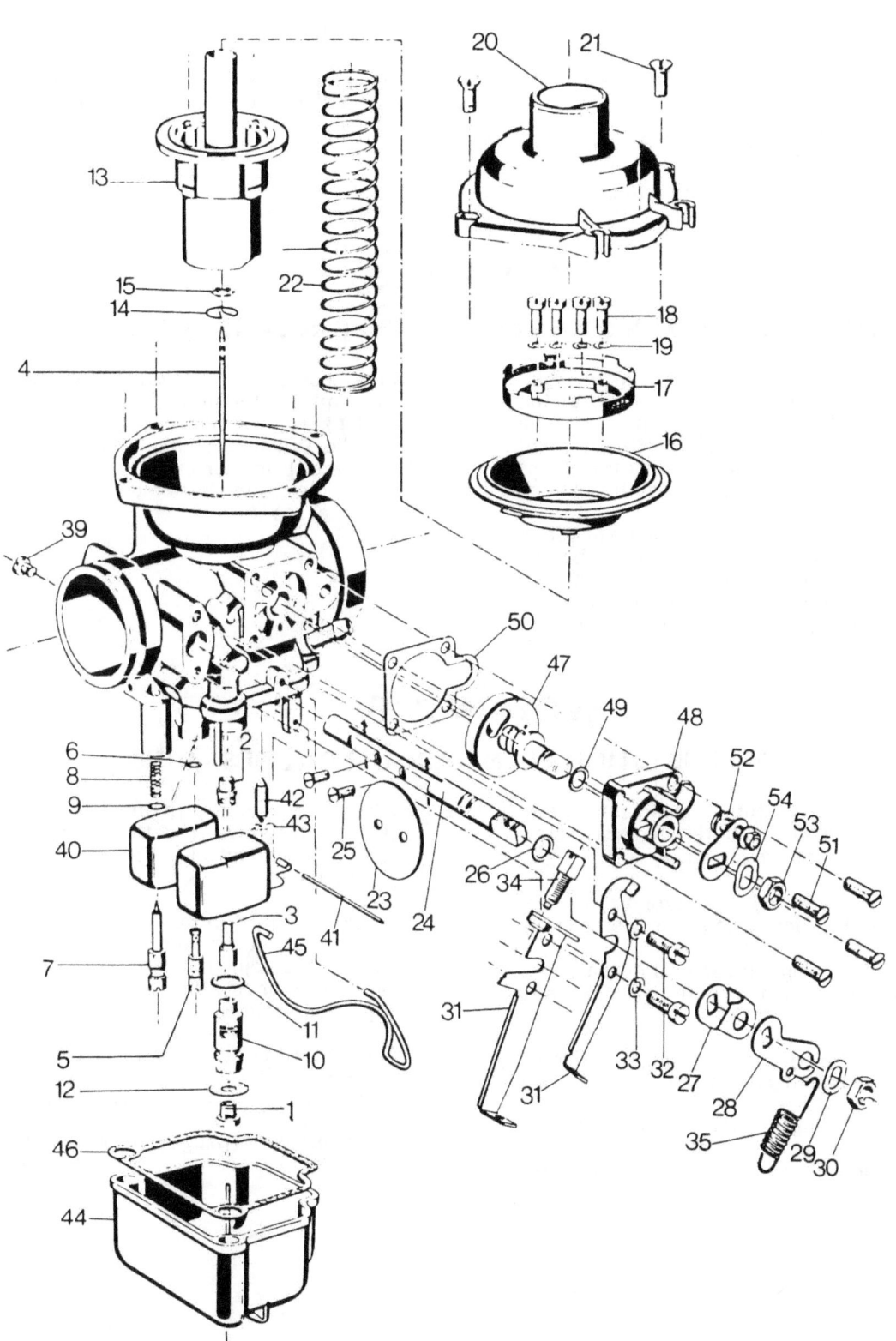

SECTION B14

REMOVING AND REPLACING THE BING CARBURETTER

Remove the petrol tank. See section E1.

Remove both side cover styling panels by releasing centre allen fixing screw.

Release both throttle and choke cables from carburettor see section E8.

Undo petrol pipe balanance at one carburettor.

Undo balance tube at one carburettor

Release jubilee clip at carburettor mounting to engine

Withdraw carburettor from mounting stub.

Replace by reversing the above procedure paying particular attention to obtaining correct Synchronisation. See section B16.

SECTION B15

STRIPPING AND REASSEMBLING THE BING CARBURETTER

The float bowl is attached by a spring clip. Pushing this clip towards the intake end of the carburettor will cause the clip to pivot and the float bowl can then be removed. When refitting the float bowl ensure that it enters the recess correctly before springing the clip into position.

Should it be necessary to remove the piston or diaphragm ensure that during reassembly the diaphragm locating segments are correctly positioned relative to the piston itself and to the carburettor body when assembling the piston.

The piston needle can be withdrawn by pinching between thumb and forefinger and partially rotating whilst keeping a gentle pulling pressure on the needle. When reassembling ensure the needle is entered in the correct groove. As this is a blind assembley count the number of clicks as the needle passes its retainer.

SECTION B16

SETTING THE IDLING WITH VACUUM GAUGES - BING

1. Screw the mixture adjustment screws fully in on both carburettors and unscrew by ¾ of a rotation on each.

2. Run Engine until normal running temperature is reached and then stop engine.

3. Remove balance pipe from both carburettors and attach vacuum gauge pipes to each of the nozzles.

4. Start engine and note the readings on both vacuum gauges.

    If one gauge reads higher, adjust the idling stop screw at the carburettor attached to that side i.e. open the throttle flap.

5. If the idling speed is too high. Unscrew the idling stop screws on both carburettors by an even amount and balance out again as under 4.

6. Check the mixture composition: The idling speed must go down when turning the mixture adjustment screw in either direction. From the best of optimum setting balance out as under 4.

7. Accelerate gently. An unbalanced reading on one side indicates that the cables are not sychronised, adjust as required.

8. Remove vacuum gauge pipes and reconnect balance pipe.

SECTION B17

REMOVING AND REPLACING THE EXHAUST SYSTEM

ALL T140 AND TR7 MODELS
To remove the complete exhaust system first slacken the two fin clip securing bolts and the balance tube clamps forward of the cylinder head. Remove the two screws from the front attachment brackets and slacken both silencer to exhaust pipe clips.

Now using a hide mallet tap both exhaust pipes away from the cylinder head so that they are removed together. This will allow the balance tube to be detached from between the pipes.

Remove the silencers from the machine by detaching the pillion footrests.

Replacement of the exhaust system is the reversal of the above instructions. Remember to assemble the exhaust pipes to the head together in one operation with the balance tube and clips in between their respective stubs. Finally tighten all nuts and bolts securely.

SECTION B18

REMOVING AND REFITTING THE CYLINDER HEAD ASSEMBLY

Proceed as detailed in Section B2 for removal of the rocker boxes and pushrods.

Remove the exhaust system as in Section B17.

Detach the carburetter(s) from the cylinder head, (see section B8), and place well clear of the cylinder head.

Unscrew the ten cylinder head bolts/nuts, a turn at a time, until the load has been released.

Remove the push rod cover tubes and note that it is essential to renew the rubber seals. Check for sharp edges on the corners of the top portion of the tappet guide blocks which could cut the new 'O' rings when reassembling. Use a file or emery cloth to smooth any such sharp edges.

REFITTING THE CYLINDER HEAD
Ensure that the junction surfaces of the cylinder block, gasket and cylinder head are clean. Grease the gasket and place it in position. Coat the tappet guide blocks with heavy grease and locate the push rod cover tubes (complete with top oil seals). Relieve any roughness at the push rod tube counterbores in the head.

Lower the cylinder head into position over the push rod cover tubes and fit the cylinder head bolts/finger tight, also, fit the central nuts finger tight.

Tighten the ten cylinder head bolts/nuts in the order given in Fig. B12 and to the torque settings given in "Technical Data". Refit the rocker boxes as detailed in Section B2.

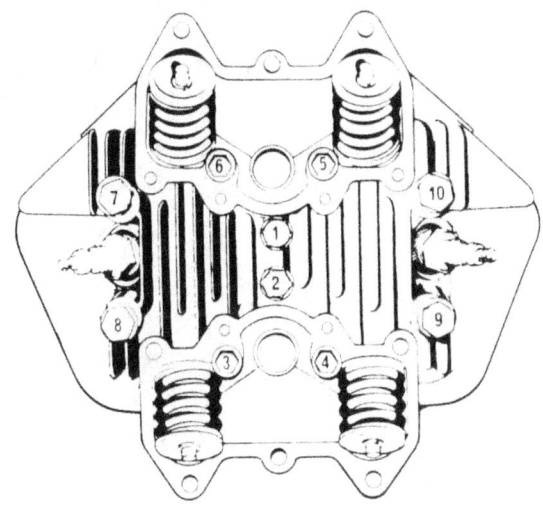

Fig. B12. Cylinder head bolt tightening sequence (T140V shown)

To facilitate torquing the inner head nuts (A) Fig B13 use service tool 61-7010.

IMPORTANT
Re-torque the cylinder head bolts/nuts after the engine has thoroughly warmed up for the first time, i.e. Run the machine for approximately 5 miles then re-torque when cool and reset tappet clearances as detailed in B5.

This procedure must also be carried out at 500 miles from fitting a replacement head gasket.

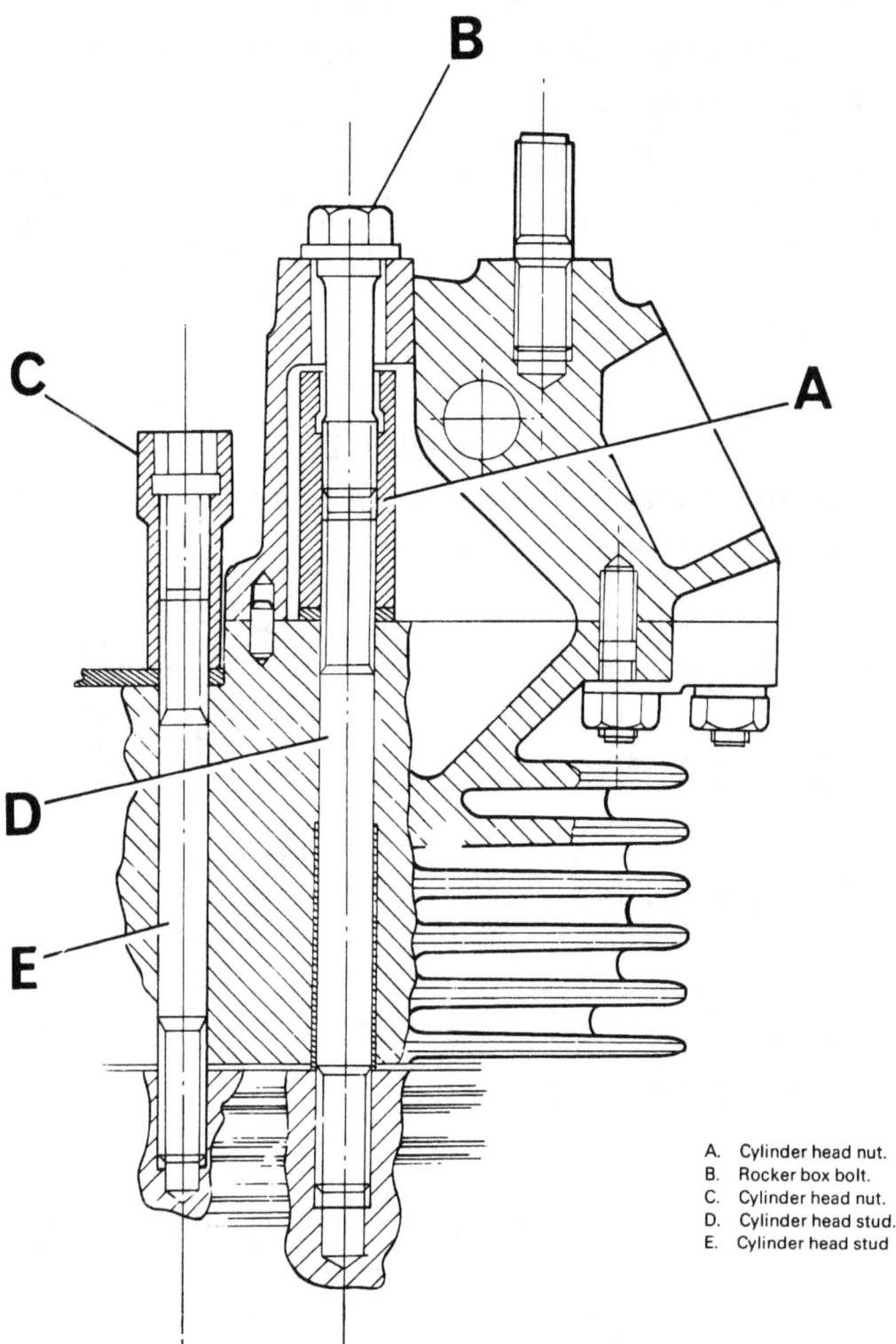

Fig. B13. Showing assembly of cylinder head studs and nuts

A. Cylinder head nut.
B. Rocker box bolt.
C. Cylinder head nut.
D. Cylinder head stud.
E. Cylinder head stud

SECTION B19

REMOVING AND REFITTING THE VALVES

Removal of the valves is facilitated by means of a "G" clamp type valve spring compressor. When the spring is compressed sufficiently, the split cotters can be removed with a narrow screwdriver, and the valve spring withdrawn when the compressor is released. As each valve is removed it should be marked so that it can be replaced in its original position.

NOTE: The inlet valves and the exhaust valves have differing head diameters and cannot be interposed.

Fitting a new or reground valve necessitates seating by the grinding in process described in Section B22, but it does not necessitate recutting the cylinder head valve seal unless new valve guides have been fitted.

The valve springs should be inspected for fatigue and cracks, and checked for wear by comparing them with a new spring or the dimension given in "Technical Data". Renew when spring is $1/8$" below given figure.

All parts should be thoroughly cleaned in paraffin (kerosene) and allowed to drain before reassembling.

Assemble the inner and outer springs and top and bottom cups over the valve guide, then slide

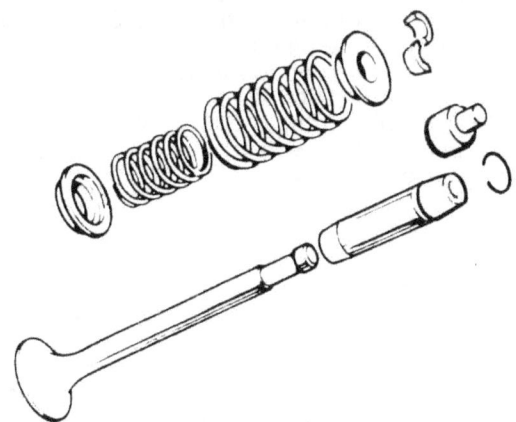

Fig. B14. Valve components

the valve into position lubricating the stem with a small amount of engine oil.

Compress the springs and slide the two halves of the split cotter into the exposed groove in the valve stem. Finally give the valve stem a sharp blow with hide mallet to seat cotters.

SECTION B20

RENEWING THE VALVE GUIDES

The valve guides can be pressed out using service tool 60-6063, with the cylinder head inverted on the bench.

The same method may be employed to fit the new guide. Lightly grease the valve guide to assist assembly. Ensure that the guide is pressed in until the circlip is flush with the cylinder head.

Bronze valve guides are fitted, the shorter ones being used in the inlet position.

Where new valve guides have been fitted it is necessary to re-cut the valve seats in the cylinder head and grind in the valves (see Section B22).

SECTION B21

DECARBONISING

It is not normally advisable to remove the carbon deposits from the combustion chamber and exhaust ports until symptoms indicate that decarbonising is necessary.

Such symptoms as falling off in power, loss of compression, noisy operation and difficult starting are all indications that decarbonising may be necessary.

When the cylinder head is removed unscrew the sparking plugs, have them grit-blasted and checked. Before fitting the plugs, check that the gap setting is correct (see "Technical Data".)

If special decarbonising equipment is not available then a blunt aluminium scraper or a piece of lead solder flattened at one end, should be used to remove the carbon deposits. Do not use a screw-driver or a steel implement of any kind on an aluminium surface.

When removing the deposits from the piston crown, a ring of carbon should be left round the periphery of the pistons to maintain the seal. Also the carbon ring round the top of the cylinder bore should not be disturbed. To facilitate this an old piston ring should be placed on top of the piston, level with the top surface of the cylinder block.

Remove the valves as shown in Section B19 then remove the carbon deposits from the valve stems, combustion chamber and ports of the cylinder head. Remove all traces of carbon dust by means of a jet of compressed air or the vigorous use of a tyre pump, then thoroughly clean the cylinder head and valves in paraffin (kerosene). Finally, check the valves for pitting. If necessary, the valves can be ground-in with carborundum paste. See B22.

SECTION B22
RE-SEATING THE VALVES

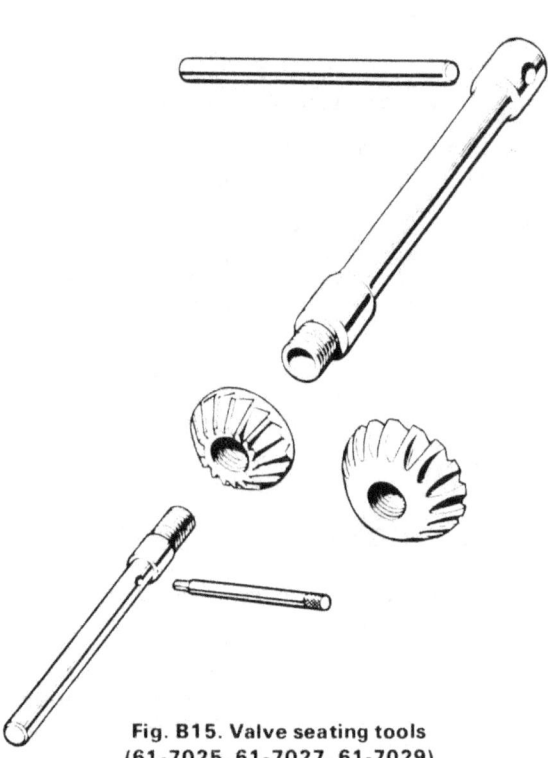

Fig. B15. Valve seating tools
(61-7025, 61-7027, 61-7029)

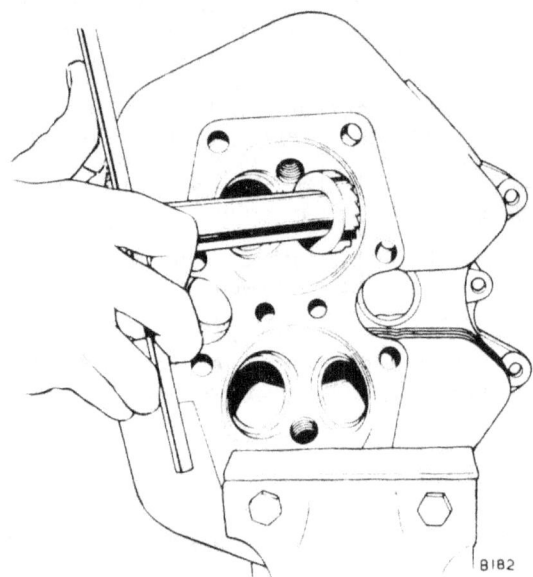

Fig. B16. Cutting a valve seat

Where the valve guides have been renewed or the condition of a valve seat is doubtful, it is advisable to re-cut the cylinder head valve seat then grind in the valve, using a fine grade grinding-in paste.

It is important that the cylinder head valve seat and the valve guide bore should be concentric. For the purpose of re-cutting the valve seats the following service tools are available.

61-7025   Valve seat cutter inlet and exhaust
61-7027   Blending cutter inlet and exhaust
61-7029   Arbour pilot and tommy bar

The valve seat cutting operation should be carried out with the greatest care, and only a minimum amount of metal should be removed.

After the seats have been re-cut, they should be blended to give an even seating of 3/32in. (2.4mm.).

Examine the face of the valve to see if it is pitted, scored or damaged. If necessary, the face can be reground, but excessive re-grinding is not advisable for this adversely affects the heat transference properties of the valve and will ultimately result in critical pocketing.

The stem of the valve should be inspected for wear or scuffing and if either is pronounced, the valve should be renewed.

To grind in the valve use a fine grade carborundum grinding paste. Place a small amount evenly on the valve seat and place the valve in its guide and a holding tool attached.

Use a semi-rotary motion, occasionally lifting the valve and turning it through 180°. Continue this process until a uniform seal results. Wash

ENGINE B

the parts in paraffin (kerosene) to remove the grinding paste. Apply a smear of "Engineer's" marking blue to the seat of the valve. Rotate the valve through one revolution and inspect both seats. Successful valve grinding will give an unbroken ring of blue on the valve seat.

Alternatively, assemble the springs and split cotters and pour a small amount of paraffin (kerosene) into the port. It should not penetrate the seating for at least 10 seconds if a good seal has been achieved.

Prior to reassembling the cylinder head, ensure that all traces of "Blue" or grinding paste are removed by thoroughly washing in paraffin (kerosene).

SECTION B23

REMOVING AND REPLACING THE CYLINDER BLOCK AND TAPPETS

Wedge a dis-used shock absorber rubber, or a suitable retainer between the inlet and exhaust tappets to prevent the tappets from falling through the tappet block into the crankcase when the cylinder block is removed. Turn the engine until the pistons are at T.D.C. then unscrew the 12 point nuts from the base of the cylinder block and remove the washers, carefully raise the block clear of the pistons.

Raise the block sufficiently to insert non-fluffy rag into the crankcase mouth. It is also advisable at this stage to fit four rubber protectors (e.g. gear change lever rubbers) over four cylinder base studs (see Fig. B17) to avoid any damage to the alloy connecting rods. Remove the cylinder and ensure that the two locating dowels are in their correct position in the crankcase.

Remove the tappets from the cylinder block storing them in the order of their removal, and thoroughly clean all parts in paraffin (kerosene). It is important that the tappets are replaced in their original positions; failure to observe this may result in subsequent excessive tappet and cam wear.

If it has been decided to fit new piston rings then the bores must be lightly honed as described in Section B27.

Lubricant is supplied under pressure direct to the exhaust tappet and camshaft working faces as described in Section A2.

When replacing the cylinder block ensure that the cylinder base gasket is not fitted in such a way that the oil feed hole incorporated in the crankcase and cylinder block is obscured, so preventing lubricants from reaching the tappets. This only applies to engines before No. EDA 30,000.

If for any reason the tappet guide block is removed, it should be refitted as described in

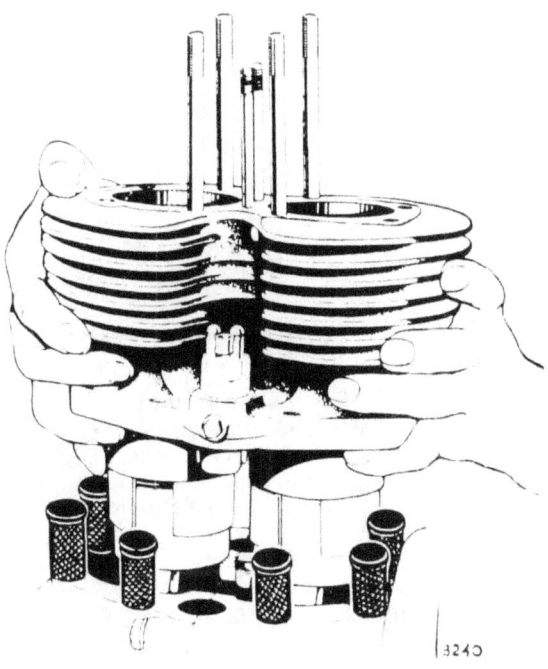

Fig. B17. Refitting the cylinder block

Section B25, but the oil feed holes should be checked to ensure that they are not blocked by foreign matter.

The correct method of assembly of the tappets is shown in Fig. B18. The machined cutaway faces (C) should be facing the outside of the tappet guide block, i.e. the tappets must not be fitted with the cutaways facing one another, otherwise the oil holes (B) drilled in the annular groove of the tappet block (A) will not be able to supply lubricant to the tappets. This only applies to engines before No. EDA 30,000

Care should be taken to ensure that the cylinder block is correctly located over the two dowels in the left half-crankcase.

The tappets should be well lubricated prior to wedging them in their original positions in the tappet guide blocks. To facilitate an easy assembly of the cylinder block over the pistons, two collars, part number 616135 are required. The collars should be placed over the pistons to compress the piston rings, and withdrawn over the connecting rods when the pistons are sufficiently engaged in the block. Refit the eight cylinder base nuts.

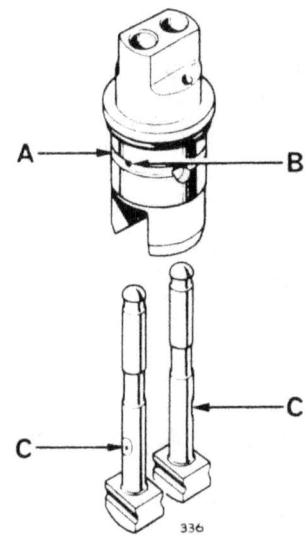

Fig. B18. Showing the correct method of assembly of the exhaust tappets
PRE Engine No. EDA 30,000

SECTION B24

INSPECTING THE TAPPETS AND GUIDE BLOCKS

The base of the tappet is fitted with a "Stellite" tip. This material has good wear resisting qualities but the centre of the tip may show signs of slight indentation. If the width of the indentation exceeds $3/32$ in. then the tappet should be renewed.

It is not necessary to remove the tappet guide blocks for inspection purposes; the extent of wear can be estimated by rocking the tappet whilst it is in position in the guide block. It should be a sliding fit with little or no sideways movement, (See "Technical Data" for working clearances).

Excessive play between the tappets and guide block may cause undesirable mechanical noise.

SECTION B25

RENEWING THE TAPPET GUIDE BLOCKS

Place the cylinder block in an inverted position on the bench. Remove the locking screw and drift out the guide block using service tool 61-6008, as shown in Fig. B19.

"O" ring oil seals are fitted between the tappet blocks and cylinder block. The seals must be replaced whenever oil leakage is noted at this point or whenever the tappet blocks are removed and refitted. Under no circumstances must the tappet guide blocks be interchanged. The exhaust tappets are pressure lubricated through the exhaust tappet guide block and the oilways must therefore be cleaned out carefully before assembly. (Only applicable to Pre EDA 30,000 engines.

To fit the new guide block, first grease the outer surface to assist assembly, then align the location hole in the guide block and cylinder block base, and drive in the guide block using 61-6008, until the shoulder is flush with the flange.

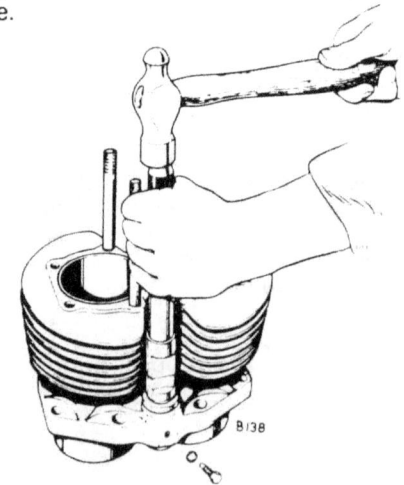

Fig. B19. Refitting a tappet guide block

ENGINE

SECTION B26

REMOVING AND REFITTING THE PISTONS

It is most important that the alloy connecting rods are not damaged by contact with the sharp crankcase edge. For this reason four gear lever rubbers should be placed over the four central cylinder base studs.

Remove the inner and outer circlips and press out the gudgeon pin. The pistons are then free to be removed.

When the pistons are removed they should be suitably scribed inside so that they can be refitted in their original positions. When refitting the pistons, first place the inner circlip in position to act as a stop, then press the gudgeon pin into position.

It is advisable to renew the four circlips; this can be done for negligible cost.

Finally, check that all the gudgeon pin retainer circlips are in position, and are correctly fitted. This is extremely important.

SECTION B27

REMOVING AND REPLACING THE PISTON RINGS

There should be little difficulty in removing piston rings, if the following procedure is adopted. Lift one end of the top piston ring out of the groove and insert a thin steel strip between the ring and piston. Move the strip round he piston, at the same time lifting the raised part of the ring upwards with slight pressure. The piston rings should always be lifted off and replaced over the top of the piston.

If the piston rings are to be refitted the carbon deposits on the inside surface of the rings must be removed and the carbon deposits in the piston ring grooves must also be removed.

When fitting new piston rings, the bores must be lightly honed with a fine-grade emery cloth so that the new piston rings can become bedded down properly. The honing should be carried out with an oscillatory motion up and down the bore until an even "criss-cross" pattern is achieved. The recommended grade of emery for this purpose is 300. Thoroughly wash the bores in paraffin (kerosene) and check that all traces of abrasives are removed.

Pistons and rings are available in ·010 and ·020 inches (·254 and ·508mm.) oversizes. When fitting new rings the gap must be checked in the lowest part of the cylinder bore. The ring must lie square to the bore for checking purposes, and to ensure this, place the piston crown onto the ring and ease it down the bore. Check the gap with feeler gauges.

Piston rings, when new, should have the following gap clearances:

Compression ring gap: 0.013 - 0.008"
(0.330 - 0.203mm)
Scraper ring gap: 0.010" - 0.008"
(0.254 - 0.203mm)

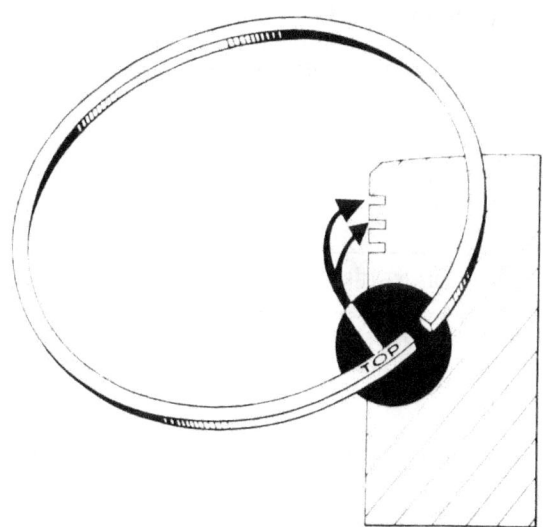

Fig. B20 Refitting a tapered piston ring

Refitting the piston rings is straight forward, but check that the two compression rings are fitted the right way up.

The two taper compression rings are marked "TOP" to ensure correct assembly, and should be fitted with the "TOP" marking towards the cylinder head (See Fig.B20).

ENGINE

SECTION B28

INSPECTING THE PISTONS AND CYLINDER BORES

PISTONS

Check the thrust areas of the piston skirt for signs of seizure or scoring.

The piston skirt is of a special oval form and is designed to have limited working clearances within the bore.

Prior to inspection, ensure that both the cylinder bores and the pistons are clean and free from dirt, etc. Any deposits of burnt oil round the piston skirt can be removed by using a petrol (gasolene) soaked cloth.

NOTE: The top lands of the piston have working clearance varying from ·016in. to ·020in. and thus allows the top piston ring to be viewed from above, and the piston to be rocked slightly. However, this is not critcal, it is the skirt clearances that are all-important.

CYLINDER BORES

The maximum wear occurs within the top half-inch of the bore, whilst the portion below the piston ring working area remains relatively unworn. A badly worn block will have a lip at the thrust faces of each bore about ¼ in. from top face. Previous symptoms such as smoking exhaust, heavy oil consumption and noisy pistons when cold also indicate that a rebore may be necessary.

CYLINDER BORE AND PISTON GRADING

Pistons and cylinder blocks are graded to suit one another during manufacturing. The pistons are identified by a letter stamped on the piston crown and the barrels by the same letter (see Fig. B21). Two different identifications are in use i.e. (L) and (H). Each letter stands for LOW and HIGH grades respectively. The grades with their corresponding dimensions are shown between the cylinder bores.

	CYLINDER BLOCK AND PISTON GRADING		
	LOW (L)	MEDIUM (M)	HIGH (H)
DIAMETER OF PISTON (ins)	2·9874/2·9871	2·9878/2·9875	2·9882/2·9879
DIAMETER OF PISTON (mm)	75·880/75·872	75·890/75·883	75·900/75·893
BORE SIZE (ins)	2·9911/2·9913	2·9914/2·9917	2·9918/2·9921
BORE SIZE (mm)	75·973/75·980	75·983/75·990	75·993/76·000

SECTION B29

TABLE OF SUITABLE RE-BORE SIZES

Piston Marking in (mm)	+·010 (·254mm)	+·020 (·508mm)	+·030 (·726mm)	+·040 (1·016mm)
Suitable bore sizes (ins)	3·0021/3·0010	3·0121/3·0110	3·0221/3·0210	3·0321/3·0310
Suitable bore sizes (mm)	76·2533/76·2254	76·5073/76·4794	76·7613/76·7334	76·9793/76·9514

ENGINE B

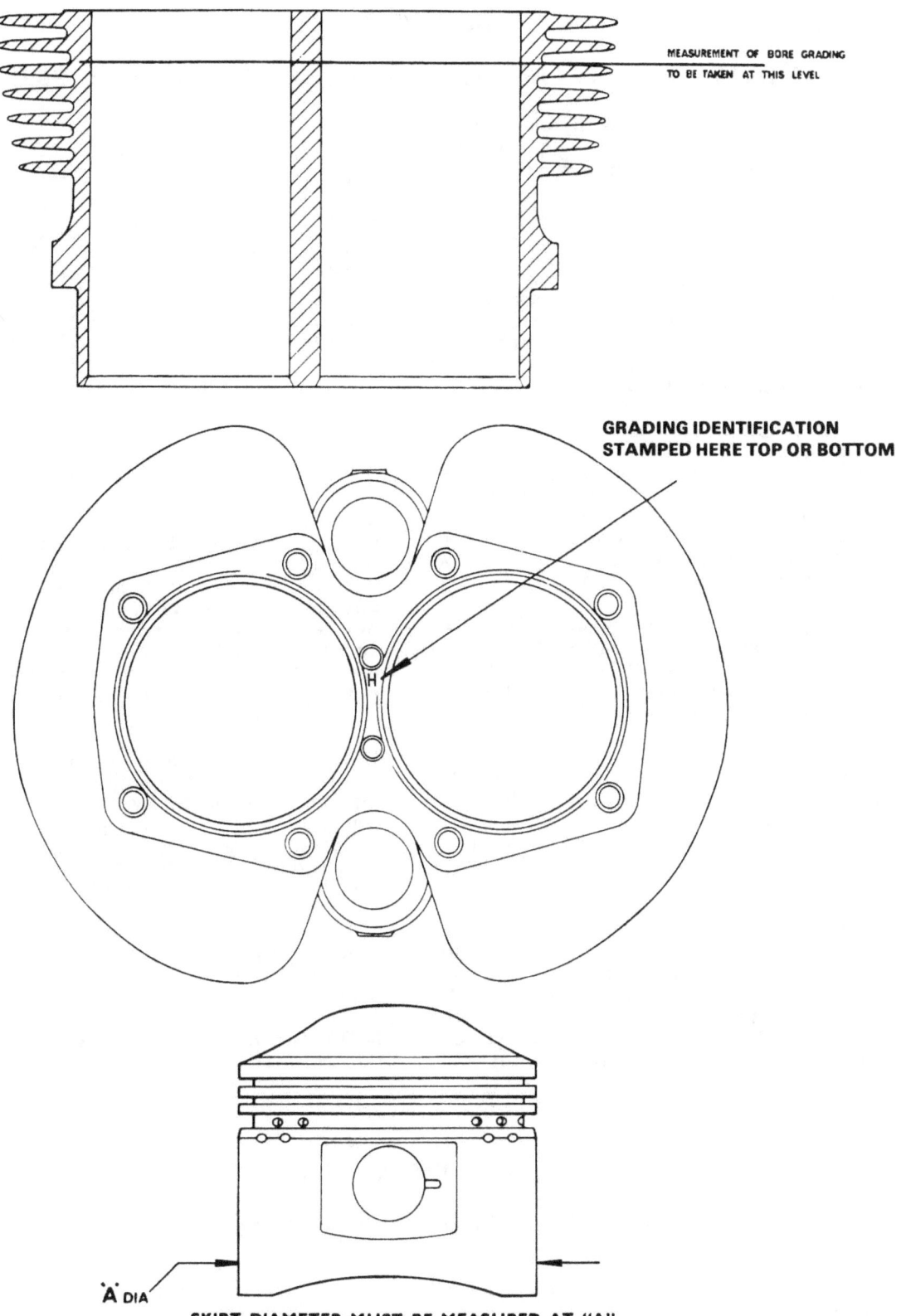

Fig. B21. Cylinder block and piston grading details

SECTION B30

RE-MOVING AND REPLACING THE CONTACT BREAKER - TR65 ONLY

The contact breaker mechanism is housed in the timing cover on the right of the engine and is driven by the exhaust camshaft. It consists of two sets of points (one per cylinder), two auxiliary backplates with cam adjustment and a fully automatic centrifugal type advance and retard mechanism. The working parts are protected by a circular cover and gasket. The engine oil is prevented from entering the contact breaker cavity by means of an oil seal fitted to the inner wall of the timing cover. The complete contact breaker unit can be removed from the timing cover with the aid of service tool 61-7023.

First, disconnect the leads from the battery terminals or remove the fuse from the holder adjacent to the battery, then remove the two screws and withdraw the outer cover and gasket. Remove the centre bolt and screw in service tool 61-7023 until the cam unit is released from it's locking taper in the camshaft. Unscrew the tool and remove the cam unit.

To completely detach the contact breaker unit it will be necessary to disconnect the two leads to the ignition coils and remove the appropriate frame clips so that the leads can be withdrawn through the holes in the crankcase and timing cover.

Prior to replacing the cam unit it is advisable to add a small drop of lubricating oil to the pivot pins only, not the cam pivot. The cam unit slot should be located on the peg in the camshaft and the centre bolt screwed in and tightened.

IMPORTANT NOTE: "Run out" on the contact breaker cam or misalignment of the secondary backplate centre hole can result in contact between the cam and backplate. This can result in the auto advance remaining retarded or the spark retarding. To check for "run-out" check the point gap with the contact nylon heel aligned with the cam scribe mark for each set of points. Should there be a discrepancy greater than 0.003in. (0.076mm.) tap the outer edge of the cam with a brass drift with the cam securing bolt tight. In cases of misalignment of the secondary backplate hole, check the cam clearance in different positions and elongate the hole only where the backplate rubs the cam.

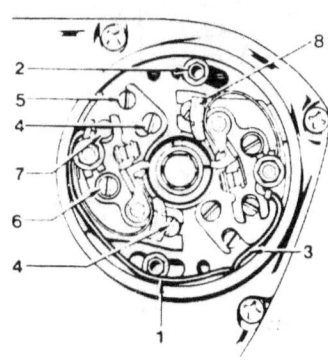

1. Black/yellow
2. Pillar bolt
3. Black/white
4. Secondary bracket screw
5. Eccentric screw
6. Contact locking screw
7. Contact eccentric adjusting screw
8. Lubricating pad

Fig. B22 Contact breaker

To adjust the contact breaker gaps, turn the motor with the starter pedal until the scribe mark on the cam aligns with the nylon heel of one set of points. Measure the point gap using a 0.015in. (0.38mm.) feeler gauge. if outside the limits, slacken the contact adjusting screw, adjust the gap by turning the eccentric screw, and re-tighten the adjusting screw.

Revolve the motor until the second set of points is lined up with the scribe line, and adjust as before.

NOTE: Setting the ignition timing is fully described in Section B32 to B33.

SECTION B31

IGNITION TIMING-INITIAL PROCEDURE-TR65 ONLY

Initial assembly of the contact breaker mechanism and auto advance unit prior to final timing of the engine:-

(1) Remove both sparking plugs and all four rocker box caps. Set the engine at T.D.C. with both valves closed in the right hand cylinder.

(2) Assemble the auto advance unit into the exhaust camshaft, locating on th camshaft peg where it is fitted.

(3) Assemble the C.B. plate taking care not to trap the C.B. leads, assembling the plate so that one set of C.B. points is located at 7 o'clock. Loosely assemble the hexagonal pillar bolts and flat washers.

ENGINE

(4) Lock the auto advance cam into the taper using the central fixing bolt. For static timing remove the bolt again, taking care not to release the taper of the cam. Temporarily fit another washer with a centre hole just large enough to fit over the cam bearing, thus allowing the washer to bear hard on the end of the cam. Rotate the cam carefully to its limit against the auto advance springs, holding in this position whilst the centre bolt is refitted and nipped up. The fully advanced position has then been located.

SECTION B32

STATIC TIMING WHERE NO STROBOSCOPE IS AVAILABLE - TR65 ONLY

Rotate the engine until the nylon heel of the C.B. points aligns with the scribe marking on the cam. At this stage set point gap to 0.015in. (0.38mm.) Rotate engine until cam has turned through 180° then set other point gap to 0.015" (0.38mm).

Locate the crankshaft at 38° B.T.D.C. using the timing marks on the rotor aligning these with the primary cover pointer Fig. B23.

It will be found easiest to start with the pistons at T.D.C. (checked through the sparking plug hole) and then, with both sparking plugs removed and top gear engaged, rotate the rear wheel backwards. As the crank is turned by this means, the rotor mark will become visible. Remove the rocker caps to establish which cylinder is on the firing stroke (i.e. which cylinder has both valves closed). Note that the timing side cylinder is operated by the contact points with the black/yellow lead and the drive side with the black/white lead.

When it has been decided which cylinder is being timed, rotate the main contact breaker backplate in its slots until the particular contact points just open. This can be checked using a battery and light or by an 0.0015in. (0.038mm.) feeler gauge between the points.

Attention should now be turned to the other cylinder. Turn the engine forwards through 360° (1 revolution) and align the rotor marks. The second set of points should now be adjusted as above but the main backplate must not be disturbed. Adjust only on the secondary backplate. Finally secure all screws, lubricate both sides of the cam with Shell Retinax A grease, replace the cover plate and the sparking plugs, finally engaging neutral gear.

SECTION B33

IGNITION TIMING BY STROBOSCOPE - TR65 ONLY

Undertake the initial procedure as in Section B31

Fig. B23. Rotor marking

Remove the screwed plug from the primary chaincase. As seen in Fig. B23 there is a marking on the outer face of the rotor which is to coincide with an ignition pointer on the primary chaincase to achieve the correct 38° ignition timing position.

NOTE: When using a stroboscope powered by a 12 volt battery as on external power source, do not use the machines own battery equipment. (A.C. pulses in the low tension machine wiring can trigger the stroboscope and give false readings).

(1) Connect the stroboscope to the right hand spark plug lead and start the engine. Read the strobo-light on the rotor marking in relation to the timing pointer with the engine running at 2,500 R.P.M. or more.

Adjust the main backplate on its slots until the marks align whereupon the timing is correct.

(2) Repeat for the L.H. plug and adjust the timing by slackening off the clamping screw on the auxilliary backplate and turning the eccentric screw (see Fig. B22) until again the markings align. Timing is then correct. Refit the primary chaincase inspection plate.

NOTE
1° = ·020" @ ₵ OF PAD.

SECTION B34

IGNITION TIMING BY STROBOSCOPE - T140 & TR7

Remove the screwed cap from the left side of the chaincase to reveal the alternator rotor. Position the transducer such that the fixing studs are approximately central in the adjustment slots. Start the engine, accelerate to 3,500 r.p.m. and observe the relative position of rotor timing slot and fixed point using an ignition controlled strobe flash gun.

If the rotor timing mark appears to the left of the fixed point, the timing is retarded and must be advanced until alignment is achieved by slackening the transducer fixing studs and turning the unit in an anti-clockwise direction or vice-versa as necessary. The transducer fixing studs must be firmly tightened to prevent subsequent movement.

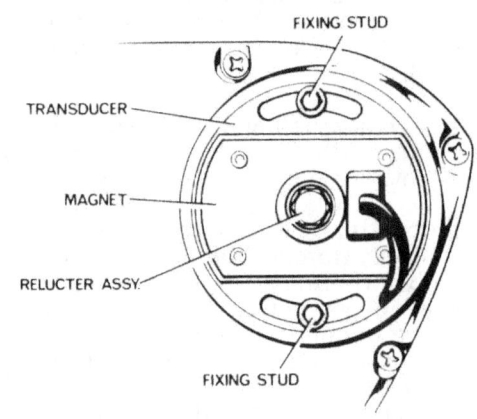

Fig. B24. Ignition timing unit

SECTION B35

REMOVING AND REPLACING THE TIMING COVER - KICKSTART MODELS

Remove the back plate and reluctor as described in Section B30.

Disconnect the oil switch lead at the spade terminal. Unscrew the eight recessed screws which serve to retain the timing cover and if necessary tap the cover on the front blanking plug with a hide mallet until the cover is free. When the cover is removed, the crankshaft and camshaft oil seals should be inspected for wear and cracks and renewed if necessary. To remove the crankshaft oil seal, the retainer circlip must first be removed by means of long-nosed pliers or a narrow screwdriver.

Unscrew the hexagonal plug from the front edge of the cover and thoroughly clean all parts in paraffin (kerosene). Clean out the oil drillings with a jet of compressed air and replace the plug and copper washer.

The oil pressure switch in the front of the timing cover has a taper thread and requires no sealant on the threads, for competition use a blanking plug is available to take the place of the switch.

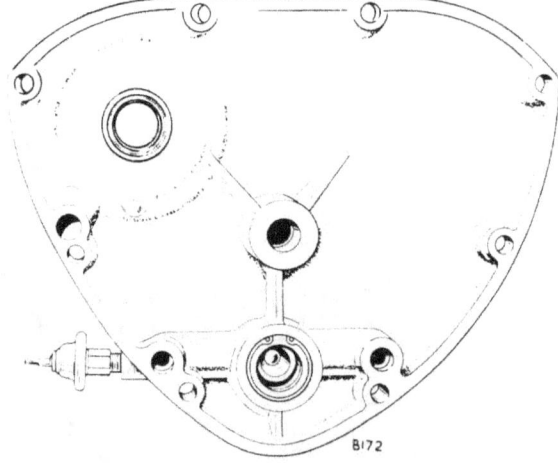

Fig. B25. Timing cover oil seal location

ENGINE

To replace the cover, first check that the oil seals are facing in the correct direction (see Fig. B25) and that the circlip is located correctly in its groove, then carefully clean the junction surfaces of the timing cover and crankcase and remove any traces of used jointing compound. Apply a fresh coat of a suitable proprietary jointing compound evenly over the timing cover junction surface. Screw the tapered adaptor pilot (service tool 61-7013) into the exhaust camshaft and smear it with oil to assist assembly. Check that both the location dowels are in their correct positions, slide the cover into position and screw in the eight recessed screws.

Finally, replace the back plate and reluctor assembly and reset the ignition timing as shown in Section 30 to 33.

NOTE: The three longer screws should be fitted in the holes marked "X"

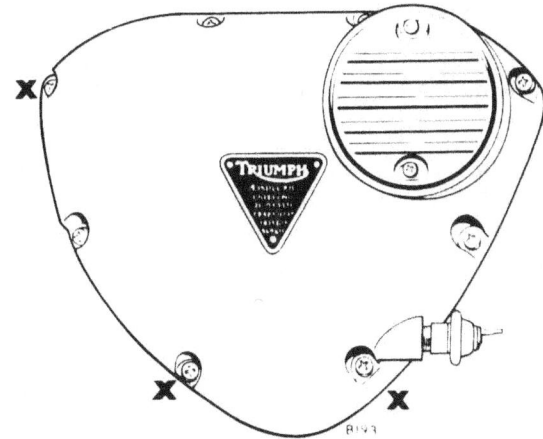

Fig. B26. Location of three long screws in timing cover

SECTION B36

REMOVING AND REPLACING THE TIMING COVER - ELECTRIC START MODELS

Remove the pulse sensor and reluctor as described in Section B30.

Disconnect the oil switch lead at the spade terminal.

Disconnect the pulse sensor leads from the main harness.

Disconnect the main battery leads at the battery.

Remove the small triangular cover on the left side of the main timing cover by undoing the three allen screws.

Remove the starter motor which is held to the timing cover by three Allen Screws. Push out the starter motor from its register and leave remaining on top of the gearbox.

Remove the outer cover screws paying particular attention to the screw situated behind the starter gear. This screw is made accessible by rotating the gear until one of the holes in the gear allow the screw to be seen. Insert screwdriver through hole in gear and remove screw in normal manner.

Feed the pulse sensor leads through the crankcase drillway and then the cover can be fully removed.

When the cover is removed the crankshaft and camshaft oil seals should be inspected for wear and cracks, and renewed if necessary. To remove the crankshaft oil seal the retainer circlip must first be removed with the aid of circlip on long nose pliers.

When reassembling the oil seal ensure that they are fitted the correct way round, that is the crankshaft seal lip and spring face inward towards the cover and the camshaft seal lip and spring face outwards towards the operator when holding the cover see Fig. B25.

To replace the cover firstly position a new gasket onto the timing cover face, threading the pulse sensor leads through the appropriate hole in the gasket. It is adviseably to lightly grease the face of the to retain the gasket in position whilst the cover is offered up.

Screw into the camshaft the tapered adaptor service tool 61-7013 to protect the camshaft seal during cover assembly.

Slide the cover into position and fit the securing screws taking note of the three longer ones and their positioning.

Replace the starter motor ensuring the sealing ring is fitted correctly and that the starter dowel enters correctly.

Fit the three alter screws to the starter motor and tighten up securely. Do not omit the locking washers.

Fit the triangular starter motor access cover using a new joint washer.

B ENGINE

Fit the reluctor ensuring that the slot in the reluctor registers with the peg in the camshaft.

Fit and reposition the pulse sensor plate approximately in the centre of the slotted adjustment holes.

Connect the pulse sensor leads and the oil switch lead, connect the battery leads to the battery.

Adjust ignition timing as per Section B34.

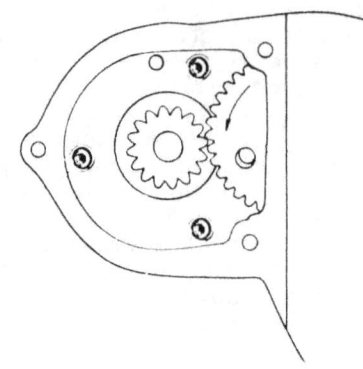

SECTION B37

REMOVING AND REPLACING THE OIL PUMP

To remove the oil pump, first remove the back plate and reluctor, and the timing cover as described in Sections B26 and B30.

The oil pump is held in position by two Allen Screws. When these are removed, the oil pump can be withdrawn. The paper gasket should be renewed.

Full details concerning inspection, testing and rectification of the oil pump are given in Section A6.

When replacing the oil pump, care should be taken to ensure that the new gasket is fitted correctly.

SECTION B38

EXTRACTING AND REFITTING THE VALVE PINIONS

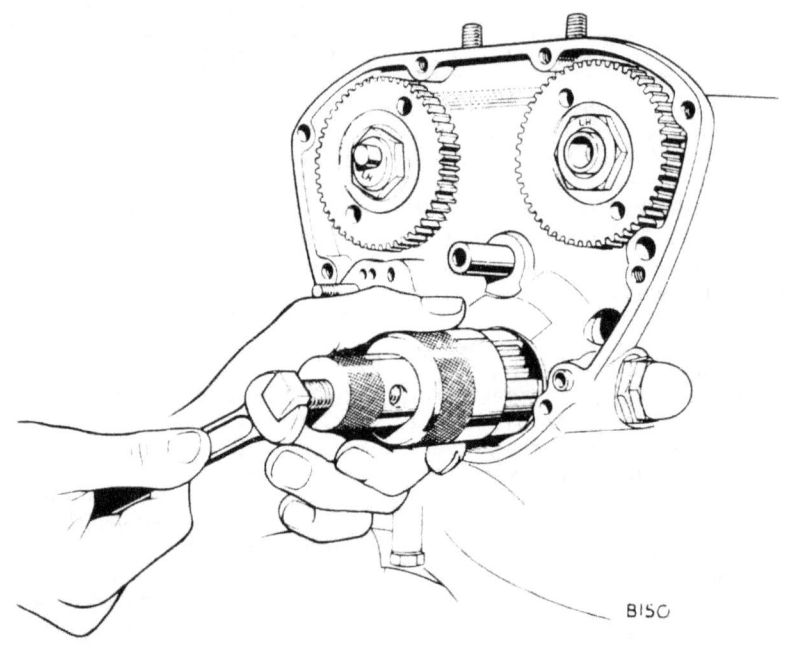

Fig. B27. Extracting the crankshaft pinion using tool 61-6019

ENGINE

Before attempting to remove any of the valve timing gears it is necessary to release the load on the camshafts caused by compressed valve springs. This should be done by removing the rocker boxes as detailed in Section B2.

Remove the reluctor as detailed in Section B26.

Remove the timing cover as described in Section B30 and the oil pump as shown in Section B31. Select 5th (top) gear, apply the rear brake and unscrew the nuts retaining the camshaft and crankshaft pinions, then withdraw the intermediate wheel.

NOTE: The camshaft pinion retainer nuts have LEFT-HAND threads. the crankshaft pinion retainer nut has a RIGHT-HAND thread.

CRANKSHAFT PINION

Removal of the crankshaft pinion is facilitated by service tool 61-6019, which consists of a protective cap and three claw extractor body, complete with extractor bolt.

To extract the pinion, first press the protection cap over the end of the crankshaft, then place the extractor over the pinion, locate the three claws behind the pinion and screw down the body to secure them. Using a tommy bar and spanner the crankshaft pinion can then be extracted (see Fig. B26). When this is achieved, the key and clamping washer should be removed and placed in safe-keeping.

When replacing the clamping washer ensure that the chamfered side is towards the crankshaft shoulder. Screw the guide onto the crankshaft. Smear the bore of the crankshaft pinion with grease to assist assembly and position it over the guide, so that the counter bore is outwards. Align the key and keyway and drive the pinion onto the crankshaft.

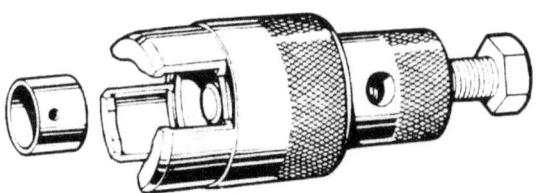

Fig. B28. Extractor tool 60-6019 showing protection cap which fits over crankshaft

CAMSHAFT PINIONS

To extract both the inlet and exhaust camshaft pinions extractor Pr. No. 61-6132 should be used. To extract pinion screw the two outriggers bolts into the camwheel and screw in the central bolt; the pinion will then be withdrawn from the camshaft. See Fig. B28.

NOTE: The camshaft pinions may be left in position if it is not intended to subsequently remove the camshafts from the crankcase. When replacing the camwheels use a suitable hollow drift and lightly drive the camwheels onto the camshaft as far as possible. They will not drive fully home because of the camshaft float, but when the retaining nuts are replaced and tightened the camwheels will then seat into position.

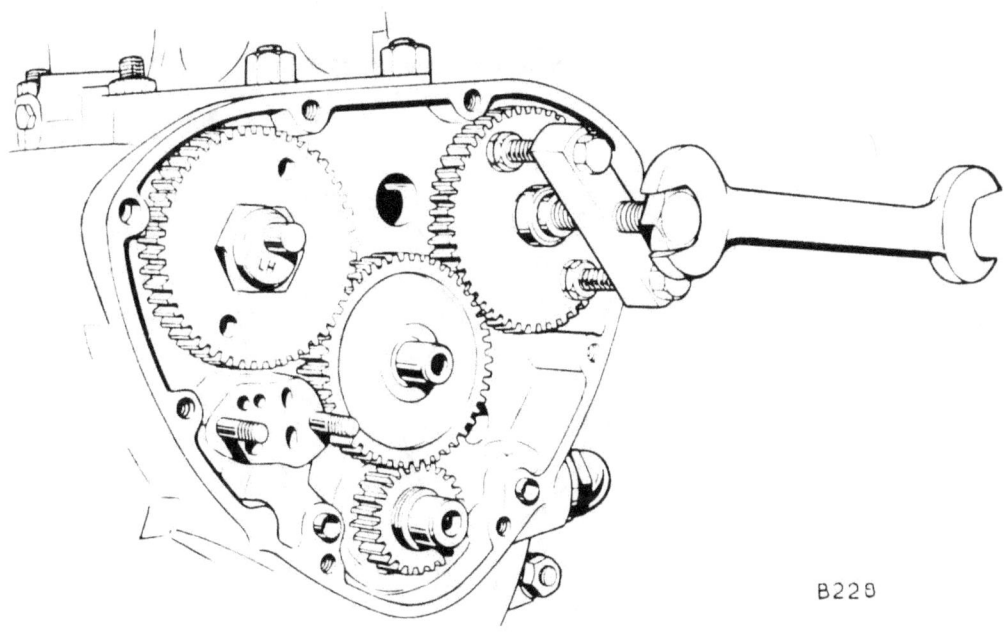

Fig. B29. Extracting the cam wheels using tool 61-6132

ENGINE

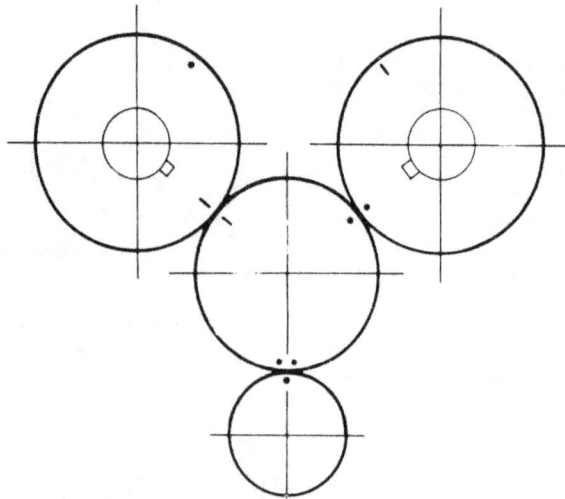

Fig. B30. Valve timing marks for T140/TR7

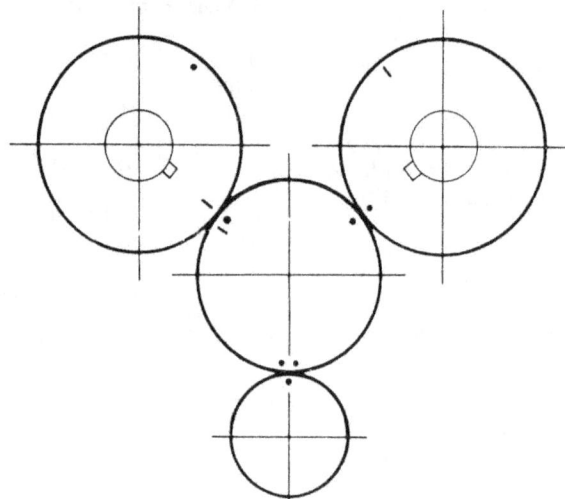

Fig. B31a. Valve timing marks for TR7T/TR65T

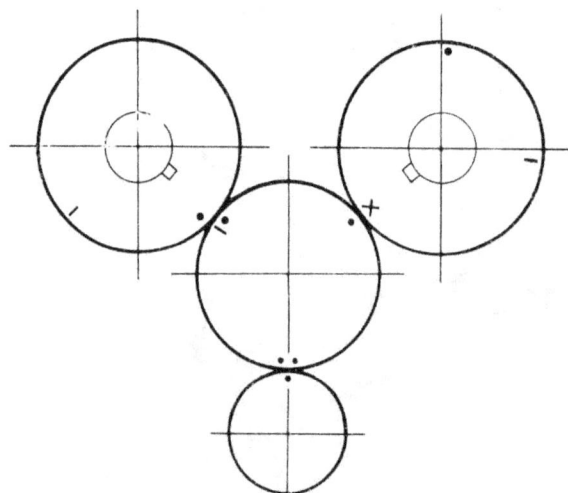

Fig. B31b. Valve timing marks for TR65

ENGINE   B

SECTION B39

VALVE TIMING

The valve timing is sufficently accurate for machines which are to be used under normal conditions, when the intermediate wheel is assembled in the position shown in Fig. B30, and the camshaft pinions are located by means of the keyway directly opposite the timing mark.

It should be noted that, due to the intermediate wheel having a prime number of teeth, the timing marks only coincide every 94th revolution, thus there is no cause for alarm if the timing marks will not readily re-align.

SECTION B40

DISMANTLING AND REASSEMBLING THE CRANKCASE ASSEMBLY

It is advisable to partially dismantle the engine unit whilst it is fixed to the motorcycle, then remove the remaining crankcase assembly and dismantle it on a work bench.

Proceed as described in Section B1 for removal of the engine unit, but leave the rear chain connected and the engine firmly mounted in the frame by means of the front and bottom engine mounting bolts. Remove the outer primary cover as sown underneath the engine (two snap connectors).

Unscrew three nuts securing the stator and withdraw it from over the mounting studs. Do not try to withdraw the leads at this stage.

Remove the pressure plate and clutch plates as detailed in Section C4. Select 5th gear and apply the rear brake, then unscrew the clutch hub securing nut and extract the clutch hub with the gearchange shaft as shown in Section C9. When the primary chain has been threaded over the stator the sleeve nut should be unscrewed and the stator leads withdrawn.

Remove the gearbox outer cover and dismantle the gearbox (see Section D) then remove the rocker boxes, cylinder head, block and pistons as shown in Sections B2, B14, B19 and B22 respectively, then disconnect the control cable(s) and remove the carburetter(s).

Remove the contact breaker, timing cover complete with oil switch and oil pump (Sections B28, B32 and B33) then extract the crankshaft pinion. If it is required to inspect or change the camshafts or bushes, the camshaft pinions should also be extracted.

Remove the front and bottom engine mounting studs, disconnect the rear chain and remove the crankcase assembly.

Remove the crankcase filter and oilway blanking plug located at the bottom of the crankcase in line with the oil pump, and catch any oil that may be present in the crankcase.

Grip the crankcase firmly in a vice by means of the bottom mounting lug and unscrew the three bolts from the left side which are situated at the cylinder barrel spigots and rear of the primary drive breather outlet. Then the remaining four studs and unscrew two nuts adjacent to the gearbox housing. The crankcase halves may now be parted. If difficulty is encountered parting the crankcase halves it will be due to the front TOP (crankcase to frame) hollow dowel which is a press fit. Prior to splitting the crankcase drift the dowel out of position using a suitable bar (an old rocker shaft is ideal for this purpose). When the halves are apart, withdraw the crankshaft assembly and store it carefully.

Remove the timing side main bearing, See Section B38.

Thoroughly clean and degrease the crankcase paying particular attention to the oilways. DO NOT DAMAGE the scavenge pipe to crankcase joint.

REASSEMBLY
Prior to reassembly, the junction surfaces should be carefully scraped clean, giving special attention to the location spigot and dowels. Replace the oilway blanking plug located at the bottom of the R/H crankcase in line with the oil pump, and crankcase filter.

Mount the left half-crankcase on its side on two wooden blocks, or a bench with a hole in for crankshaft clearance, lubricate the main bearings and camshaft bushes. Assemble the crankshaft into position ensuring that it is right home in the bearing by giving it a sharp blow with a hide mallet.

Apply a fresh coat of jointing compound to the junction surface of the left half-crankcase then lubricate the main bearings and camshaft bushes in both halves of the crankcase. Position the con-rods centrally and lower the right half-crankcase into position over the crankshaft. When the halves are mated, check the crankshaft and camshafts for freedom of rotation. The crankshaft should revolve freely whilst the camshafts should offer little or no resistance to rotation by hand.

Refit the crankcase securing bolts and studs, and tighten them until they are just "pinched-up".

Check that the cylinder block junction surface of the crankcase is level.

If there is a slight step between the two halves, this should be corrected by tapping the front and rear of the crankcases as required, until a level surface is achieved. The crankcase securing bolts should then be tightened, a turn at a time, to the torque figures given in "Technical Data".

Reassembly then continues as a reversal of the dismantling instructions. Prior to refitting the cylinder block, pour approximately ¼ pint (0.14 litres) of oil into the crankcase.

SECTION B41

SERVICING THE CRANKSHAFT ASSEMBLY

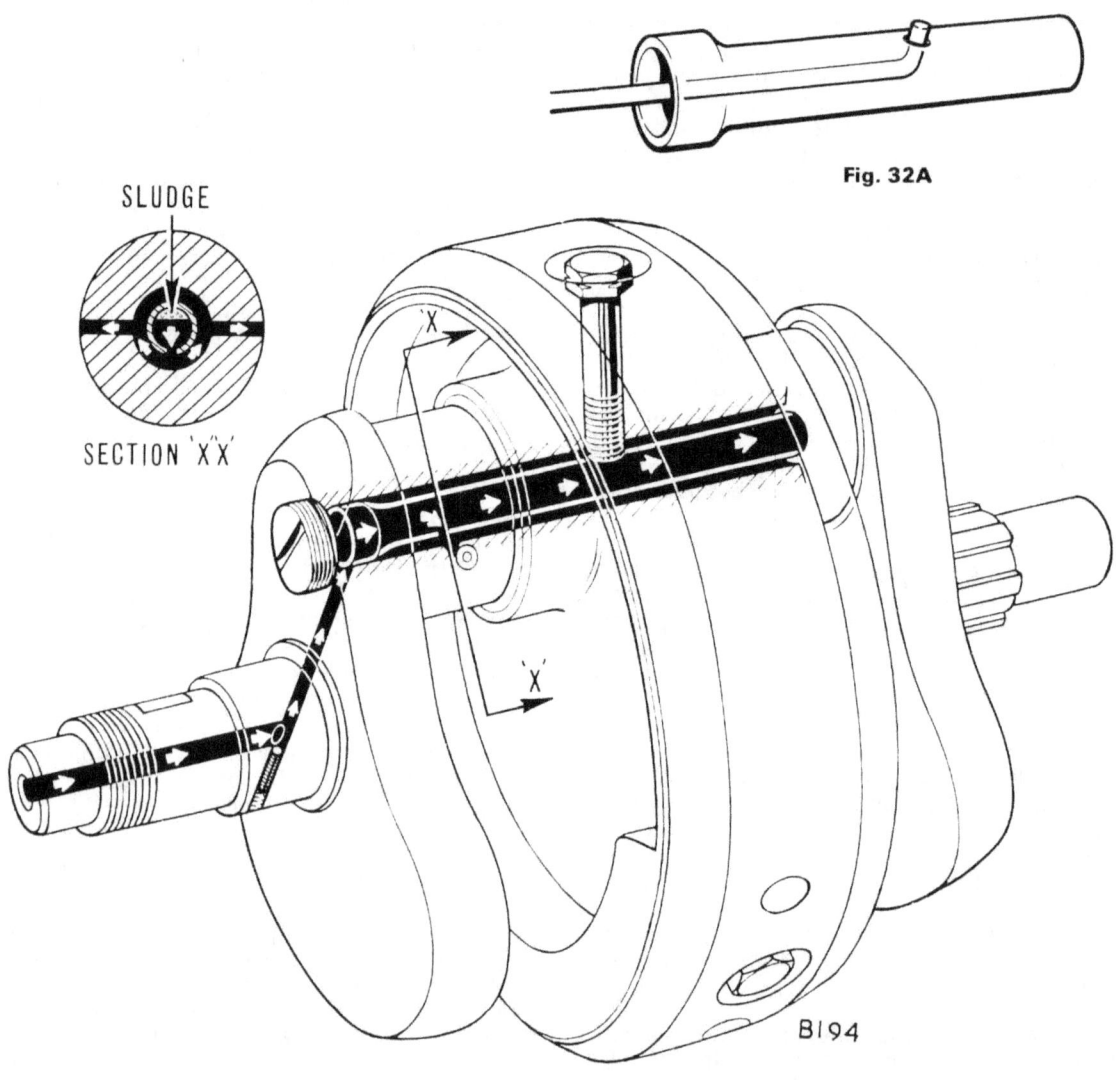

Fig. B32. Sectional view of crankshaft - showing oil tube.

ENGINE

Grip the crankshaft conveniently in a suitable vice and place rag over any sharp edges to avoid the connecting rods becoming damaged. Mark the connecting rods, caps and crankshaft so that they can be replaced in their original positions.

Unscrew the cap retainer nuts, a turn at a time to avoid distortion, then remove the caps and connecting rods. Refit the nuts to their respective bolts to ensure correct reassembly.

Using a large impact screwdriver, unscrew the oil tube retainer plug from the right end of the big-end journal. If difficulty is encountered, drill a 1/8 in. (3mm.) dia. hole to 1/8 in. (3mm.) depth in the crankshaft, to remove the centre punched identation which locks the oil tube retainer plug in position.

Unscrew the flywheel bolt adjacent to the big-end journal, then withdraw the oil tube using a hooked rod located in the flywheel bolt location (See Fig. 32A).

Thoroughly clean all parts in paraffin (kerosene) then clean the oil drillings using a jet of compressed air. Particular attention should be given to checking that each oil drilling is free from blockage.

REGRIND
Crank shafts can be reground to the following dimensions it is not advisable to reduce the crankshaft below the recommended figs as this could weaken the crankshaft with subsequent failure.

BIG END JOURNAL

SIZE	IN	MM
STD	1.6235	41.237
	1.6240	41.250
−.010"	1.6135	40.983
	1.6140	40.996
−.020"	1.6035	40.729
	1.6040	40.742

OIL FEED DIA

	IN	MM
STD	.622	15.799
	.623	15.824
−.020	.602	15.291
	.603	15.361

NOTE:
Use oil seal part No. 70.6387
For −.020" condition

SECTION B42

REFITTING THE CONNECTING RODS

First, ensure that the connecting rod and cap and both the front and rear of the bearing shells are scrupulously clean, then offer the shells to the rod and cap to their original journals, ensuring that the tab location slots are adjacent (see Fig. B33).

Refit the bolts and screw on the nuts to the given torque figure.

Finally, force oil through the drilling at the right end of the crankshaft with a pressure oil can until it is expelled from both big-end bearings, thus indicating that the oil passages are free from blockage and full of oil.

NOTE: The connecting rod, cap and nut are centre punched on initial assembly so that the cap may be refitted correctly relative to the connecting rod.

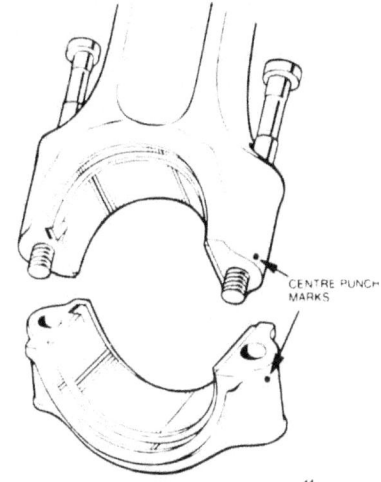

Fig. B33. Refitting the connecting rods

SECTION B43

INSPECTING THE CRANKCASE COMPONENTS

In preparation for inspection, thoroughly clean the crankcase-halves, main bearings, crankshaft and connecting rods, etc., in paraffin (kerosene) and allow them to drain. If there is an air pump accessible, then dry the components with a jet of compressed air and examine them as follows:-

(1) BIG-END BEARINGS

The extent of wear to the big-end journals can be determined by inspecting the bearing surfaces for scoring and by measuring the diameter of the journals. Light score marks can be reduced with smooth emery cloth but ensure that all parts are carefully washed after this operation.

Where a journal has been slightly scored the big-end shell bearings should be renewed. If the scoring and wear is extensive the big-end journals should be reground to a suitable size as given in B37.

NOTE: The replaceable white metal big-end bearings are pre-finished to give the correct diametral clearance. Under no circumstances should the bearings be scraped or the connecting rod and cap joint faces filed.

(2) MAIN BEARINGS

Clean the bearings thoroughly in paraffin (kerosene), then dry them with a jet of compressed air. Test the bearing for roughness by spinning. check the centre race for side-play and inspect the rollers and tracks for any signs of indentation and pocketing. Examine the main bearing diameters on the crankshaft for wear. The bearings should be a tight push fit on the crankshaft and a press fit in the crankcase. A loose fitting bearing would tend to cause crankcase "rumble". The correct diameters of the main bearing journals are given in "Technical Data".

(3) CAMSHAFTS AND BUSHES

The camshaft bushes normally show very little sign of wear until a considerable mileage has been covered. A rough check on the wear can be made by inserting the camshaft into the bearing and feeling the up and down movement. An exact check can be made by measuring the chamshaft with a micrometer and measuring the camshaft bushes with calipers. The working clearance figures are given in "Technical Data". Wear on the cam form will be mainly centred on the opening flank of the cam and on the lobe of the cam. Particular attention should be given to these areas when examining the cam form for grooving. In a case where there is severe grooving the camshaft and tappet followers should be renewed.

A method of estimating the extend of wear on the cam form is that of measuring the over-all height of the cam and the base-circle diameter. The difference is the cam lift. if all other aspects of the camshaft are satisfactory and the wear on the cam form does not exceed 0.010in. (0.25mm.) then the camshaft may be used for further service.

(4) CRANKCASE FACES AND DOWELS

Ensure that the faces of the crankcases are not damaged in any way and that any dowels are in position,

SECTION B44

RENEWING THE MAIN BEARING

To remove the timing side ball journal bearing heat the crankcase to approximately 100 C and drive the bearing inwards. A suitable drift can be made from a piece of 1 ¼ in. (31mm.) diameter mild steel bar, about 6in. (150mm.) long by turning it to 1 ⅛ in. (28.6mm.) diameter for ½ in. (12mm.) at one end.

On engines fitted with roller bearings the inner portion will be withdrawn with the crankshaft. The outer spool however will still involve heating the crankcase and if it is very tight in the case will require the use of special tool 61-7017 which expands to grip the outer spool.

The roller and spool can be removed from the crankshaft using a suitable extractor.

To assemble the new bearings first ensure that the main bearing housing is clean, then heat the crankcase to approximately 100°C and drive in the bearing using a tubular drift onto the outer race. Ensure that the bearing enters its housing squarely. If possible, use a press. Suitable dimensions for the drift are 2 ¾ in. (70mm.) outside diameter x 6in. (150mm.) long.

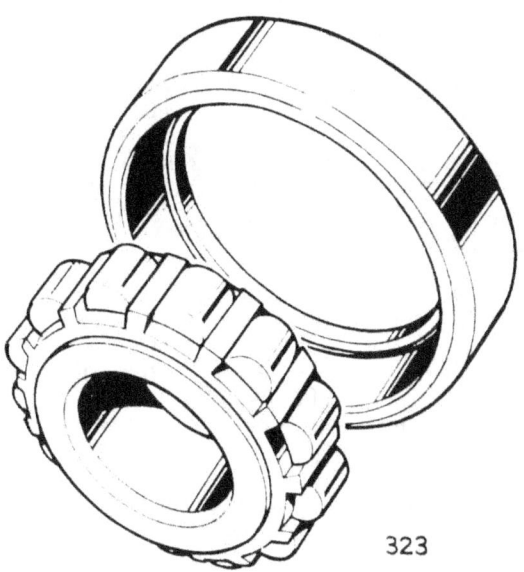

Fig. B34. Roller main bearing

SECTION B45

RENEWING CAMSHAFT BUSHES

To remove the camshaft bushes in the RIGHT half-crankcase heat the crankcase to 100°C and drive the bush out from the outside, using a suitable drift. While the crankcase is still hot, drive in the new bush, ensuring that the oil feed holes in the bush and the crankcase drilling are aligned. A suitable drift for this purpose can be made from a 6in. (150mm.) long piece of M.S. bar of 1⅛ in. (28.6mm.) diameter, by machining a pilot on one end ⅞ in. (22.2mm.) x 1in. (25mm.) long.

To remove the camshaft bush from the LEFT half-crankcase, a tap is necessary. An ideal size is ⅞ in. diameter x 9 Whit. When a good thread has been cut in the old bush, heat the crankcase (100°C.) and screw in a suitable bolt. Grip the bolt in a vice and drive the crankcase with a hide mallet until the bush is removed. Do not attempt to lever the bush out of position with the bolt, or the case may be damaged. If the tap is used in place of the bolt, care must be taken not to give too hard a knock to the crankcase or the brittle tap may break.

The sintered bronze camshaft bushes are machined to size before pressing in, therefore they will not need to be machined when they are renewed. See "Technical Data" for sizes and working clearances.

SECTION B46

REMOVING AND REPLACING THE TACHOMETER DRIVE

Where the tachometer is fitted, there is a right angled drive gearbox as shown in Fig B35. It is not necessary to part the crankcases to remove the drive gearbox. When the large slotted end cap is removed and the engine turned over quikkly the drive gear should be ejected. If this is not so, the gear can be withdrawn with long-nosed pliers. The left-hand threaded centre bolt holding the drive gearbox to the crankcase will then be seen. A thin box spanner is needed to release this and the box will then come away from the crankcase.

NOTE: The securing nut has a L.H. thread.

It will be noted that a spade in the back of the tachometer gearbox fits into a slot in the end of the exhaust camshaft. Take care to engage this when reassembling.

The reassembly procedure for the drive gearbox is the reversal of the above.

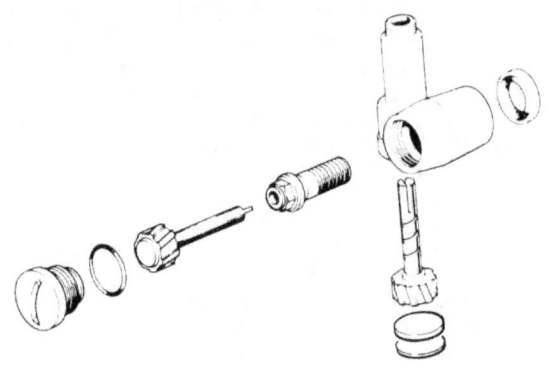

Fig. B35. Exploded view of tachometer gearbox

WORKSHOP MANUAL
SUPPLEMENT

FOR

T140W-TSS MODEL

TRIUMPH MOTORCYCLES (MERIDEN LTD)
MERIDEN WORKS · ALLESLEY · COVENTRY · CV5 9AU · ENGLAND

TELEPHONE MERIDEN 22331   TELEX TRUSTY GB 311672

99-7089R Published May 1983

ENGINE

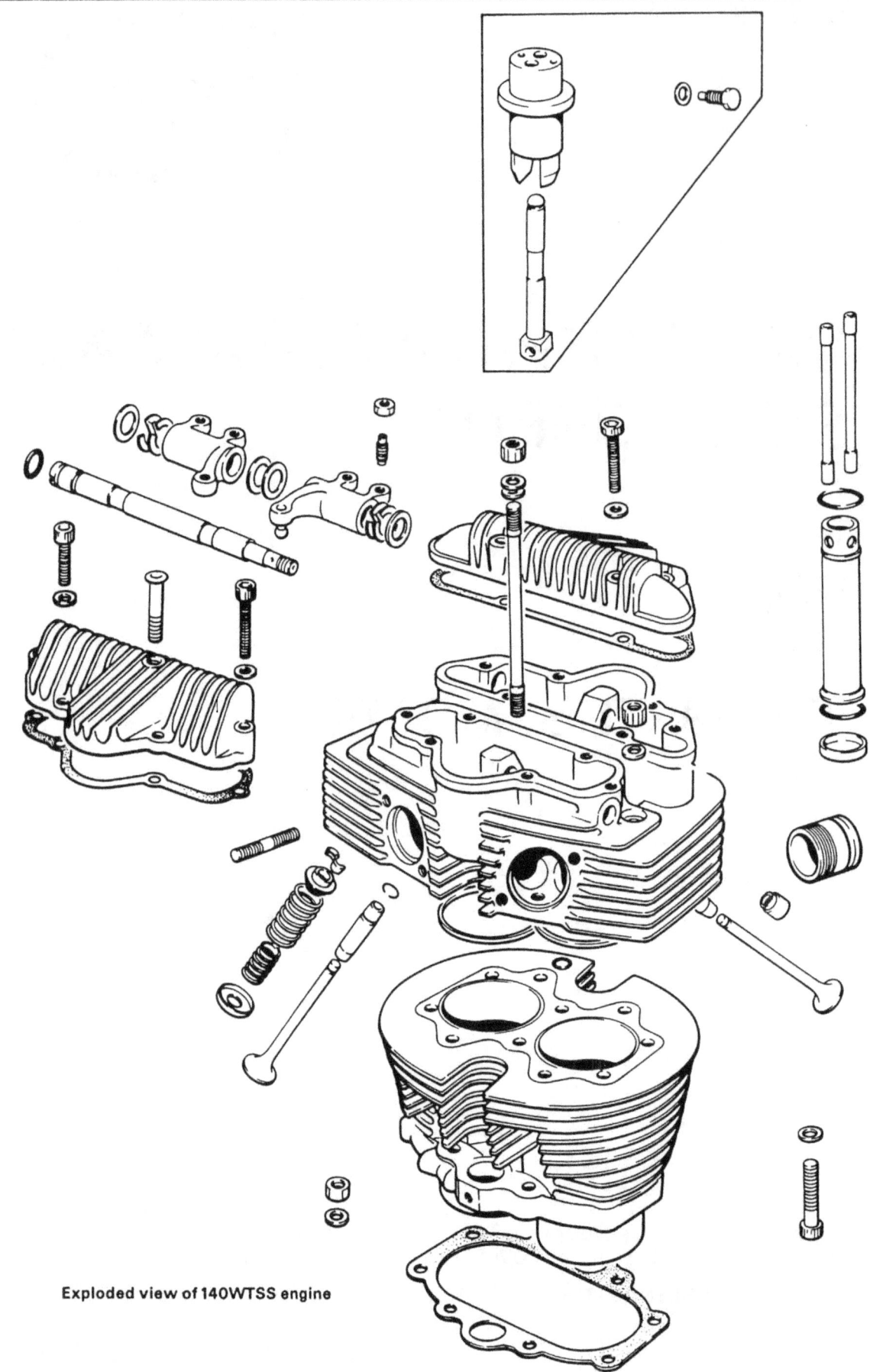

Exploded view of 140WTSS engine

ENGINE

STRIPPING & REASSEMBLING THE ROCKERS

Removal of the rocker spindles from the cylinder head is best achieved by driving them out, using a soft metal drift applied to the threaded end.

Before attempting to remove the rocker spindle ensure both valves are closed and therefore there is no load on the rockers via the push rods.

When the rocker spindle has been withdrawn the rockers and spacing washers can be removed.

NOTE the positioning of the rockers to ensure that they are refitted correctly, if in doubt mark each before removal as this will ensure correct replacement.

If it is required to replace the rocker ball pins, the old ones can be removed by a suitable drift and new ones pressed in.

When reassembling the rocker spindle always renew the 'O' ring and use tool No. 61-7048 to aid the compressing of spindle 'O' ring.

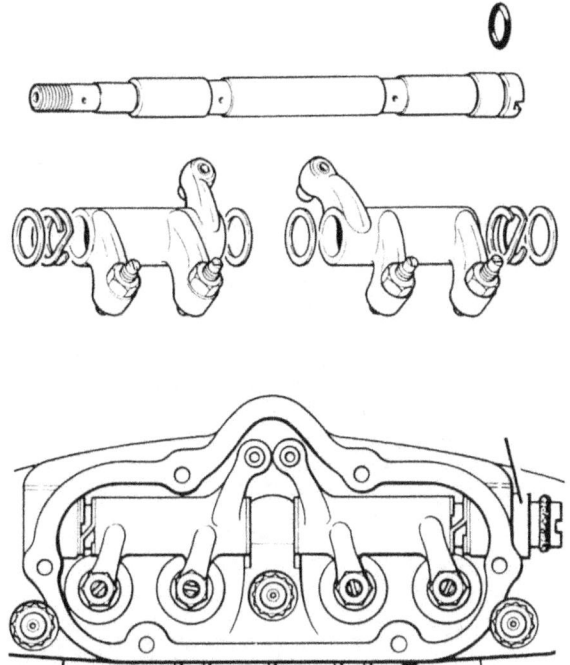

ADJUSTING THE VALVE ROCKER CLEARANCE

The valve rocker clearances should be checked and adjusted if necessary every 3,000 miles (4,800KM). The correct clearances are given in the technical data section.

NOTE Adjustment must only be made what the engine is cold.

There are four adjusters on the rockers which are accessible after removing the inspection covers from the cylinder head. A feeler gauge can then be inserted between the adjuster and valve when the engine position is correct. To enable this engine position to be readily obtained place the motor cycle on the centre stand and engage fifth gear. By revolving the rear wheel slowly the crankshaft will be turned and the valves can be positioned.

INLET
Revolve the rear wheel until one of the inlet rockers moves downwards thus opening the valve. When this valve is fully open the opposite inlet valve can be adjusted using the feeler gauge of the correct thickness.

The clearance is correct when the feeler gauge is a tight sliding fit between the valve tip and the

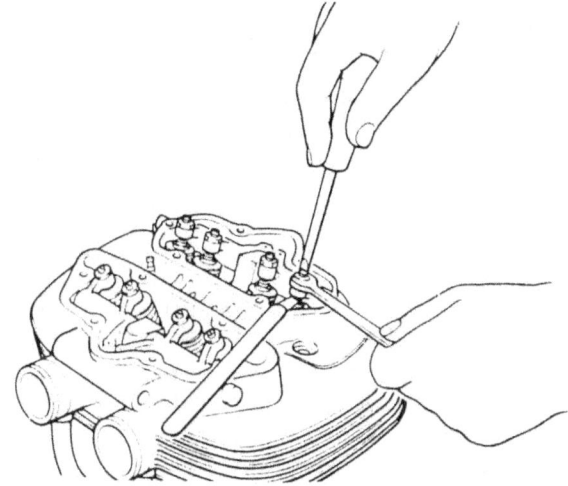

adjuster. After tightening the adjuster locknut recheck the clearance. Having adjusted one set of inlet valves turn the rear wheel until the valve which you have adjusted is now fully open and repeat the procedure for the other inlet valves.

ENGINE

EXHAUST
Proceed in the same way as for the inlet valves having one valve fully open whilst checking the opposite one. See technical data for settings.

Replace the inspection covers ensuring the gaskets are in good condition if in doubt renew.

REMOVING & REPLACING THE EXHAUST SYSTEM

To remove the exhaust pipes first slacken the clamps nuts securing the balance pipe on both sides. Undo the brass nuts holding the finned clip to the cylinder head.

Remove the bolts holding the front brackets to the exhaust pipe. Slacken the clamps which secure the silencer to exhaust pipe. Using a rubber hammer tap both exhaust pipes away from the cylinder head so that they are removed together. This will allow the balance tube to be removed from between the pipes. Remove the silencers by detaching the pillion footrest.

Before refitting the exhaust pipes inspect the copper asbestos sealing joint for condition and if necessary renew.

Replacement of the system is a reversal of the above instructions remembering to assemble the pipes together in one operation with the balance tube.

REMOVING & REFITTING THE CYLINDER HEAD

Proceed as detailed in Section 4 Relating to exhaust system.
Remove the fuel tank as detailed in Section E1.
Remove the carburettors as detailed in Section B8.
Unscrew the cylinder head torque stay fixing bolt upper.
Unscrew the nut retaining the torque stay to head and withdraw the bolt. Remove the torque stay completely.
Remove the tappet inspection covers by unscrewing the allen fixing screws.
Remove the rocker oil feed pipe by undoing the large Dome nuts.
Remove the rocker sindles as detailed in 2 and remove the Push Rods.
Undo and remove the four allen screws securing the cylinder head to barrel.
Undo the cylinder head securing nuts a turn at a time, until the load has been released.

Lift cylinder head clear of through studs and remove. Remove push rod cover tubes and sealing rings.

Refitting the Cylinder Head
Fit new push rod cover tube seals and fit push rod covers to cylinder barrel.

Ensure that the cylinder head and cylinder barrel faces are clean.
Position new sealing rings in the head recesses -grease may be used to retain these rings whilst fitting the cylinder head.
Offer cylinder head over fixing studs taking care that sealing rings are not disturbed whilst head is slid into position.

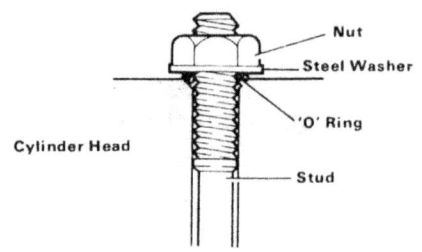

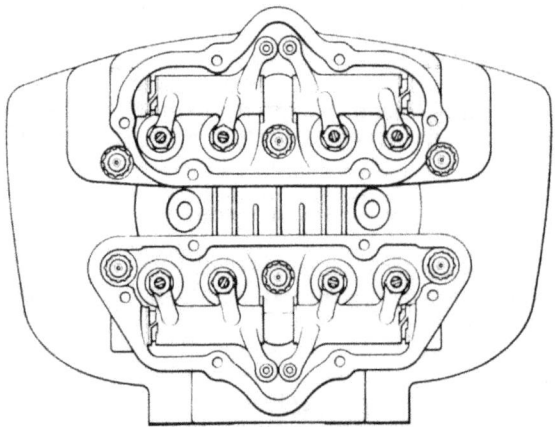

Fit washers and nuts to all upper fixing studs and very lightly tighten down. Fit new seals to the two inside fixing studs,

ENGINE

Fit the four Allen Screws which retain the head to the barrel and lightly tighten.

Finally tighten all fixing screws and nuts observing the tightening procedure and the torque settings TD5.

Refit the push rods rockers and rocker spindles along with the spacing washers.

Adjust tappets as 3.
Refit Rocker covers as 3.
Refit exhaust system as 4.
Refit the cylinder head torque stay.
Refit the carburettors B8.
Refit fuel tank as sec E1.

REMOVING & REPLACING THE CYLINDER BLOCK & TAPPETS

Proceed as sec 5 until cylinder head is removed.

Secure the inlet and exhaust tappet by wedging a suitable retainer between them. This will prevent the tappets from falling into the crankcase. Remove the four cylinder to crankcase retaining nuts followed by removal of the long through studs. Note two studs are locating doweled.

Turn the engine until the pistons are at the bottom of the cylinder and gently remove the cylinder block.

When reassembling note that the dowel through studs are fitted R.H. rear and L.H. front. Reassemble in reverse order and for further information see sections B19 to B27 T140.

IGNITION TIMING

Initial Setting
To enable the engine to be started and run so that the timing can be set stroboscopically, the following procedure should be adopted.

(1) Set engine at full advance firing position by aligning the rotor mark with the pointer situated in the primary cover.

(2) Fit reluctor into camshaft. Taper aligning front edge with line marked in the housing (this line will be located at approximately the 2 o'clock position). Tighten reluctor retaining bolt.

(3) Fit pulse sensor plate positioning radial adjustment slots centrally about the threaded holes. Fit retaining bolts and tighten.

The engine will now be ready to start and run.

Note
Never fail to finally check ignition timing with a stroboscope as correct setting is essential.

ENGINE

For data not given refer to T140 1980/81

Bore	mm	76	
	in	2.993"	
Stroke	mm	82	
	in	3.228"	
Capacity	cc	747	
	in	45	
Compression Ratio		9.5:1 STD	8.5:1 alternative

VALVE TIMING – CHECKED WITH NIL CLEARANCE AT T.D.C.

Inlet in 0.150" (3.810 mm)
Exhaust in 0.130" (3.266 mm)

TAPPET CLEARANCE – COLD

Inlet in 0.008" (0.203 mm)
Exhaust in 0.008" (0.203 mm)

CRANKSHAFT

Big End Journal Diameter	1.8765"/1.8760"	(47.6631/47.6504 mm)
Main Bearing Journal Diameter		
Drive Side	1.1247"/1.250"	(28.576/28.575 mm)
Timing Side	1.1812"/1.1808"	(30.00/29.99 mm)
Balance Factor	69% STD	55% AV

CONNECTING RODS

Big End Diameter   2.0215"/2.0210"   (51.3461/51.3334 mm)

CYLINDER BLOCK

Material   ALUMINIUM ALLOY WITH CAST IRON LINERS

		Low (L) Grade	High (H) Grade
Bore Size	in	2.9898"/2.9893"	2.9904"/2.9899
	mm	75.941/75.928	75.957/75.943

CYLINDER HEAD

Valve Guide Bore	0.4985"/0.4980"	(12.661/12.649 mm)
Valve Seat Interference	0.0055"/0.005"	(0.1397/0.1270 mm)
Valve Seat Angle	45°	

VALVES

Stem Diameter	Inlet	0.2797"/0.2794"	(7.1043/7.0967 mm)
	Exhaust	0.2790"/0.2787"	(7.0866/7.078 mm)
Head Diameter	Inlet	1.152"/1.148"	(29.26/29.159 mm)
	Exhaust	0.995"/0.990"	(25.273/25.146 mm)

VALVE GUIDES

Bore Diameter	Inlet		
Bore Diameter	Exhaust	0.2816"/0.2813"	(7.1526/7.1449 mm)
Outside Diameter		0.501"/0.5005"	(12.795/12.712 mm)
Length	Inlet	1.435"	(36.413 mm)
Length	Exhaust	1.475"	(40.455 mm)

VALVE SPRING

	OUTER	INNER
Free Length	1.378" (35.00 mm)	1.161" (29.489 mm)
Total No. of Coils	5.4	6.5
Rate	75 lb/in (5.273 kg^{2}cm)	41.41 lb/in (2.918 kg^{2}cm)

ROCKERS

Bore Diameter	0.5317"/0.5312"	(13.469/13.4564 mm)
Spindle Diameter	0.5290"/0.5285"	(13.4366/13.4239 mm)

ENGINE

IGNITION TIMING

Crankshaft Position – full advance	30°
Engine rpm when full advance occurs	3500

SPARK PLUG

Type	Champion G63
Gap Setting	0.25 (0.635 mm)
Thread Size	10 mm
Reach	¾" (19.06 mm)

PISTONS

	LOW (L) GRADE	HIGH (H) GRADE
Diameter	75.887/75.877 mm	75.900/75.890 mm
	2.9876"/2.9872"	2.9882"/2.9878"

PISTON RINGS

Compression Rings

Width	0.0586"/0.0581"	(1.49/1.478 mm)
Thickness (Radial)	0.127"/0.120"	(3.23/3.07 mm)
Fitted Gap	0.013"/0.008"	(0.330/0.203 mm)
Clearance in Groove	0.0035"/0.0015"	(0.089/0.038 mm)

OIL CONTROL

Width	0.159"/0.158"	(3.937/3.925 mm)
Thickness (Radial)	0.109"/0.103"	(2.78/2.62 mm)
Fitted Gap	0.010"/0.008"	(0.254/0.203 mm)
Clearance in Groove	0.0025"/0.0015"	(0.063/0.038 mm)

CARBURETTOR

Make	AMAL	BING
Type	2934/2934/	64 CD
Bore Size	34 mm	36 mm
Main Jet	220	140
Needle Jet	0.106	2.66
Neddle Type	2C3	STD
Needle Position	—	1
Throttle Valve	—	—
Piston	—	3
Pilot Jet	20	45
Starter Jet	35	—

GEARBOX

RATIOS

INTERNAL

5th Top	1.00:1
4th	1.19:1
3rd	1.40:1
2nd	1.837:1
1st Bottom	2.585:1

OVERALL

5th	4.40:1
4th	5.24:1
3rd	6.16:1
2nd	8.08:1
1st	11.37:1

Engine rpm at 10 mph in 5th Gear	626

SPROCKET DETAILS

Engine	29
Gearbox	20
Clutch	58
Rearwheel	44

GEARBOX

CHAIN DETAILS
Primary   Triplex endless ⅜" pitch x 84 links
Secondary   Single ⅜" x 1⅝" x 10 links Renold Grand Prix

ELECTRICAL

BULBS
Headlight   12 volt 60/55 Quartz Halogen H4 Lucas 472

TORQUE WRENCH SETTINGS (DRY)
Cylinder Head Fixing Nuts   22 lb ft   (3.0 kg m)
Cylinder Head Fixing Screws   12 lb ft   (1.659 kg m)
Cylinder Barrel Fixing Nuts   14 lb ft   (1.936 kg m)
Con-Rod Nuts   22 lb ft   (30 kg m)

SECTION C
TRANSMISSION

DESCRIPTION	Section
ADJUSTING THE CLUTCH OPERATING MECHANISM	C1
ADJUSTING THE PRIMARY CHAIN TENSION	C2
REMOVING AND REPLACING THE PRIMARY COVER	C3
REMOVING AND REFITTING THE CLUTCH PLATES	C4
INSPECTING THE CLUTCH PLATES AND SPRINGS	C5
ADJUSTING THE CLUTCH PRESSURE PLATE	C6
RENEWING SHOCK ABSORBER RUBBERS	C7
REMOVING AND REPLACING THE STATOR AND ROTOR	C8
REMOVING AND REPLACING THE CLUTCH AND ENGINE SPROCKETS	C9
INSPECTION OF THE TRANSMISSION COMPONENTS	C10
CLUTCH AND ENGINE SPROCKET ALIGNMENT	C11
REAR CHAIN ALTERNATIONS AND REPAIRS	C12

TRANSMISSION

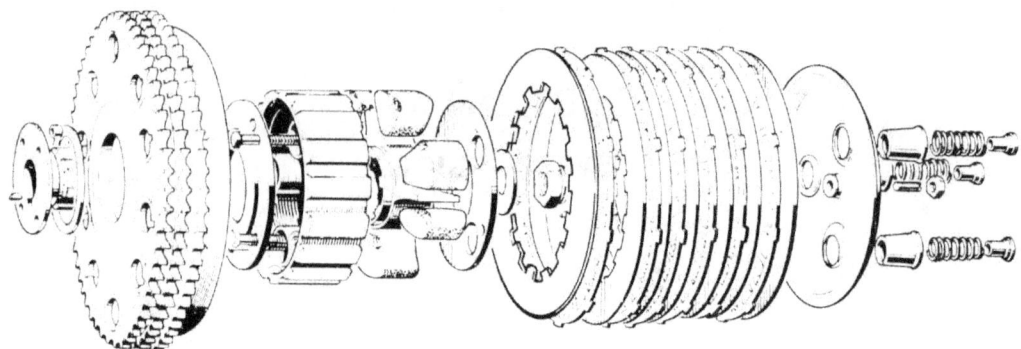

Fig. C1. General arrangement of clutch and shock absorber unit

DESCRIPTION

The clutch is of a multiplate type, using synthetic friction material on the bonded drive plates and incorporating a transmission shock absorber. The pressure on the clutch plates is maintained by three springs held in position by three slotted nuts.

The clutch is designed to operate in oil and this is automatically catered for in conjunction with the engine oiling system.

The shock absorbing unit transmits the power from the clutch sprocket via the clutch plates to the gearbox mainshaft. Within the shock absorber unit the drive is transmitted through three large rubber pads to the three-armed spider which is splined to the clutch centre; this in turn is located to the gearbox mainshaft by means of a locking taper and key. In addition, there are three rubber rebound pads. The total effect of the rubber pads is to reduce the variations in engine torque at low speeds, providing an extremely smooth transmission of power to the gearbox.

SECTION C1

ADJUSTING THE CLUTCH OPERATING MECHANISM

The clutch, which is situated within the outer primary cover to the left of the machine, can be adjusted by means of the handlebar adjuster, pushrod adjuster and the pressure plate springs, the latter only being accessible for adjustment when the outer primary cover is removed. Section C4 fully describes adjusting the springs and pressure plate.

The clutch operating rod should have $1/16$ inches (1.5mm.) clearance between the clutch operating mechanism and the pressure plate. To achieve this remove the inspection cap from the centre of the primary cover, then slacken the clutch cable handlebar adjustment right off.

Unscrew the hexagonal lock nut and screw in the slotted adjuster screw in the centre of the pressure plate until the pressure plate just begins to lift. Unscrew the adjuster one half turn and secure it in that position by re-tightening the lock-nut.

The clutch operating cable should then be re-adjusted, by means of the handlebar adjuster, until there is approximately $1/8$ inches (3mm.) free movement in the cable.

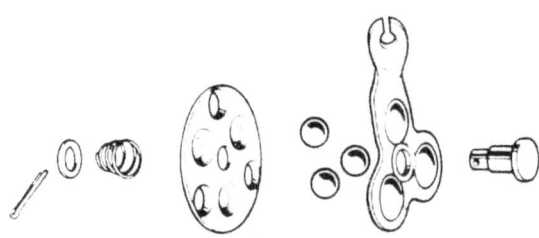

Fig. C2. Exploded view of clutch operating mechanism

If the clutch is dragging and normal adjustment of the operating rod and operating cable produces no improvement, it will be necessary to remove the outer primary cover and check the pressure plate for true running as shown in Section C6.

To maintain a smooth and easy clutch operation, particular attention should be given to the recommended primary chaincase oil change periods (see "Routine Maintenance") and clutch cable lubrication (see Section A17).

TRANSMISSION

SECTION C2

ADJUSTING THE PRIMARY CHAIN TENSION

The primary chain is of the triplex type and is non-adjustable as the centres of the engine main-shaft and gearbox mainshaft are fixed. Provision for take-up of wear in the primary chain is made by means of a rubber faced tension slipper blade below the lower run of the chain. The free movement in the chain can be felt with the finger after removing the top inspection plug adjacent to the cylinder block, with the engine stopped, of course.

The correct chain adjustment is $3/8$ in. (9.5mm.) free movement. To adjust the chain tension first remove the L.H footrest and slacken locknut on (6) threaded bolt Fig. C4. Screw in bolt to tighten chain. Fig C4, 5. When correct adjustment is obtained tighten locknut and replace footrest.

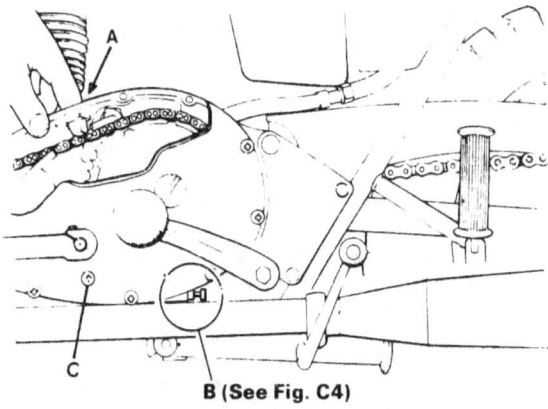

Fig. C3. Adjusting the chain tensioner

SECTION C3

REMOVING AND REPLACING THE PRIMARY COVER

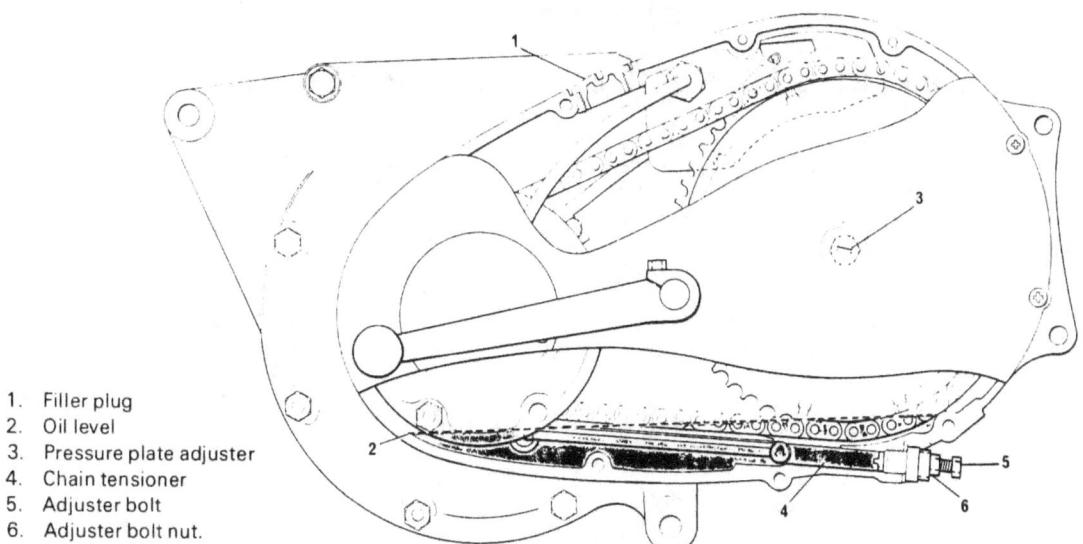

1. Filler plug
2. Oil level
3. Pressure plate adjuster
4. Chain tensioner
5. Adjuster bolt
6. Adjuster bolt nut.

Fig. C4. Section through primary chaincase

Slacken the left finned clip bolt, left silencer clip bolt and remove the nut and bolt securing the left exhaust pipe bracket forward of the engine. Remove the exhaust pipe as in Section B17.

Unscrew the left footrest securing bolt and withdraw the footrest.

Place a drip tray underneath the primary cover and remove the Allen screw directly under the change shaft and allow the oil to drain from the chaincase.

Remove the two domed nuts and copper washers and unscrew eight recess screws from the periphery of the primary cover. Withdraw the cover and paper gasket.

Refitting the cover is the reversal of the above instructions but fit a new paper gasket and if necessary, replace the 'O' ring on the gearchange spindle. Take care when replacing the cover so as not to damage or displace the 'O' ring. Later models are fitted with oil seal in outer cover which should be checked for damage.

Finally, replace the drain plug and 'prime' the chaincase with approximately $1/4$ pint of fresh engine oil. (See Section A1).

SECTION C4

REMOVING AND REFITTING THE CLUTCH PLATES

Remove the outer primary cover as described in Section C3.

The three pressure plate springs are locked in position by means of location "pips" in the cups and on the drive adjuster nuts. To facilitate removal of the slotted adjuster nuts, insert a knife blade under the head of the nut whilst the nut is unscrewed (using a screwdriver of the type shown in Fig. C5). Withdraw the springs, cup and pressure plate assembly. Removal of the clutch plates is facilitated by means of two narrow hooked tools which can be made from a piece of $1/32$ in. dia. wire by bending to form a hook at one end. Thoroughly clean all parts in paraffin (kerosene) and inspect the clutch springs and plates for excessive wear (see section C5). When replacing the clutch plates remember that the bottom position is occupied by a bonded plate.

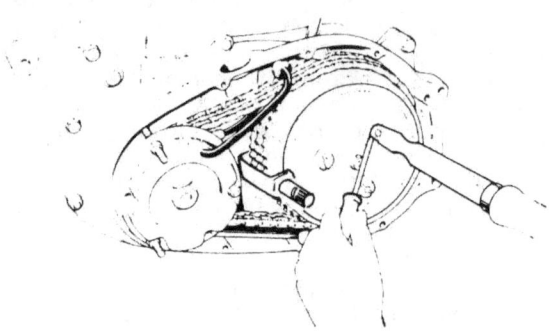

Fig. C5. Unscrewing the clutch spring nuts

Ensure that the cups are located correctly and assemble the springs and nuts, then adjust the pressure plate for true running as described below. Reassembly then continues as the reversal of the above instructions.

SECTION C5

INSPECTING THE CLUTCH PLATES AND SPRINGS

The bonded friction plates should be examined for excessive wear to the driving tags and the overall thickness of the clutch plates should be measured to determine the wear to the friction faces. If the bonded insert measures less than 0.020" thick when measured from the clutch plate face the friction plate should be renewed. Check the fit of the driving tags in the clutch housing. The clearance should not be excessive.

Check the plain steel driven plates for flatness by placing the plates horizontally on a perfectly flat surface such as a thick piece of plate glass.

Original finish on the driven plates is a phosphoric acid etched surface and hence the plates need not be polished. Check the fit of the plate on the shock absorber housing. the radial clearance should not be excessive.

Inspect the clutch springs for compressive strength by measuring the length of the spring and comparing it with the dimensions given in "Technical Data". If a spring has shortened more than 0.1 in. (2.5mm.) the complete set should be renewed. It is not advisable to renew just one or two springs as this may ultimately result in the pressure plate running unevenly.

SECTION C6

ADJUSTING THE CLUTCH PRESSURE PLATE

When the pressure plate is refitted or requires adjustment, the following procedure should be observed. With neutral selected, sit astride the machine, disengage the clutch, then depress the kickstart-pedal and observe the rotation of the pressure plate; it should revolve true relative to the clutch housing. If it does not do so, the three slotted nuts must be initially adjusted so the ends of the clutch pins are flush with the heads of the nuts. The nut is prevented from unscrewing by a "pip" on the underside and to unscrew a nut, a narrow screwdriver should be used to hold the spring away from the "pip" of the nut as shown in Fig. C5.

When the nuts are flush with the ends of the pins depress the kickstart again and mark the "high-spot" with chalk, then screw in the nearest nut(s) about half a turn and try again. Repeat this procedure until the plate rotates evenly without "wobbling".

TRANSMISSION

SECTION C7

RENEWING THE SHOCK ABSORBER RUBBERS

When the primary cover and clutch plates are removed, access is gained to the shock absorber unit, which consists of a housing, paddle or spider, inner and outer cover plates and shock absorbing rubbers.

To remove the rubbers for inspection or renewal, first unscrew the three bolts which serve to retain the shock absorber plate and lever the plate free, using a suitable small lever.

The shock absorber rubbers can be prised out of position, using a sharp pointed tool, commencing by levering out the small rebound rubbers first.

When the three small rebound rubbers are removed the large drive rubbers will be free to be withdrawn.

If the rubbers show no signs of punctures or cracking, etc., they can be refitted, but remember that a slight puncture in the rubber can ultimately result in the rubber disintegrating.

To replace the shock absorber drive and rebound rubbers, first install all three of the larger drive rubbers in position as shown in Fig. C6. Follow through by inserting and replacing the smaller rebound rubbers. It may prove necessary to lever the shock absorber spider arms using a small tommy bar or similar to facilitate assembly, but this operation can be accomplished 'in situ' on the machine without the need for special tools or equipment, or necessity for removing the complete unit from the machine.

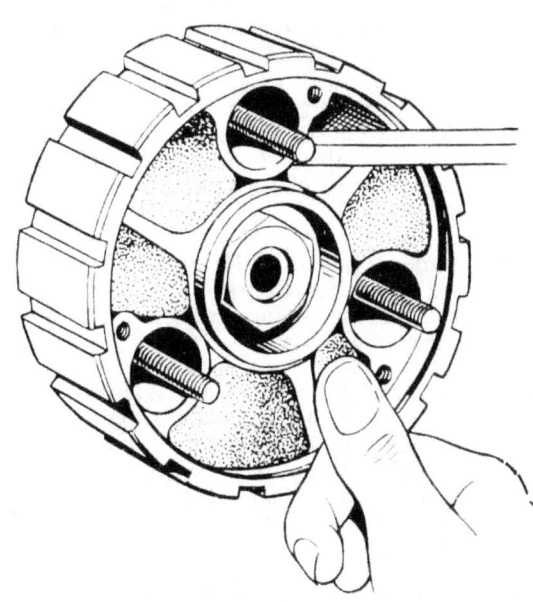

Fig. C6. Replacing the shock absorber rubbers.

Although the rubbers are of an oil resistant type, it is not advisable to use oil or grease as an aid to reassembly as this may shorten the working life of the rubber.

Ensure that the three outer cover bolts are tighten then 'peen' the protruding threads thereby preventing the bolts from unscrewing during service.

SECTION C8

REMOVING AND REPLACING THE STATOR AND ROTOR

First disconnect the stator leads at the top rear of the primary chaincase then, with the primary cover removed, unscrew the three stator retaining nuts and withdraw the stator from over the mounting studs and withdraw the lead from the sleeve nut. If any difficulty is encountered, unscrew the sleeve nut and the lead can then be withdrawn easily. To remove the rotor unscrew the mainshaft nut using a box spanner and mallet, or, alternatively, select 5th (top) gear and apply the rear brake, then unscrew the nut.

Check the rotor carefully for signs of cracking or fatigue failure. Store the rotor within the stator to prevent metal particles adhering.

When replacing the rotor ensure that the key is located correctly, then tighten the nut to the torque figure given in "Technical Data".

It is advisable to renew the lockwasher before refitting the rotor securing nut.

When refitting the stator, ensure that the side of the stator with the leads connecting the coils together is outermost, then tighten the retaining nuts to the torque figure given in Technical Data Section. Insert the lead into the sleeve nut and connect the wires to those of the same colour code from the main harness.

Check that the position of the lead is such that it cannot foul the chain.

Finally, rotate the crankshaft and ensure that the rotor does not foul the stator. It should be possible to insert a feeler gauge of at least 0·008 in. (0.2mm.) thickness between each of the stator pole pieces and the rotor.

SECTION C9

REMOVING AND REPLACING THE CLUTCH AND ENGINE SPROCKETS

Remove the primary cover as shown in Section C3, then remove the pressure plate and clutch plates, as shown in Section C5. Insert the locking plate 61-3768 into the clutch housing and remove the stator and rotor as described in Section C8. Remove the rotor key and distance piece and slacken off the chain tensioner. Unscrew the clutch hub self locking nut then remove the plain washer.

As the primary chain is of the endless type, the clutch and engine sprockets have to be extracted simultaneously using extractor tool 61-7014 as shown in Fig. C8.

Screw the body of the clutch extractor into the clutch hub until the maximum depth of thread is engaged, then tighten the centre bolt until the hub is released. When this is achieved, assemble the engine sprocket extractor, No. 61-6014 and screw in the centre bolt and extract the engine sprocket.

Press out the hub from the shock absorber to release the sprocket, thrust washer, rollers and threaded pins.

Finally, remove the key from the gearbox mainshaft and check that the oil seal in the primary chain inner cover is a good fit over the high gear. To renew this oil seal the circular cover should be removed. When replacing the cover, use a new gasket and ensure that the oil seal is pressed in with the lip relative to the cover as shown in Fig. C9.

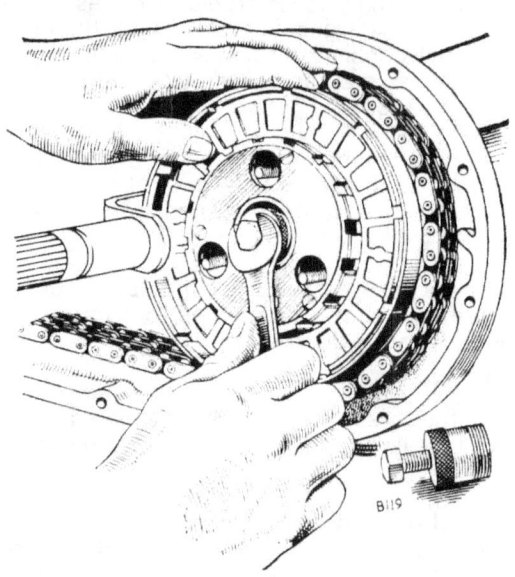

Fig. C8. Extracting the clutch centre, using extractor 61-7014 and locking plate 61-3768

SECTION C10

INSPECTION OF THE TRANSMISSION COMPONENTS

(1) Inspect the primary chain for excessive wear of the rollers and pivot pins and check that the elongation does not exceed 1 ½ %. To do this first scribe two marks on a flat surface exactly 12in. (30.5cm.) apart, then after degreasing or washing the chain in paraffin (kerosene), place the chain opposite the two marks. When the chain is compressed to its minimum free length the marks should coincide with the centres of two pivot pins 32 links apart. When the chain is stretched to its maximum free length the extension should not exceed ¼ in. (6.25mm.).

Inspect the condition of the sprocket teeth for signs of hooking and pitting.

A very good method of indicating whether the chain is badly worn or not is to wrap it round the clutch sprocket and attempt to lift the chain from its seating at various points round the sprocket. Little or no lift indicates that both the sprocket and chain are in good condition.

(2) Check the fit between the shock absorber spider and the clutch hub splines. The spider should be a push fit onto the clutch hub and there should not be any radial movement.

Similarly check the fit of the engine sprocket splines onto the crankshaft. Again, there should not be any radial movement.

If either the spider or the engine sprocket are tight fitting on the clutch hub and crankshaft respectively, there is no cause for concern as such a fit is to the best advantage.

(3) Check the clutch hub roller bearing diameter, the rollers themselves and the bearing of the clutch sprocket for excessive wear and pitting etc. Measure the rollers, clutch hub and clutch sprocket bearing diameters and compare them with the dimensions given in "Technical Data".

If the diameters of the rollers are below the bottom limit, they should be renewed. When purchasing new rollers ensure that they are in accordance with the dimensions given in "Technical Data". In particular, check that the length is correct.

(4) Check that the shock absorber spider is a good working fit in the inner and outer retaining plates and that the arms of the spider have not caused excessive score marks on the inner faces of the retaining plates. A good idea is to check the working clearance by assembling the shock absorber unit without the rubbers.

(5) Inspect the clutch operating rod for bending, by rolling it on a flat surface such as a piece of plate glass. Check that the length of the rod is within the limits given in "Technical Data". This component should not be replaced with anything other than a genuine Triumph spare part. The ends of the rod are specially heat treated to give maximum wear resistance.

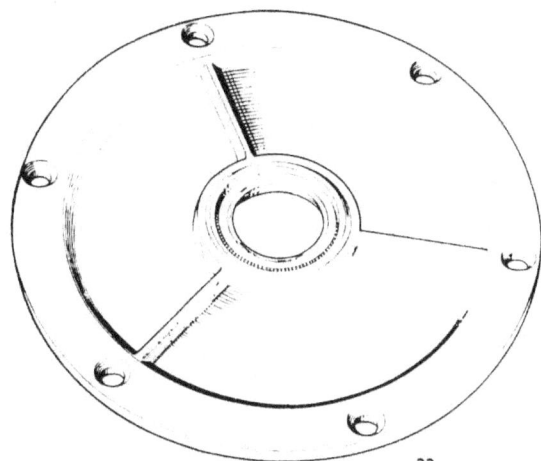

Fig. C9. Oil seal in gearbox sprocket detachable cover

Thoroughly clean all parts in paraffin (kerosene) and inspect them for wear or fatigue as shown in Section C5.

Grease the clutch hub and fit the thrust washer and 20 of the correct rollers.

Do not use ¼in. x ¼in. bright ended rollers

Place the sprocket in position and press on the shock absorber complete with the three threaded pins. If the splines are loose use "LOCTITE" 207

When replacing the primary chain and sprockets, ensure that the taper ground boss of the engine sprocket is towards the crankshaft main bearing. With the gearbox mainshaft key carefully in position, locate the clutch hub onto the mainshaft taper and tap it slightly to lock it onto the taper.

Place the primary chain over the engine sprocket and drive the sprocket onto the crankshaft.

Offer the clutch locking tool 61-3768 into the clutch plate housing and then refit the plain washer, and clutch self-locking nut.

Engage fourth gear, apply the rear brake and tighten the clutch securing nut to the torque figure given in "Technical Data".

Do not forget to fit the distance piece between the engine sprocket and rotor and remember to refit the rectangular section rotor locating key. Reassembly then continues as a reversal of the above instructions. Finally, replenish the chaincase with the recommended grade of oil (see Section A1).

Note.-Alternatively, the clutch sprocket may be removed by prising out the twenty roller bearings and allowing the sprocket to move both outwards and forwards until it can be unmeshed from the primary chain. This alternative only applies if the shock absorber assembly can readily be detached from the hub to allow access to the rollers.

SECTION C11

CLUTCH AND ENGINE SPROCKET ALIGNMENT

It is important that the engine and gearbox sprockets are accurately in line, otherwise rapid wear of the primary chain and sprockets will occur. This will result in the chain rollers fracturing and the chain breaking. This would almost certainly cause irreparable damage to the crankcase.

Correct alignment of the sprockets is easily effected by the use of spacing shims removed or replaced from behind the engine sprocket. the alignment can be initally checked by placing a straight edge alongside both sprockets (e.g. a steel rule) after first removing the primary chain (See previous section). If any gap produced is in excess of 0.005" (0.127mm.) maximum tolerance, then the engine sprocket must be shimed accordingly. Place the appropriate shim between the engine sprocket and the spacer that sits up against the roller bearing.

Shims are available as follows:-

0.010" thick-Part Number 70-8038

0.030" thick-Part Number 71-2660

SECTION C12

REAR CHAIN ALTERATIONS AND REPAIRS

If the chains have been correctly serviced, very few repairs will be necessary. Should the occasion arise to repair, lengthen or shorten a chain, a rivet extractor, as shown in Fig. C11, and a few spare parts will cover all requirements.

RIVET EXTRACTOR

The rivet extractor can be used on all motorcycle chains up to 3/4in. pitch, whether the chains are on or off the wheels.

Fig. C10. Rear chain alterations

To SHORTEN a chain containing an EVEN NUMBER OF PITCHES remove the dark parts shown in (1) and replace by cranked double link and single connecting link (2).

To SHORTEN a chain containing an ODD NUMBER OF PITCHES remove the dark parts shown in (3) and replace by a single connecting link and inner link as (4).

To REPAIR a chain with a broken roller or inside link, remove the dark parts in (5) and replace by two single connecting links and one inner link as (6).

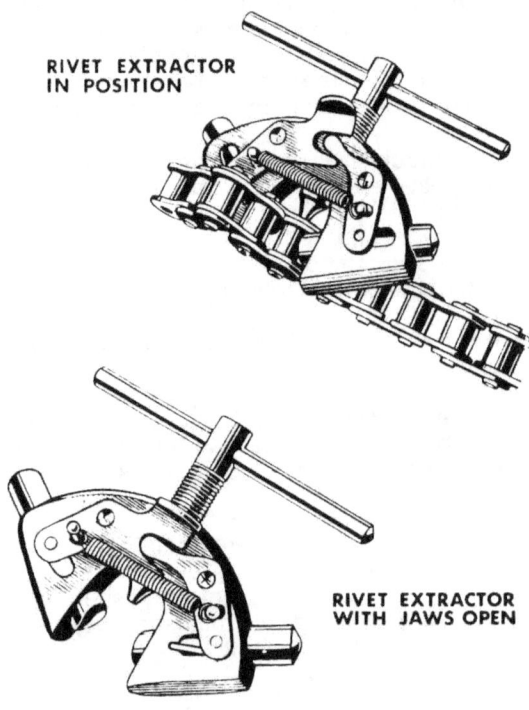

Fig. C11. Chain link rivet extractor

When using the extractor:-

(1) Turn screw anti-clockwise to permit the punch end to clear the chain rivet.

TRANSMISSION

(2) Open the jaws by pressing down the lever (see below).

(3) Pass jaws over chain and release the lever. Jaws should rest on a chain roller free of chain link plates (see below).

(4) Turn screw clockwise until punch contacts and pushes out rivet end through chain outer link plate. Unscrew punch, withdraw extractor and repeat complete operation on the adjacent rivet in the same chain outer link plate. The outer plate is then free and the two rivets can be withdrawn from opposite sides with the opposite plate in position. Do not use the removed part again.

When the alterations are finished the chain should be lubricated as shown in Section A12.

SECTION D

FIVE SPEED GEARBOX

INDEX

DESCRIPTION	Section
SEQUENCE OF GEARCHANGING	D1
REMOVING AND REPLACING THE OUTER COVER ASSEMBLY	D2
DISMANTLING AND REASSEMBLING THE KICKSTART MECHANISM	D3
DISMANTLING AND REASSEMBLING THE GEARCHANGE MECHANISM	D4
INSPECTING THE GEARCHANGE AND KICKSTART COMPONENTS	D5
RENEWING KICKSTART AND GEARCHANGE SPINDLE BUSHES	D6
CLUTCH OPERATING MECHANISM	D7
DISMANTLING THE GEARBOX	D8
INSPECTION OF THE GEARBOX COMPONENTS	D9
RENEWING MAINSHAFT AND LAYSHAFT BEARINGS	D10
REASSEMBLING THE GEARBOX	D11
CHANGING THE GEARBOX SPROCKET	D12

GEARBOX

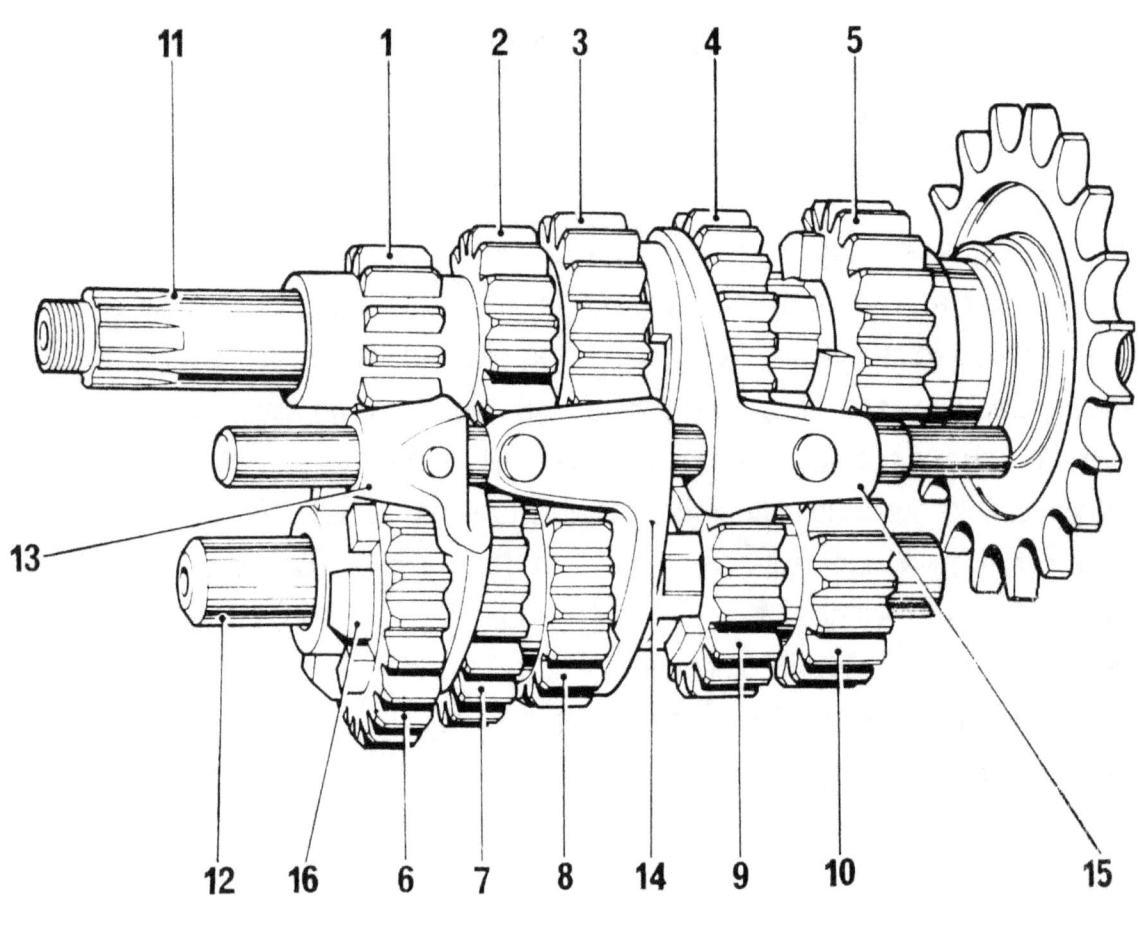

1. Low gear
2. Second gear
3. Third gear
4. Fourth gear
5. Fifth gear
6. Low gear
7. Second gear
8. Third gear
9. Fourth gear
10. Fifth gear
11. Mainshaft
12. Layshaft
13. First gear layshaft selector fork
14. Third gear layshaft selector fork
15. Mainshaft selector fork
16. Layshaft engaging dog

Fig. D1. Plan of gear components

GEARBOX

SECTION D1

SEQUENCE OF GEARCHANGING

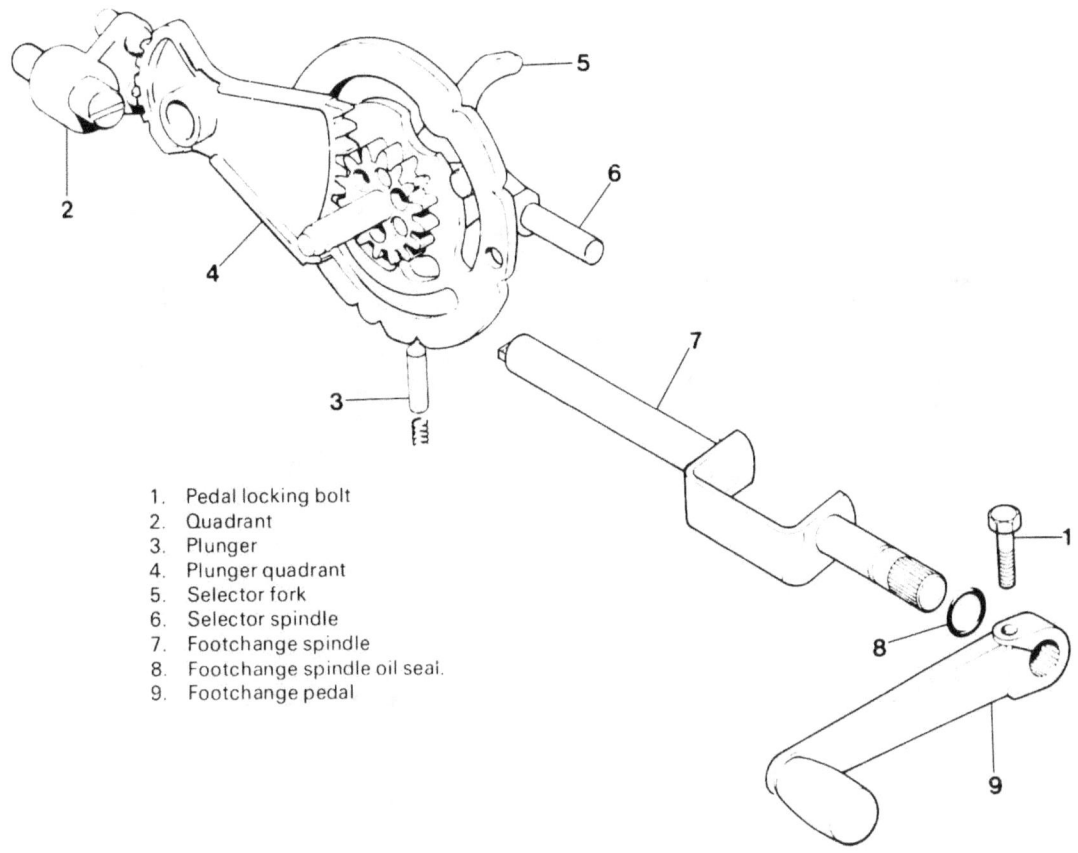

1. Pedal locking bolt
2. Quadrant
3. Plunger
4. Plunger quadrant
5. Selector fork
6. Selector spindle
7. Footchange spindle
8. Footchange spindle oil seal.
9. Footchange pedal

Fig. D2. Gear selection components

The gearbox is operated by the pedal on the left-hand side of the machine, the pedal being splined to the gear change spindle. (Prior to engine no. HN62501 the gearbox is operated from the right-hand side). Two chamfered plungers with springs fit into the housing in such a way that as the gear pedal is moved up and down the plungers locate in the teeth at the outboard end of the quadrant. The quadrant is pivoted in the centre and the inboard end is formed to mate with the captive pinion of the camplate. See Fig. D2.

Figs. D3 (i) to D3 (vi) illustrate the camplate with its plunger and the three engaging pins of the selector forks which can be seen in the camplate track. The three sliding pinions are moved along the mainshaft and layshaft by the selector forks. The neutral positions of the camplate and gears are shown in Fig. D3 (ii).

When the pedal is depressed to engage low gear (first) the camplate is turned anti-clockwise moving the layshaft selector fork to mesh the sliding first gear with the engaging dog on the end of the layshaft. (The engaging dog is illustrated in Fig. D1.)

As second gear is selected by lifting the pedal, the second layshaft selector fork brings the sliding third gear into mesh with the layshaft second gear, while the previous selector fork disengages first gear from the engaging dog.

Movement of the gear lever in the same direction will select third gear by moving the mainshaft sliding gear into mesh with the mainshaft third gear. At the same time the second layshaft selector disengages second gear.

D GEARBOX

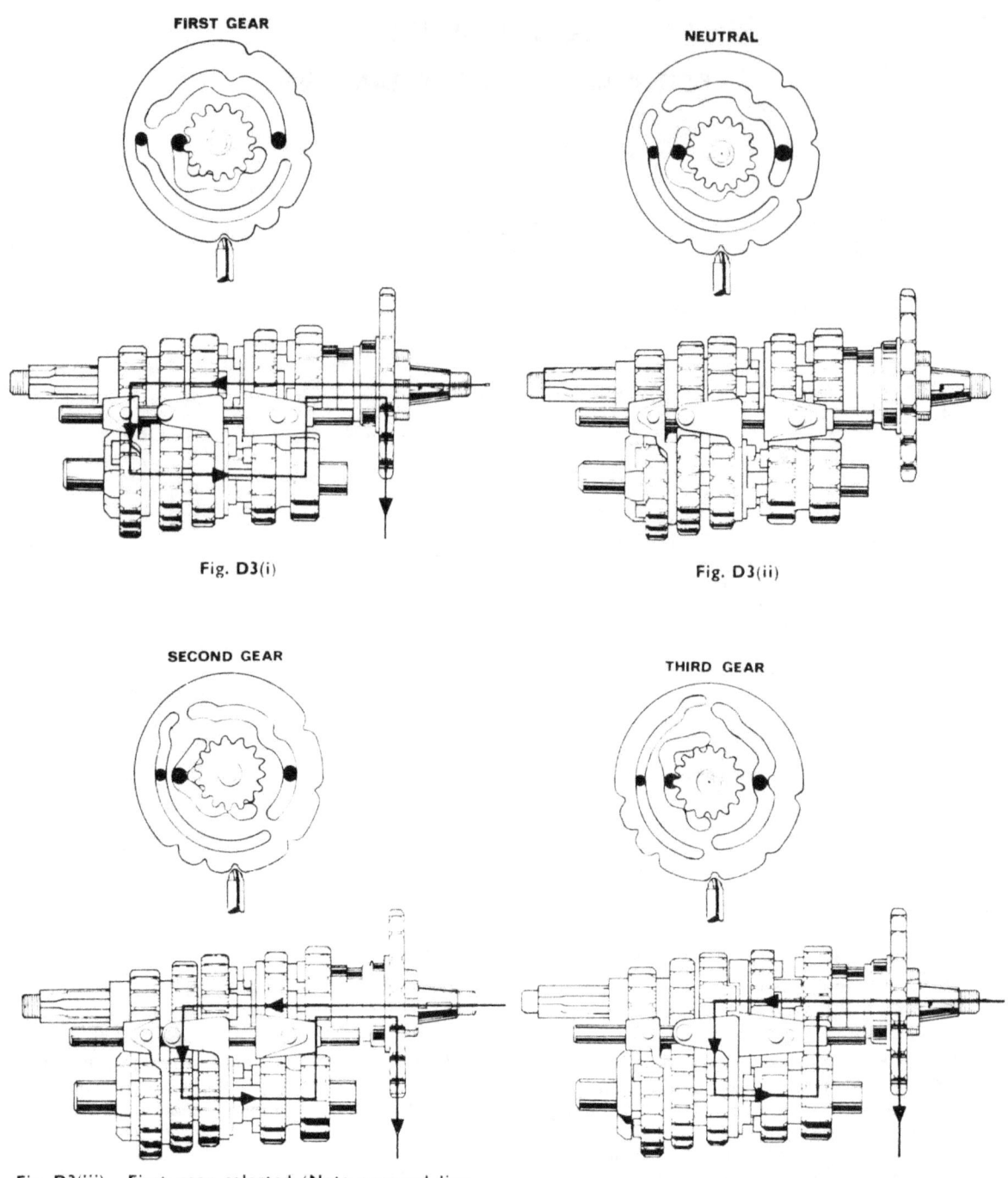

Fig. D3(i).

Fig. D3(ii).

Fig. D3(iii). First gear selected (Note arrowed line showing power being transmitted through the gear cluster)

Fig. D3(iv).

Further movement of the gear lever will select fourth gear by moving the sliding layshaft third gear into mesh with the layshaft fourth gear while the mainshaft fourth gear is moved into a neutral position.

Finally, fifth gear is obtained by a final movement of the lever in the same direction. The mainshaft selector fork will bring the mainshaft sliding gear (fourth gear) into mesh with the mainshaft fifth gear. At the same time the second layshaft sliding gear (third gear) is moved into neutral position.

It should be noted that throughout the range of gear pedal movements the gear pedal spindle and plunger housing return to the original position ready for the next selection.

GEARBOX

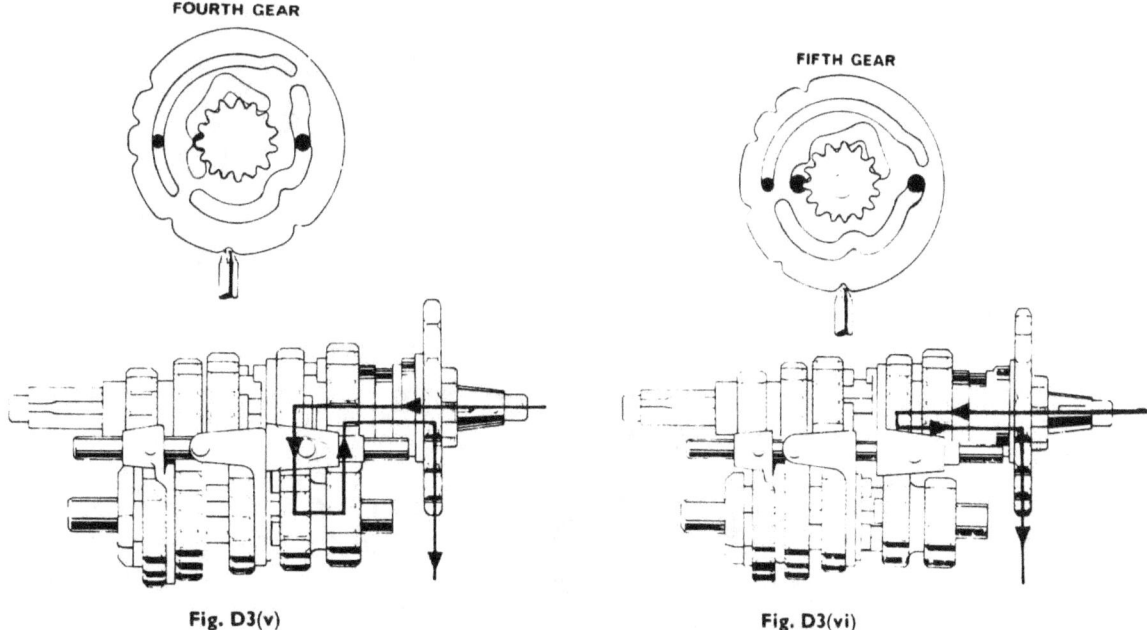

Fig. D3(v) **Fig. D3(vi)**

SECTION D2

REMOVING AND REPLACING THE GEARBOX OUTER COVER ASSEMBLY

Remove the right hand exhaust system. See section B17.

Remove the right footrest by detaching the fixing bolt.

Slacken off the clutch cable adjustment and slip out the cable nipple at the handlebar control. Slide the rubber cover up away from the abutment for the cable at the gearbox end and unscrew the abutment.

Remove the large slotted plug from the gearbox outer cover and access will be gained to the clutch operating arm. It is only necessary then to release the cable nipple from the arm with the finger.

Place a drip tray underneath the gearbox and unscrew the gearbox filler plug and drain plug.

Engage 5th (top) gear. This will allow several otherwise difficult nuts to be unscrewed by subsequently applying the rear brake when required.

Unscrew the top and bottom hexagonal nut and the recess screws from the periphery of the gearbox cover. Depress the kickstart lever slightly and tap the cover until it is free.

When the cover is removed, the gear-change mechanism, kickstart mechanism and clutch operating mechanism will be accessible.

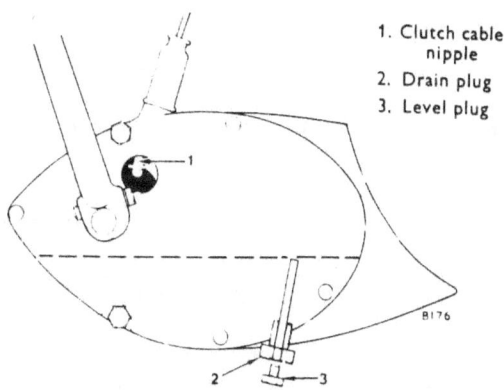

1. Clutch cable nipple
2. Drain plug
3. Level plug

Fig. D4. Showing gearbox oil level and oil drain plugs

Prior to refitting the outer cover ensure that the junction surface is clean and free from any deposits. Always renew the joint face gaskets before refitting cover.

Turn the kickstart pedal until it is halfway down its operational stroke and offer the cover to the gearbox. Check that the kickstart pedal returns to its normal fully-returned position. Reassembly then continues as reversal of the above instructions. Finally, refill the gearbox to the correct level with the recommended grade of oil (see Section A1).

D

GEARBOX

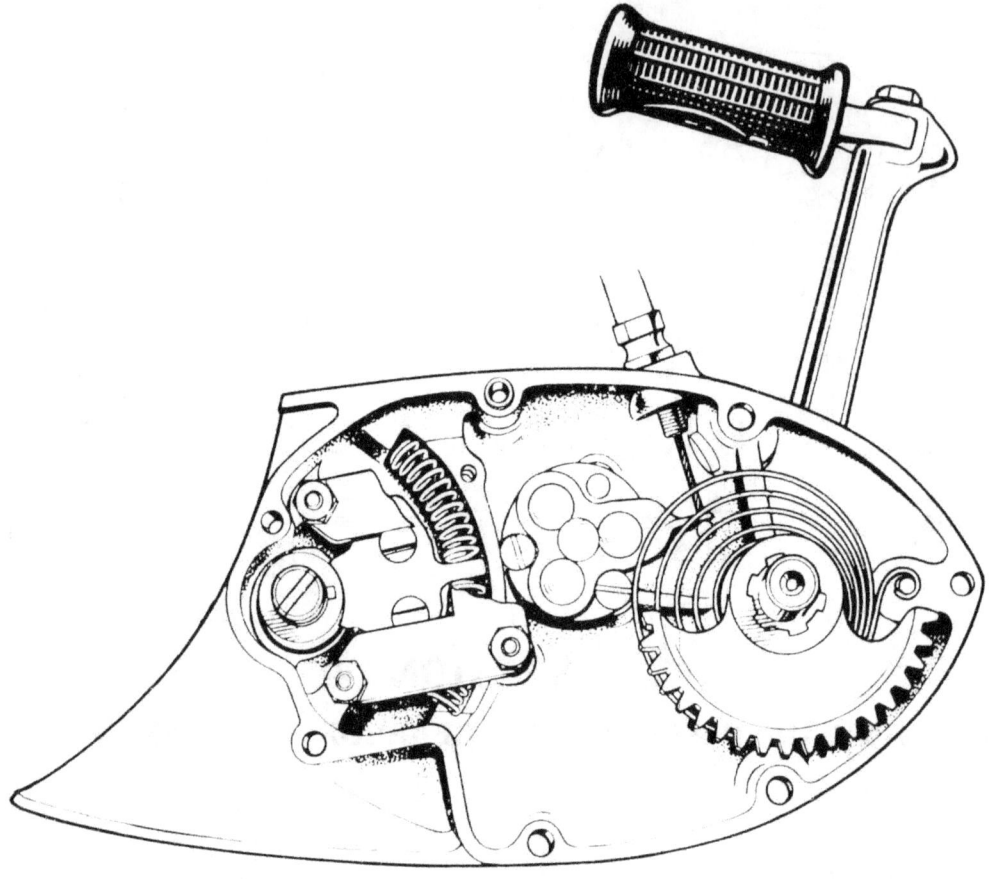

Fig. D5. Gearbox outer cover, showing gearchange mechanism, clutch operating mechanism and kickstart quadrant

SECTION D3

DISMANTLING AND REASSEMBLING THE KICKSTART MECHANISM

Slacken the kickstarter crank cotter pin nut about two or three turns and release the cotter pin from its locking taper by using a hammer and a soft metal drift. Slide the pedal off the shaft and withdraw the quadrant and spring assembly. Apply the rear brake, bend back the tab on the lock washer and unscrew the kickstart ratchet pinion securing nut from the gearbox mainshaft. Withdraw the pinion, ratchet, spring and sleeve, then thoroughly clean all parts in paraffin (kerosene) and inspect them for wear etc., as shown in Section D5.

If the kickstarter quadrant is to be renewed the spindle should be driven out using a hammer or press and the gear quadrant pressed onto the spindle so that the kickstart crank location flat is positioned correctly relative to the quadrant (see Fig. D6).

To reassemble the mechanism, first refit the thin walled steel sleeve, spring, pinion and ratchet to the gearbox mainshaft and assemble the tab

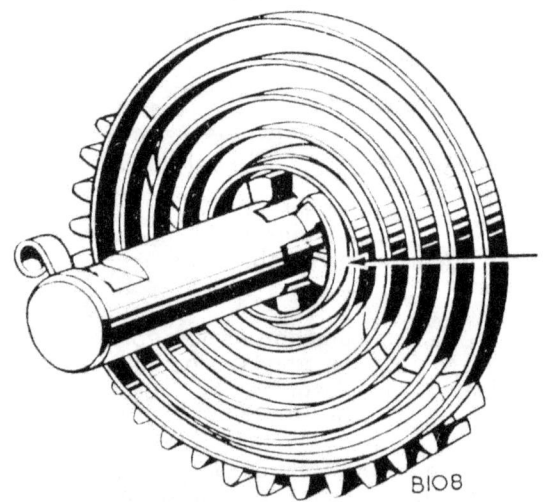

Fig. D6. Kick start quadrant and spring. Arrow indicates correct spring location

GEARBOX D

washer, then screw on the retaining nut to the torque figure given in "Technical Data". **Do not over-tighten the retaining nut as this may result in failure of the thin walled inner steel sleeve.**

Fit the return spring to the kickstart quadrant as shown in Fig. D6. Offer the spindle into the kickstart bush and locate the return spring onto the anchor peg at the rear of the cover. Fit the oil seal over the spindle and assemble the kickstart crank, locking it into position with the cotter pin from the rear. Refit the outer cover as shown in Section D2. Do not forget to refit the oil seal. Refill the gearbox with the correct grade of lubricant (Section A1).

SECTION D4

DISMANTLING AND REASSEMBLING THE GEARCHANGE MECHANISM

Remove the four bolts and locking washers securing the guide plate. Withdraw the guide plate, plunger quadrant and curved return springs. Thoroughly clean the parts in paraffin (kerosene) and inspect them for wear etc., as shown in Section D5.

To reassemble the mechanism, offer it to the outer cover bush then refit the two quadrant return springs and ensure that they locate correctly over the step in the cover.

Refit the retainer plate, not forgetting the lokking washers which fit one under each of the four bolts. Finally, refit the springs the plungers, taking care that they are not suddenly ejected from their seats during assembly.

SECTION D5

INSPECTING THE GEARCHANGE AND KICKSTART COMPONENTS

GEARCHANGE:

(1) Inspect the gearchange plungers for wear and ensure that they are a clearance fit in the quadrant. Check the plunger springs by comparing their lengths with the figures given in "Technical Data".

(2) Examine the plunger guide plate for wear and grooving on the taper guide surfaces. Renew the plate if grooving has occurred.

(3) Inspect the footchange return springs for fatigue and if they shown signs of corrosion due to condensation, they should be renewed.

(4) Examine the gearchange quadrant bush for wear and possible ovality by inserting the quadrant into the bush and feeling the amount of play.

(5) Check the tips of the plungers and the teeth of the camplate operating quadrant for chipping and wear. To remove the camplate quadrant, first remove the inner cover as shown in Section D8, then withdraw the spindle.

KICKSTART:

(1) Examine the kickstart quadrant for chipped or broken teeth or looseness on the spindle and the kickstart return spring for fatigue cracks and signs of wear, particularly at the centre where it engages on the splines of the spindle.

(2) Examine the kickstart spindle bush for wear. If the required measuring instruments are not available, use the spindle as a gauge and feel the amount of play.

(3) Examine the kickstart ratchet mechanism for wear, giving particular attention to the ratchet teeth ensuring that they have not become chipped or rounded. Check that the thin walled steel bush is a clearance fit in the kickstart pinion and that the spring is not badly worn.

(4) Finally, check that the kickstart stop peg is firmly pressed into the inner cover and is not distorted.

SECTION D6

RENEWING KICKSTART AND GEARCHANGE BUSHES

If it is found necessary to renew the kickstart spindle bush this should be done by completely stripping the outer cover of its assembly parts and heating it to 100°C., then driving the bush out using a suitable shouldered drift. Press in the new bush while the cover is still hot.

The gearchange spindle and plunger assembly are supported in four cast iron bushes. One in the gearbox outer cover, one in the inner cover, one in the L.H. crankcase and one in the primary cover.

Remove the outer cover, see Sections D2 and D4. Using a suitable tap (e.g. ¾ in. dia. U.N.C.) cut a thread in the bush to a depth of ½ in. (12mm.) heat the cover to 100°C, then insert a suitable bolt. Grip the bolt firmly in a vice then drive the cover away using a hide mallet. A suitably shouldered drift is required to drive in the new bush, which should be done whilst the cover is still hot.

Remove the inner cover see Section D8. Heat the cover to 100°C and remove the bush using a suitable drift. Press in the new bush whilst the cover is still hot.

Remove the primary cover, see Section C3 and remove and replace the bush as above.

The L.H. crankcase bush is not prone to wear even after considerable mileage. However, if necessary, remove the L.H. crankcase half, see Section B40 and using a suitable tap (e.g ¹³⁄₁₆ in. dia. x UNC) cut a thread in the bush to a depth of ¾ in. (18mm.). Insert a suitable bolt and remove the bush. Drift in the new bush whilst the case is still hot.

SECTION D7

CLUTCH OPERATING MECHANISM

The clutch operating mechanism, which is situated in the gearbox outer cover, consists of two spring loaded plates held apart by three balls, which are seated in conical indentations in the plates.

Wear in this mechanism is negligible, even after excessive mileage has been covered, so long as the gearbox oil level is maintained at the recommended level. The mechanism is removed as a unit by unscrewing two slotted screws and is then easily dismantled. The parts are arranged as shown in Fig. D7, which should be referred to when reassembling the mechanism.

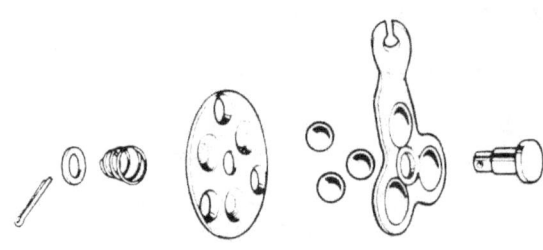

Fig. D7. Exploded view of clutch operating mechanism

SECTION D8

DISMANTLING THE GEARBOX

Remove the gearbox outer cover as shown in Section D2, leaving the gearbox with 5th (top) gear selected.

Remove the two short bolts, two long bolts and a centre nut which serves to retain the rear right engine mounting plate, then withdraw the plate.

Bend back the tags on the lock washer and unscrew the kickstart pinion ratchet retainer nut from the end of the gearbox mainshaft. this should be easily achieved with 5th (top) gear selected and the rear brake applied.

Remove the outer primary cover and dismantle the transmission as shown in Section C, not forgetting, finally to remove the key from the gearbox mainshaft.

The gearbox inner cover is retained by two socket screws, and a hexagonal bolt (See Fig. D8). When these are removed the cover can be released by tapping it outwards with a hide mallet.

GEARBOX

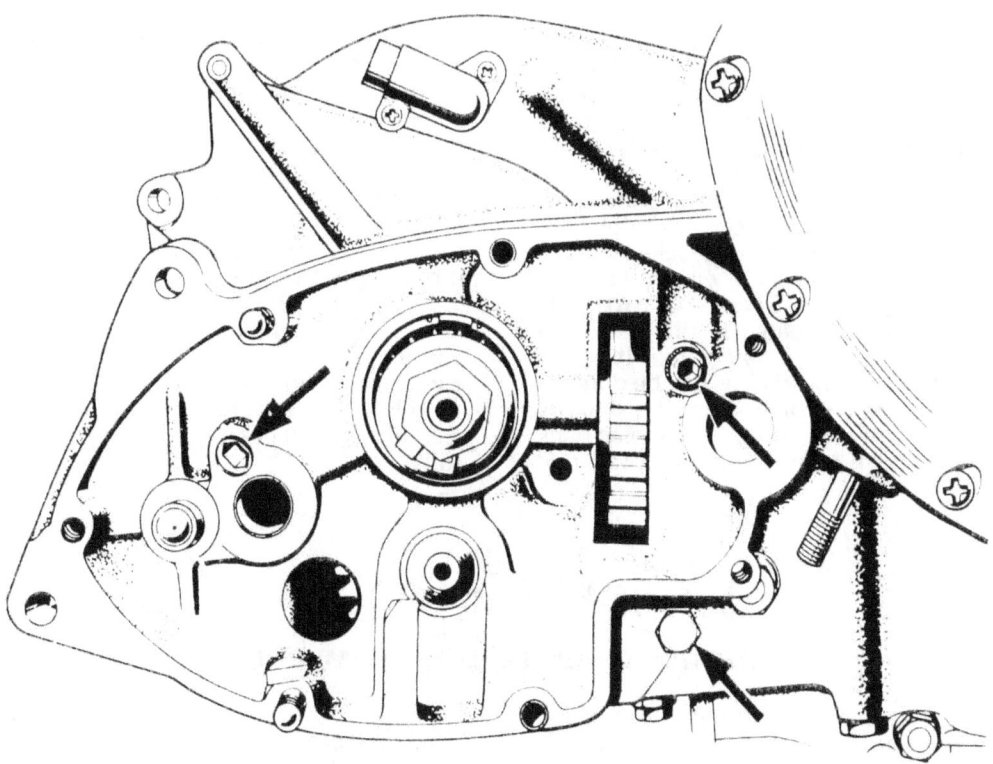

Fig. D8. Gearbox inner cover retaining screws

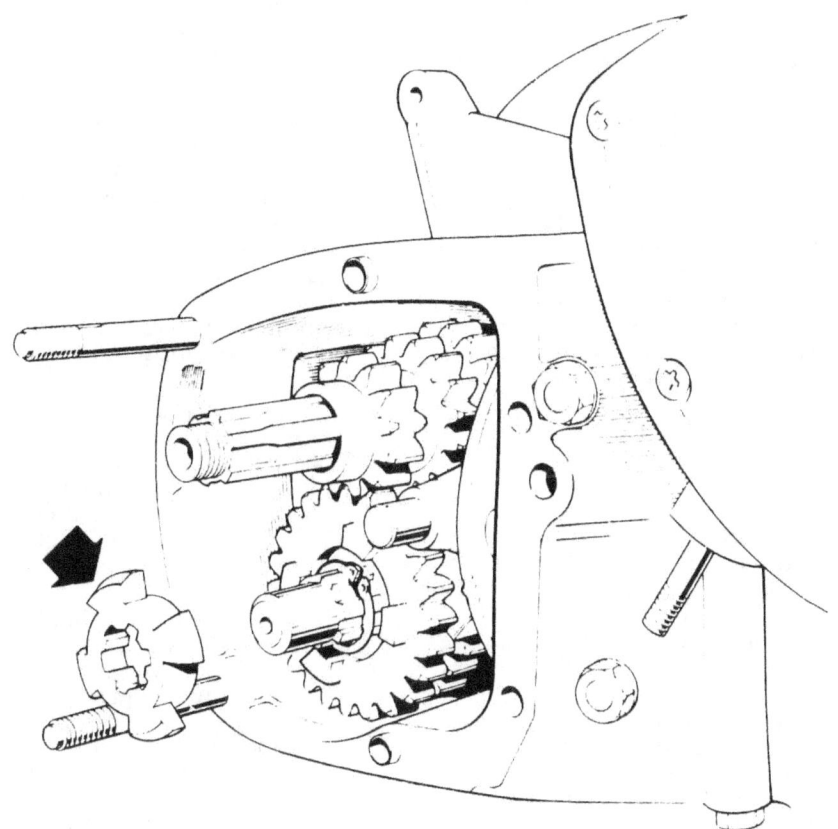

Fig. D9. Showing removal of engaging dog

D   GEARBOX

Withdraw the engaging dog from the layshaft. See Fig. D9, then remove the circlip from the end of the layshaft with a pair of circlip pliers. Pull the selector rod out and then remove the layshaft first gear with its selector fork. Withdraw the second gear from the layshaft and then remove the mainshaft complete with first, second and third gears in position. Remove the mainshaft fourth and layshaft third gears with their selector forks and then withdraw the layshaft with the fifth and fourth gears in position. Detach the two brass thrust washers which locate over the needle roller bearings. Remove the camplate if the high gear needs to be removed. This can be done by removing the circular plate from the primary inner cover at the rear of the clutch, tapping back the bent-over portion of the locking plate and unscrewing the large hexagonal gearbox sprocket nut (1.875" across the flats) and remove the 'O' ring. To facilitate removal of the nut, Workshop Tool number 61-6125 is available. When the nut has been removed, tap the high gear into the gearbox using a hide mallet or a soft metal drift. To remove the gearbox sprocket, disconnect the rear chain and remove it from around the sprocket which can now be easily withdrawn through the aperture.

The oil is prevented from leaving the gearbox through the main bearing by an oil seal which runs on a ground boss on the gearbox sprocket. Check the oil seal for cracking and wear (see Section D10 for bearing and oil seal removal details).

SECTION D9

INSPECTION OF THE GEARBOX COMPONENTS

Thoroughly clean all parts in paraffin (kerosene) and check them for wear and fatigue, as follows:-

(1) Inspect the gearbox housing and inner cover for signs of cracking and damage to the joint faces. Check that the location dowels are in position correctly in the gearbox and inner cover (2 dowels each). In preparation for reassembly, clean th junction surfaces of the gearbox, inner cover and outer cover of any old deposits of jointing compound.

(2) Examine both the mainshaft and layshaft for signs of fatigue, damaged threads and badly worn splines. Check the extent of wear to the bearing diameters of both shafts by comparing them with the figures given in "Technical Data". Examine the shafts carefully for signs of seizure.

Excessive friction resistance and seizure will be indicated by local colouring on the shaft.

(3) Check the layshaft needle roller bearing by inserting the layshaft and feeling the amount of play.

(4) Inspect the gearbox mainshaft bearings for roughness due to pitting or indentation of the ball/roller tracks. Note that the high gear bearing operates directly in a roller bearing pressed into the right hand side crankcase half. If wear is apparent at the high gear bearings (check general data for high gear spigot dimensions), it will be necessary to replace the roller bearing and the high gear. Under no circumstances should the bearing or the high gear be replaced independently.

Check the inner cover bearing by feeling the amount of side play of the centre track. It should not be possible to detect any movement by hand if the bearing is in good condition. The mainshaft should be a push fit into the inner cover bearing.

(5) Examine the gears thoroughly, for chipped, fractured or worn teeth. check the internal splines, dogs and bushes. Make sure that the splines are free on their respective shafts with no tendency to bind, and the bushes in the mainshaft third gear, layshaft second gear and layshaft first gear are not loose or excessively worn. Again, reference should be made to the dimensions given in "Technical Data".

(6) Check that the selector fork rod is not grooved and that it is a good fit in the gearbox casing and the inner cover. Inspect the selector fork running faces for wear. This will only have occured if the gearbox is being continually used with a badly worn mainshaft bearing.

(7) The gear selector camplate should be inspected for signs of wear in the selector tracks. Excessive wear will occur if the mainshaft main bearing has worn badly. Check the fit of the camplate spindle in its housing. Examine the camplate gear wheel for excessive wear. Difficulty will be encountered in gear selection, causing subsequent damage to the gears, if this gear is badly worn.

GEARBOX

(8) Inspect the mainshaft high gear needle roller bearings for roughness or fracture. Check the mainshaft diameter with the "Technical Data" and check for surface pitting or damage due to scoring.

SECTION D10

RENEWING MAINSHAFT AND LAYSHAFT BEARINGS

MAINSHAFT

The mainshaft bearings are a press fit into their respective housings and are retained by spring circlips to prevent sideways movement due to end thrust. To remove the right bearing, first lever out the circlip, then heat the cover to approximately 100°C and drive out the bearing using a suitably shouldered drift. The new bearing should be pressed or drifted in whilst the cover is still hot using a suitable tubular drift onto the outer race (2 ½ in. (62mm.) outside diameter x 6in. (150mm.) long). Do not forget to refit the circlip.

To remove the high gear bearing on the left of the machine, first lever out the large oil seal (which must be renewed), then remove the retainer circlip. Carefully heat the casing locally to approximately 100°C., then drive out the bearing from the inside by means of a suitably shouldered drift. Whilst the casing is still hot, drive in the new bearing, using a suitable tubular drift onto the outer race, then refit the circlip and press in the new oil seal.

MAINSHAFT HIGH GEAR BEARINGS

Two caged needle bearings are fitted into each end of the high gear and they can be both pressed out together using a drift of the dimensions shown in Fig. D10.

LAYSHAFT

The right needle roller bearing should be removed by heating the cover to approximately 100°C, then pressing or drifting out the bearing using a tool similar to that shown in Fig. D12.
The new bearing should be pressed in, plain end first, whilst the cover is still hot, from the inside of the cover, until ·073/·078in. (1·85/1·98mm.) of the bearing protrudes above the cover face (see Fig. D12)

The left needle roller bearing is of the closed-end type and is accessible from the left, through the sprocket cover plate aperture. The casing should be heated to approximately 100°C and the bearing driven through into the gearbox using a soft metal drift, taking care not to damage the bore into which the bearing fits. The new bearing must be carefully pressed in whilst the casing is hot, until ·073/·078in. (1.85/1·98mm.) protrudes above the spot face surface inside the gearbox. Do not use excessive force or the needle roller outer case may become damaged, resulting in the rollers seizing, or breaking up.

Finally, the outer portion of the bore into which the bearing fits, should be sealed with a suitable proprietary sealant.

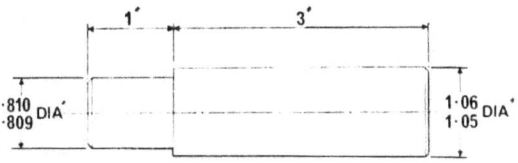

Fig. D10. Drift dimensions

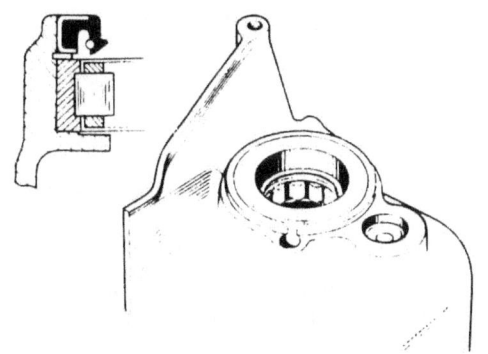

Fig. D11. Section through gearbox mainshaft oil seal

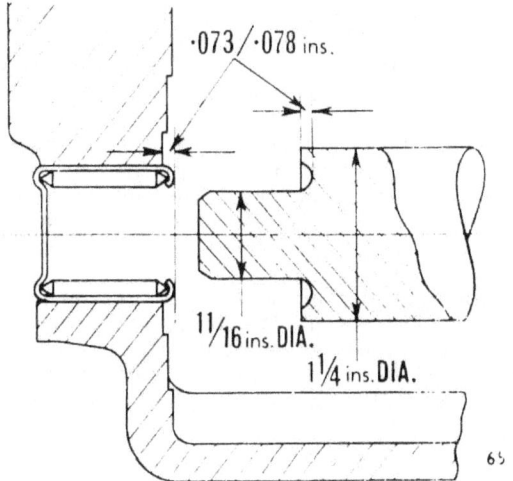

Fig. D12. Sketch of needle roller and drift

SECTION D11

REASSEMBLING THE GEARBOX

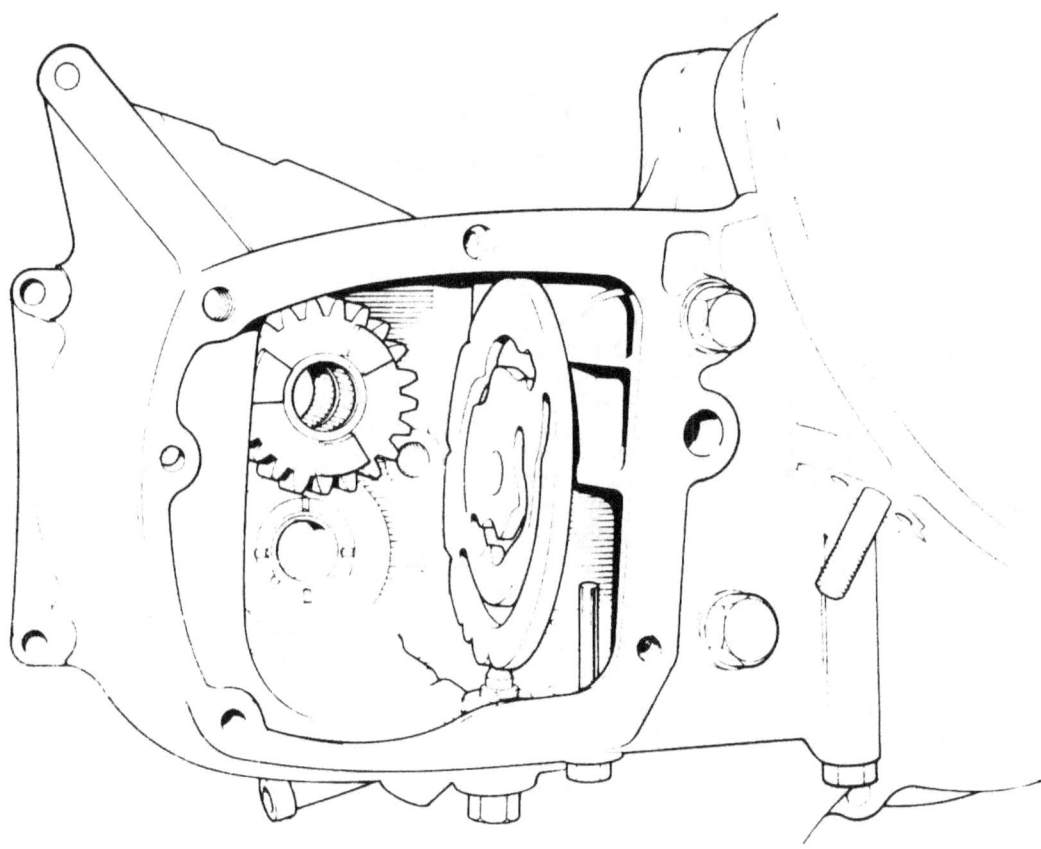

Fig. D13. Reassembling the gearbox

Lubricate the camplate spindle and offer it into the spindle housing within the gearbox.

Drive the new oil seal up to the main bearing with the lip and spring towards the bearing. Insert the high gear into the bearing. Lubricate the ground tapered boss of the sprocket with oil and slide it onto the high gear. Fit a new 'O' ring and screw on the securing nut finger tight.

Re-mesh the rear chain with the sprockets and replace the connecting link. Apply the rear brake and tighten the sprocket securing nut using service tool 61-6125 to the torque figure given in "Technical Data".

Locate the bronze thrust washer over the inner needle roller bearing. The thrust washer can be held in position by smearing its rear surface with grease. Note that the grooved surface of the thrust washer is towards the layshaft. (See Fig. D13).

Set the camplate in the first gear position (See Fig. D13). Lubricate the needle roller bearings in the high gear (use oil recommended in Section A2) and layshaft bearing. Place the mainshaft fourth gear with its respective selector fork onto the mainshaft. See Fig. D1. This selector fork has a large engaging pin and no cuttaway on the housing. assemble the shaft into the high gear using a heavy grease to retain the selector fork on the gear and in the camplate track. Replace the layshaft assembly with fifth and fourth gears into the gearbox and engage with the mainshaft fifth and fourth gears (note that with the gearbox in the neutral position none of the sliding dogs will be engaged).

Replace the layshaft third gear with its respective selector fork (See Fig. D1). this selector fork has a large engaging pin and a cuttaway on the selector housing. Then replace the mainshaft third gear and engage with the layshaft third. Replace the layshaft second gear after first lu-

GEARBOX D

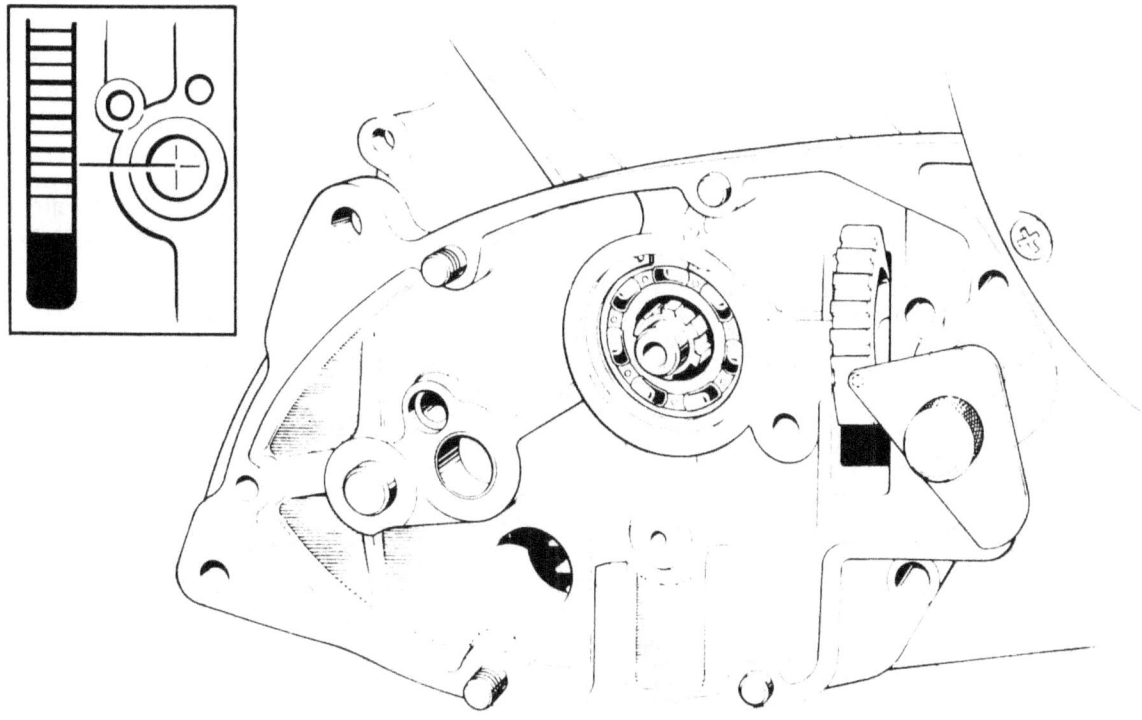

Fig. D14. Refitting the gearbox inner cover using tool 61-7011

bricating the bush with oil. Replace the combined first and second gear onto the mainshaft. Replace the layshaft bottom gear with is selector fork (this selector fork has a small diameter engaging pin and a cutaway to match the previous selector fork. See Fig. D1. Replace the selector rod. Fit the circlip onto the end of the layshaft and the engaging dog up against the circlip. Turn the camplate towards the inner cover from the top thereby placing the gearbox into the first gear position (note engaging dog on layshaft will be in mesh with the dogs on the layshaft first gear).

Check the camplate operating quadrant is moving freely in the inner cover and position the bronze layshaft thrust washer over the needle roller bearing in the inner cover. Again, use grease to hold the thrust washer in position during assembly.

Using a pressure oil can, lubricate all the moving parts in the gearbox, then apply a fresh coat of jointing compound to the gearbox junction surface.

Ensure that the two location dowels are in position offer the inner cover assembly to the gearbox. When the cover is approximately 1/4in. (6mm.) away from the gearbox junction face, position the camplate quadrant as detailed in Fig. D14 and position service tool 61-7011 as shown. If this tool is not available line up the top edge of the second tooth on the qudrant with the centre line passing through the footchange spindle housing. See insert Fig. D14.

Screw in the socket screw, recessed screw and the bolt, then temporarily assemble the outer cover gearchange lever and check that the gearchanging sequence is correct by simultaneously operating the gearchange pedal and turning the rear wheel. During this checking ensure that the mainshaft is pulled home into the R.H. bearing.

In the event of any problem of selection it must be assumed that the quadrant teeth are not engaged accurately with the camplate pinion. To rectify this, remove the inner cover again and check that the camplate has been set as shown in Fig. D14. Offer up the inner cover and repeat as previous.

When correct gearchanging is established, reassemble the kickstart pinion and ratchet, replace the tab washer and screw on the securing nut to the torque figure given in "Technical Data". To facilitate this, the rear brake should be applied with fifth gear selected.

Refit the gearbox outer cover as shown in section D2 then reassemble the transmission, referring to section A1 for the correct grades of lubricant for the primary chaincase and gearbox. See "Technical Data" for the correct quantities.

SECTION D12

CHANGING THE GEARBOX SPROCKET

To gain access to the gearbox sprocket, first remove the left footrest, exhaust pipe and the gearchange pedal and then remove the outer primary cover as shown in Section C3.

Remove the pressure plate, clutch plates and withdraw the shock absorber unit, clutch sprocket and footchange shaft as shown in Section C9. Remove the key from the gearbox mainshaft and unscrew the six screws which serve to retain the circular cover.

Apply the rear brake, then unscrew the gearbox sprocket securing nut using service tool number 61-6125. The rear chain may now be disconnected and the gearbox sprocket withdrawn through the aperture.

Before fitting the new sprocket check that the gearbox oil seal is in good condition and that the rear chain is not excessively worn. If the old chain is to be retained for further use it should be thoroughly cleaned in paraffin (kerosene) and lubricated.

Slide the sprocket over the gearbox mainshaft and high gear. When the sprocket is located on the splines fit the 'O' ring and locking plate. Screw on the securing nut finger tight, then reconnect the chain. With the rear brake applied tighten the nut to 100 lbs ft and tap over the lockplate.

When replacing the circular cover plate, use a new paper gasket. Reassembly then continues as a reversal of the above instructions.

SECTION E

FRAME AND ATTACHMENT DETAILS

INDEX

DESCRIPTION	Section
REMOVING AND REFITTING THE FUEL TANK	E1
REMOVING SIDE PANELS AND FILTER HOUSING	E2
REMOVING PROP STAND	E3
REMOVING THE CENTRE STAND	E4
REMOVING BRAKE PEDAL - DRUM BRAKE	E5
REMOVING AND SERVICING THE BRAKE PEDAL AND SPINDLE ; HYDRAULIC BRAKE	E5
REMOVING TWINSEAT	E6
CHAINGUARD REMOVAL	E7
CONTROL CABLE REPLACEMENT	E8
REMOVING COIL PLATE	E9
REMOVING REAR LIGHT UNIT	E10
REMOVING HORN	E11
REMOVING REAR STOP SWITCH	E12
REMOVING AND REPLACING THE BATTERY CARRIER ASSEMBLY	E13
REMOVING AND REPLACING FLASHER UNIT	E14
REMOVING AND REPLACING THE MUDGUARDS	E15
ADJUSTING THE REAR SUSPENSION	E16
REMOVING AND REFITTING THE REAR SUSPENSION UNITS	E17
STRIPPING AND REASSEMBLING THE SUSPENSION UNITS	E18
REMOVING AND REFITTING THE SWINGING FORK	E19
RENEWING THE SWINGING FORK BUSHES	E20
FRAME ALIGNMENT	E21
REPAIRS	E22
PAINTWORK REFINISHING	E23
FITTING REPLACEMENT SEAT COVERS	E24

E · FRAME

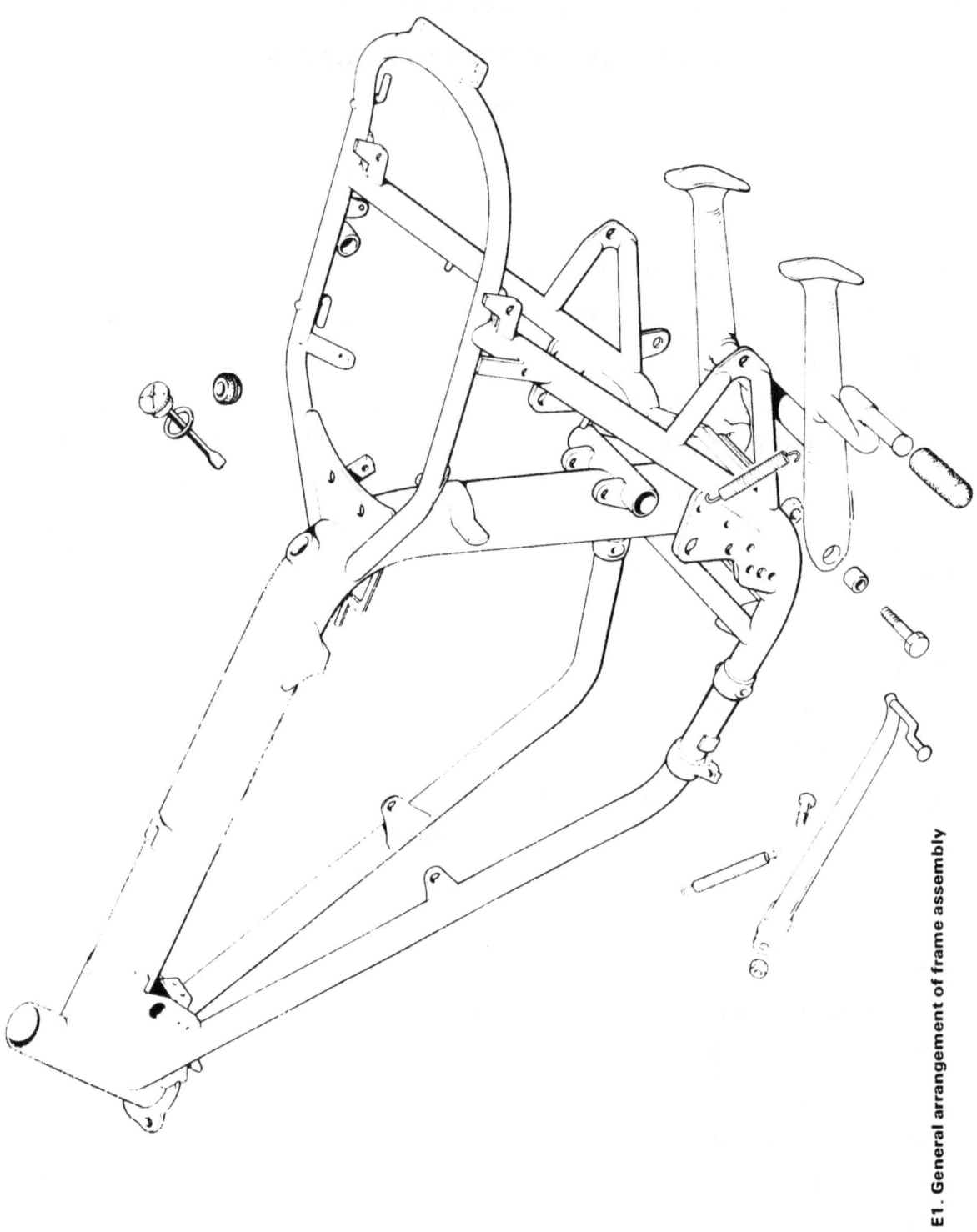

Fig. E1. General arrangement of frame assembly

FRAME

SECTION E1

REMOVING AND REPLACING THE FUEL TANK

Ensure that the fuel taps are in the "OFF" position and disconnect the feed pipes. Remove the rubber grommet from the centre of the fuel tank and unscrew the sleeve nut revealed below.

Unscrew the two bolts which retain the tie strap at the forward end of the tank.
Note the positioning of the spacing washers.

The tank can now be pulled away from the frame. Note assembly of rubber sleeve and washers securing the tank. See Fig. E2.

Drain the tank and unscrew the fuel tap assemblies and clean the mesh filters at the intervals stated in "Routine Maintenance".

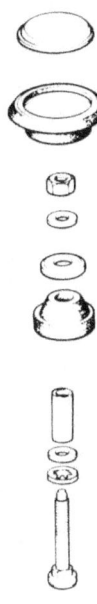

Fig. E2. Fuel tank mounting

SECTION E2

REMOVING SIDE PANELS AND FILTER HOUSING

Remove the outer trim panels by disconnecting the two retaining Springs or the centre fixing sleeve nut.
Detach filter cover by removing the single bolt situated in the centre. Undo the two bolts contained inside the housing that retain the side panel. The rearmost end of the panel is secured to the frame by rubber bushes integral with the panel and pushed onto spigots welded to the frame.

To remove the filter housing remove two securing bolts retaining the housing to the frame and the two 4BA bolts and nuts that secure the two halves of the housing. These are contained in the well at the foremost part of the housing.

E
FRAME

SECTION E3
REMOVING THE PROP STAND

The prop stand leg is secured to a lug on the frame by means of a bolt and locking nut. Remove the bolt, pull the bolt away from the lug and disconnect the return spring.

When reassembling, attach the spring to the frame and leg, then push the leg onto the lug and fit the bolt.

SECTION E4
REMOVING THE CENTRE STAND

The centre stand is secured to the frame by two bolts passing through welded brackets. Remove the bolts when the stand is in the raised position (i.e. when the return spring is slackest).

When reassembling, bolt the stand to frame and while holding the stand in the raised position stretch the return spring with the aid of a "pozidrive" headed screwdriver (or similar) and attach the spring into position.

SECTION E5
REMOVING THE BRAKE PEDAL - DRUM BRAKE ONLY

Detach the rear brake stop light switch by removing the two cross-head screws. Fig E4.

Remove the spindle locknut and washer situated on the inner of the engine plate. Remove the split pin and washer securing the brake rod. The pedal can now be removed; Assembly is a reversal of the above, ensuring to liberally grease spindle beforehand.

Note: A new split pin should always be used when reassembling.

REMOVING THE BRAKE PEDAL & SPINDLE - HYDRAULIC BRAKE

Detach the rear brake stoplight switch by removing the two cross-head screws. Fig E4
Remove the inner spindle retaining nut and washer. Fig E3.
Using a suitable drift break the taper fit of the trunnion lever on the spindle and then withdraw the spindle and pedal from the R.H. side.
Refer to E3.
Remove the brake pedal return spring and the distance piece.

NOTE: The recess in the distance piece faces the R.H. side.

Check the brake pedal spindle and the sleeve nut for damage, scoring or excessive play. If necessary replace the spindle and/or sleeve nut.

Liberally grease spindle prior to reassembly.

Replace the sleeve nut and tighten to torque shown in GD and insert pedal spindle complete with brake pedal.

Replace the distance piece with the recess located in the protruding sleeve nut. Locate the brake pedal return spring on the frame see Fig. E4.

Reconnect the lever to the spindle and refit the nut and washer finger tight ONLY.
Make up a simple hook with wire or string and connect the spring to the lever. See Fig. E5.

Tighten the nut and washer securely.

Refit the brake lever and the nut and washer.

NOTE: Do not operate the rear brake while the rear wheel is removed.

Check the rear brake pedal adjustment. See section F1.

Replace the brake light stop switch assembly. If necessary adjust the movable stop on the brake pedal such that the rear brake light is illuminated (ignition 'ON') when the rear brake is operated.

FRAME E

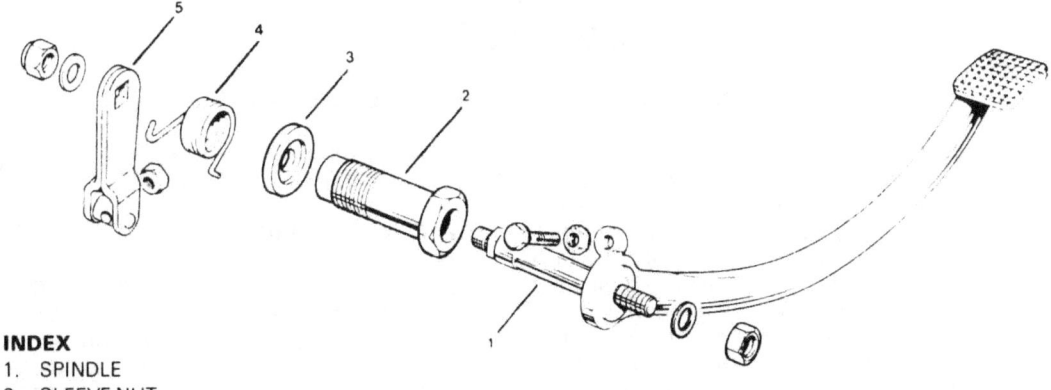

INDEX
1. SPINDLE
2. SLEEVE NUT
3. DISTANCE PIECE
4. BRAKE PEDAL RETURN SPRING
5. TRUNNION LEVER

Fig. E3. Rear brake pedal spindle assembly - exploded

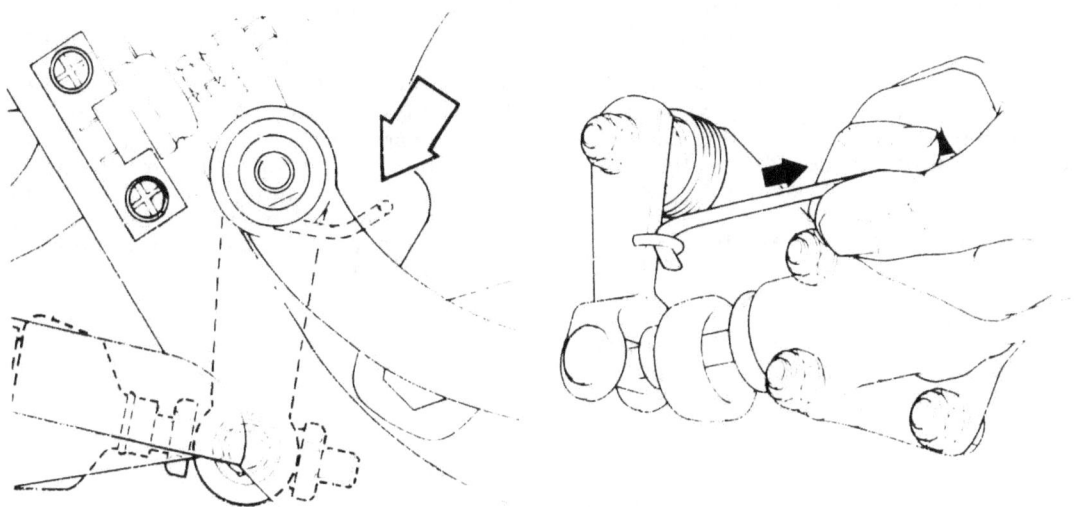

Fig. E4. Brake pedal return spring - frame location

Fig. E5. Refitting the brake pedal return spring (Shown with rear wheel removed)

SECTION E6

REMOVING TWINSEAT

Detach check strap from the underside of the seat by removing the small "pozidrive" screw.

Then remove the attachment bolts at the front seat hinge and slide the seat away towards the rear of the machine.

SECTION E7

CHAINGUARD REMOVAL

Removing the fixing bolt at the front of the chainguard and loosen the left side lower suspension unit bolt.

The chainguard mounted is slotted at the suspension unit bolt fixing and the chainguard can now be lifted clear and withdrawn from the rear of the machine.

SECTION E8

CONTROL CABLE REPLACEMENT

Clutch Cable
Slacken off the clutch cable adjustment and slip out the cable nipple at the handlebar control. Slide the rubber cover away from the abutment at the gearbox end and unscrew the abutment. Remove the large slotted plug from the gearbox outer cover and access will be gained to the clutch operating arm. It is then only necessary to release the cable nipple from the arm with the finger. Replacement is the reversal of the above instruction. Refer to D4 for illustration.

Throttle Cable(s) Amal.
To remove the throttle cable(s) first of all remove the fuel tank. See Section E1. Remove the top cap(s) from the carburetter(s). It will be found easier to disconnect the cable from the throttle slide and remove the needle and needle clip. With the spring still retracted push the cable through the slide and when the nipple is clear pull it across the figure of eight slot and withdraw the cable. The cables can be detached from the junction box by unscrewing the two halves of the casing and releasing the nipples.

When reassembling the box grease the internals liberally.

Note: When reassembling the throttle slides into the carburetter do not apply any form of lubricant to the bearing surface; this will undoubtedly cause the slide to stick.

When the cables have been replaced readjust them as detailed in Section B12.

Air Control Cable - TR7 & TR65 Models Only
Remove the top caps of the carburetter as for the throttle cables. To disconnect the air valve, push the valve guide tube and spring along with the air cable until the cable nipple protrudes sufficiently out of its counterbore to be pushed out of its slot. The cable, spring and guide can now be pulled clear of the valve. Disconnect the cable from the control lever by unscrewing the centre fixing nut, removing the lever arm and detaching the nipple.

Throttle Cables - Bing
To remove the throttle cables firstly remove the fuel tank see section E1.
Detach the cable from the twist grip. Undo the adjuster locknuts and screw out the adjuster from the carburettor body. Release the cable from the body by passing cable through slot. Release cable from operating arm by rotating cable nipple until cable aligns with slot in operating arm, the cable can now be removed. Refitting is a reversal of the above.

SECTION E9

REMOVING AND REPLACING THE COIL PLATE

The pressed steel plate holding the two ignition coils, is situated beneath the twinseat. Disconnect all the wiring from the components at the respective terminals. The front of the plate is attached to the rear battery carrier fixing bolts. Remove the two retaining nuts and then detach the two remaining nuts and bolts which attach the rear of the plate to the mudguard. The plate assembly can then be lifted clear of the machine.

Replacement is the reverse of the above instructions. Refer to the wiring diagram for the correct re-wiring procedure. (See Section H19).

SECTION E10

REMOVING AND REPLACING REAR LIGHT UNIT

Three bolts attach the unit to the mudguard and these are accessible from underneath the mudguard blade. As the unit is removed disconnect the snap connectors from beneath the housing. See Section H16 for the dismantling procedure of the tail light.

FRAME

E

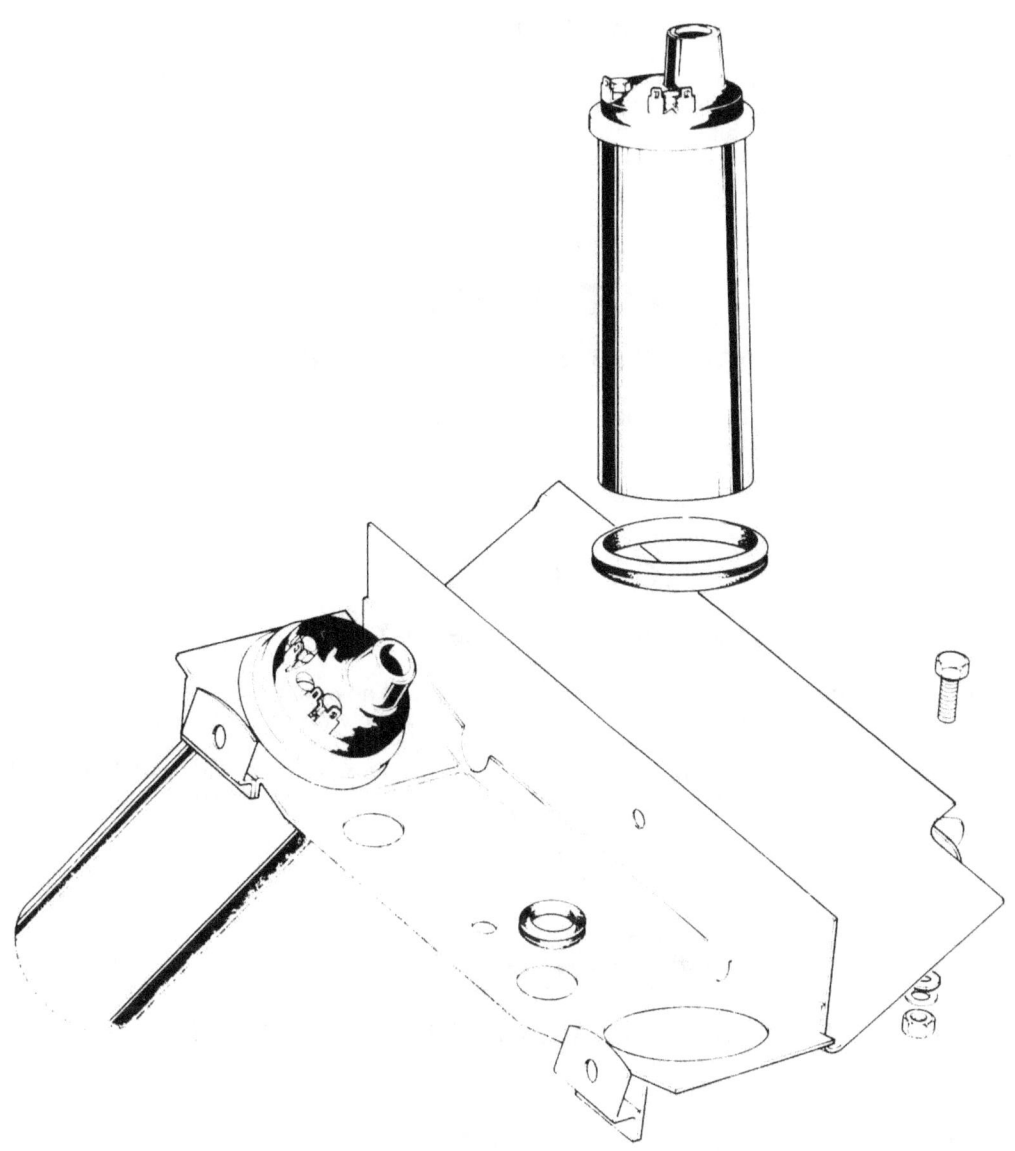

Fig. E6. Coil plate mountings

E7

SECTION E11

REMOVING THE HORN

The horn can be removed from the frame without detaching the fuel tank, but if difficulty is encountered remove the fuel tank as detailed in section E1.

Two nuts and bolts secure the horn to a bracket below and behind the head lug.

SECTION E12

REMOVING REAR STOP SWITCH

Two pozidrive screws secure the stop switch assembly to the rear frame member.

Release these screws and disconnect the electrical connections.

SECTION E13

REMOVING AND REPLACING THE BATTERY CARRIER

Remove the nuts from the three slotted constant diameter bolts that sit in the rubber retaining bushes that secure the carrier to the frame. The front mounting point has a locking nut on the right side and earth connecting wire underneath. It will now be possible to lift the battery carrier vertically clear of the machine. Replacment is the reversal of the above. Ensure that the earth connection is clean and tight. Replace the battery and note route of breather pipe.

SECTION E14

REMOVING AND REPLACING THE FLASHER UNIT

The flasher unit is contained behind the left side panel. See Section E2 for removing panel. The unit is attached to a damping spring which is in turn bolted to a bracket on the frame. Detach both lucar connectors and release the unit from the spring or remove the assembly of spring and flasher unit. See Fig. E7 for correct mounted position.

Fig. E7. Showing position of flasher unit

FRAME

SECTION E15
REMOVING AND REPLACING THE MUDGUARDS

Rear Mudguard
First disconnect the three snap connectors found under the seat, two leading to the flashers and the other leading to the rear brake light. Pull back the narness retaining clips found on the inside rim of the muguard. (Withdraw green flasher wires through the appropriate grommets.)

Detach the rear light unit by removing the three attachment bolts from underneath the mudguard blade, two of which act as bracket holders for the number plate. Lift the light away from the mudguard and withdraw the wires through the grommet. Detach the two nuts and bolts at the from mounting bracket. Remove the two nuts and bolts at the top of the mudguard. Remove the two nuts and bolts at the rear frame loop and those connecting the grab rail to the mudguard. Remove rectifier from guard and withdraw mudguard.

Front Mudguard
To remove the front mudguard detach the four bols securing the mudguard stay to the fork legs. Also detach the two bolts situated on either wheel spindle cap. Withdraw the mudguard rearwards.

SECTION E16
ADJUSTING THE REAR SUSPENSION

The movement is controlled by Girling or Marzocchi combined coil spring and hydraulic or gas damper units. The hydraulic or gas damping mechanism is completely sealed but the static loading of the spring is adjustable.

A multi position cam ring is concealed beneath a sleeve with a castellated adjuster ring. Rotation in the direction shown increases the load and vice versa.

Adjusting spanner 60-2184 found in tool kit is needed for this adjustment. Both units must be adjusted equally and a quick visual check can be made on the adjusted positions by comparison from the rear of the machine.

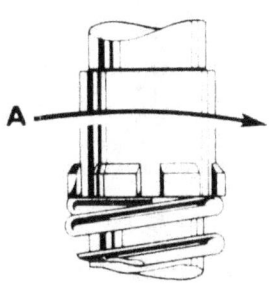

Fig. 8A. Adjusting the rear suspension unit - gas filled units only. Note the arrow showing direction of rotation to increase the spring rating.

The standard lowest position is for solo riding, the intermediate positions is for heavier solo riders or when luggage is carried on the rear of the machine and the highest position is for use when a pillion passenger is being carried.

NOTE: On some models fitted with the MARZOCCHI unit additional air assistance cylinders are fitted. In these cases the correct air pressure is 28lbs sq. in.

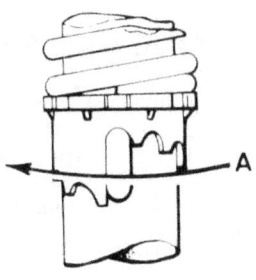

Fig. 8B. Adjusting the rear suspension unit Marzocchi type

E FRAME

SECTION E17

REMOVING AND REFITTING THE REAR SUSPENSION UNITS

Lift the twinseat by releasing the catch on the right side.

Remove the top two suspension unit bolts. Then remove the lower fixing bolts. Note that the left side fixing bolt secures the rear portion of the chainguard. When replacing the units notice that the top fixing bolts also secure the grab rail.

NOTE: If a unit is inadvertently fitted the wrong way up irreparable damage will be caused to the damping mechanism within the unit.

WARNING
Pre 1979 Triumphs were produced with Girling oil hydraulic rear suspension damper units and must not be mixed with the later gas filled girling type, nor should they be fitted incorrectly. The gas filled type must be fitted with the castellated load adjusting ring at the TOP of the unit and the oil hydraulic unit with the adjuster ring at the BOTTOM of the unit.

If in doubt the units can be identified as follows:
Gas filled units have a $7/16$" dia. damper rod whereas oil type have $3/8$" dia. damper rod.

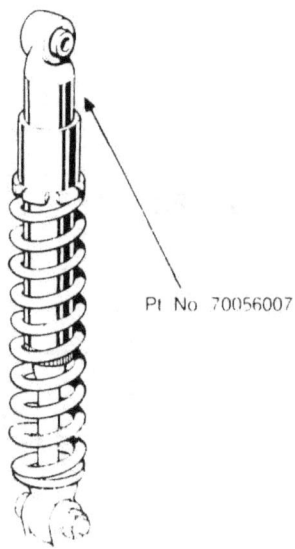

Fig. 10A. Gas filled suspension unit Girling type

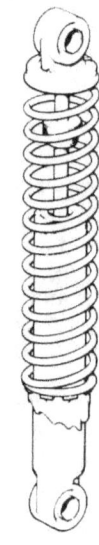

Fig. 10B. Oil hydraulic suspension unit Marzocchi type

SECTION E18

STRIPPING AND REASSEMBLING THE SUSPENSION UNITS

The suspension unit consists of a sealed hydraulic/gas damper unit, and outer coiled spring. The static loading on the spring is adjustable and should be set according to the type of conditions under which the machine is to be used (see Section E16).

To dismantle the suspension unit and remove the spring, it is required to compress the spring whilst the retaining collar is removed. To do this first turn the cam until it is in the "LIGHT-LOAD" position, then compress the spring using suitable spring clamps. Remove the spring retainer and withdraw the spring.

The damper unit should be checked for bending of the plunger rod and damping action. Check the bonded pivot bushes for wear.

The bushes can be easily renewed by driving out the old one and pressing in the new one using a smear of soapy water to assist assembly. Under no circumstances should the plunger rod be lubricated.

Note:- For information concerning suspension units or spare parts, the local Girling or Marzocchi agent should be consulted.

Reassembly is a reversal of dismantling. Check that the cam is in the light load position before compressing the spring.

FRAME

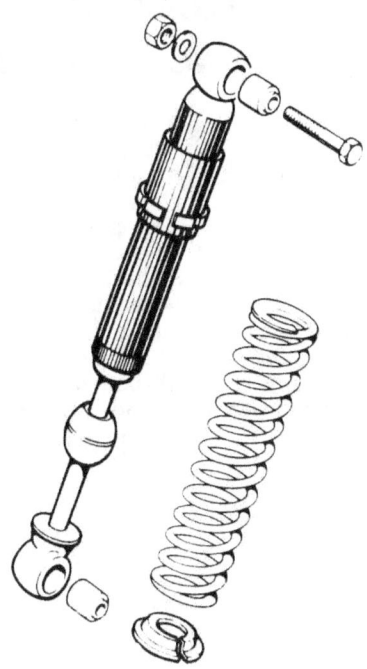

Fig. 9A. Exploded view of the rear suspension unit (Girling gas unit)

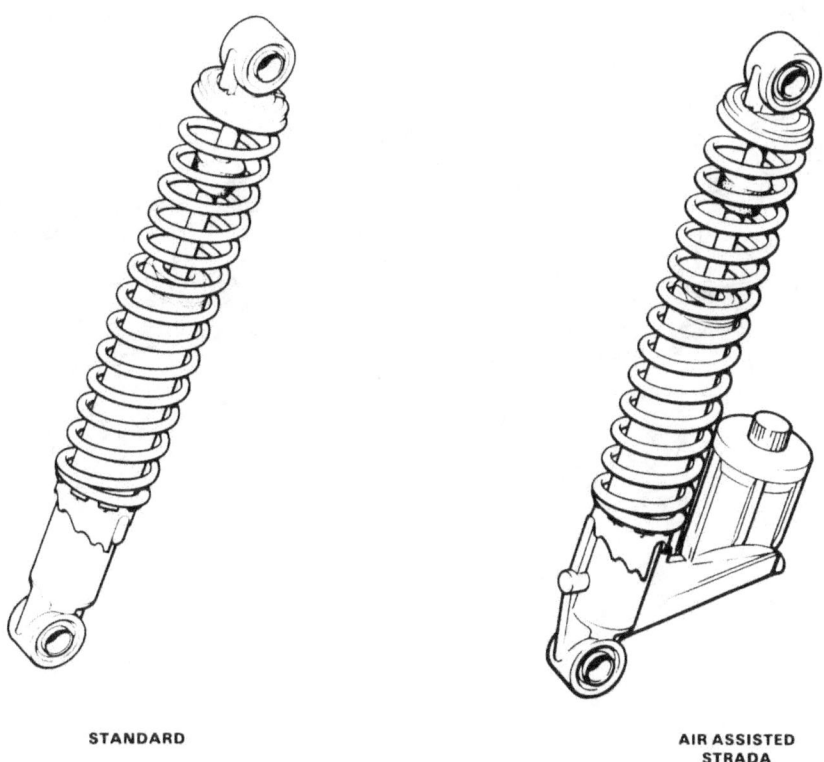

STANDARD

AIR ASSISTED STRADA

Fig. 9B. Marzocchi rear suspension unit

SECTION E19

REMOVING AND REFITTING THE SWINGING FORK

Remove the rear wheel. See Section F.14. Slacken the lower left side suspension unit fixing bolt and remove the front securing bolt. Withdraw the chainguard from the machine. Remove the rear suspension units. See Section E17.

Unscrew the swinging arm spindle nut from the right side and withdraw the spindle from the left side. The swinging arm can now be pulled away from the frame. Note the four rubber dust covers on the pivot housing. Remove the sleeve spindles from the pivot ends and thoroughly wash all parts in kerosene (paraffin). Inspect the bore of the bushes and the diameter of the sleeve spindles for excessive wear. Check the dimensions with the sizes given in "TECHNICAL DATA. If the working clearance is excessive the bushes will require renewing. See Section E20.

The parts should be reassembled in the order shown in Fig. E11 with a sufficient supply of grease as recommended in Section A1. Assemble the spindle sleeves into their housing and offer the swinging arm up to the frame with the rubber dust covers in position. Refit end thrust washers and replace the spindle. The spindle should be tightened to the correct torque fig. See Technical Data.

1. Swinging arm
2. Grease nipple
3. Sealing washer
4. Bush
5. Spacer tube
6. Thrust washer (narrow)
7. Thrust washer (wide)
8. Dust cover
9. Nut
10. Washer
11. Spindle

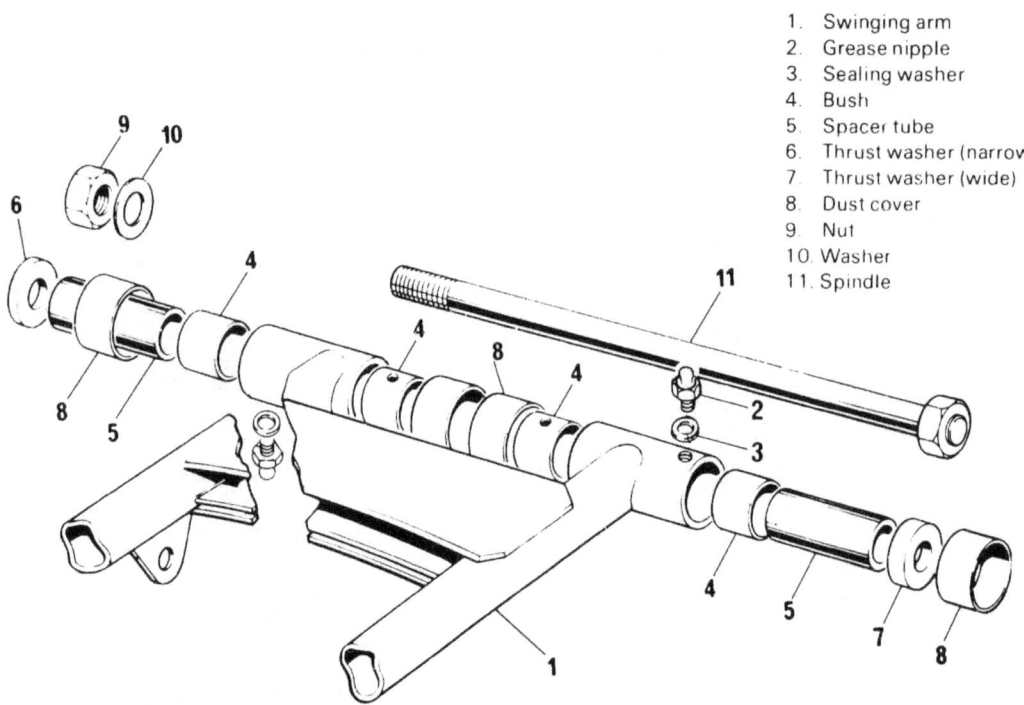

Fig. E11. Swinging arm components

FRAME

E

SECTION E20

RENEWING THE SWINGING FORK BUSHES

The bushes can be removed from their respective housings using service tool 61-6117. Assemble the tool into the housing as shown in Fig. E12 (bottom) and by turning the bolts nut it will be possible to extract the bushes into the spacer tube. Reassemble new bushes as shown in Fig. E12(top). Press in one bush at a time from each end of the housing using a little grease to assist assembly.

The new bushes are of the steel backed pre-sized type and when pressed in will give the correct diametral working clearance.

Alternatively the bushes can be removed using a mild steel shouldered drift of suitable diamensions (i.e. 1in. dia. and 1 $\frac{1}{8}$ in. dia.). It will be possible to drift one bush through the housing thereby knocking out the second bush at the same time.

REPLACING

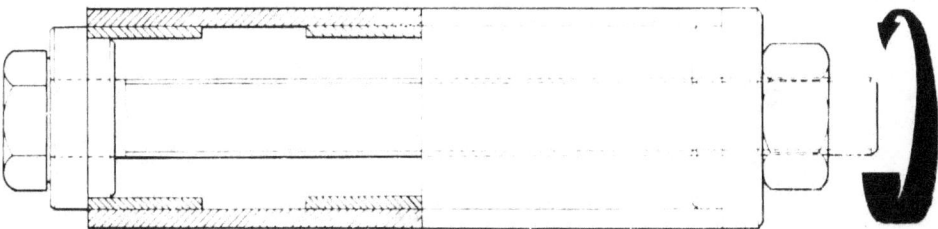

REMOVING

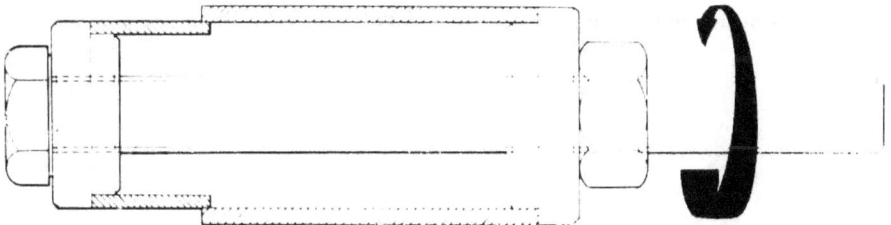

Fig. E12. Removing and replacing the swinging arm bushes using Service Tool 61-6117

SECTION E21

FRAME ALIGNMENT

If the machine has been damaged in an accident the frame must be checked for breakage or fracture at all the welded seams. Due to the design of the frame providing an extremely rigid structure, it is highly unlikely that the frame will bend or twist to any degree without fracture occuring. Under no circumstances should any attempt be made to re-align or reshape the frame as this will cause high stress concentration which can only result in further fracture taking place.

Fracture is likely to occur at the head lug gussets, (particularly in the case of a head-on collision). The frame must be completely stripped down and the steering head races removed. Note the areas at the webs joining the head lug to the main frame tube and at the lower bearing housing in the head lug itself.

See Figs. E13 and E14. Also carefully check the front down tubes for any deforming or splitting. If necessary remove all the paint from the suspected area and check again.

In cases of side collision etc. if the damage is not immediately apparent a simple check can be made by attempting to place spindles or bolts of suitable length and diameter through the swinging arm pivots and engine mounting positions. Mis-alignment will be apparent if the spindle or bolt fouls its exit hole.

Note Fig. E15 for the critical dimensions of the frame. If possible check these if any doubt is revealed.

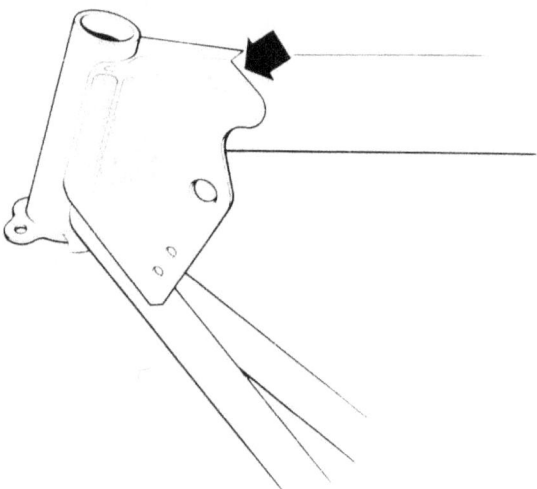

Fig. E13. Fracture at rear of head lug

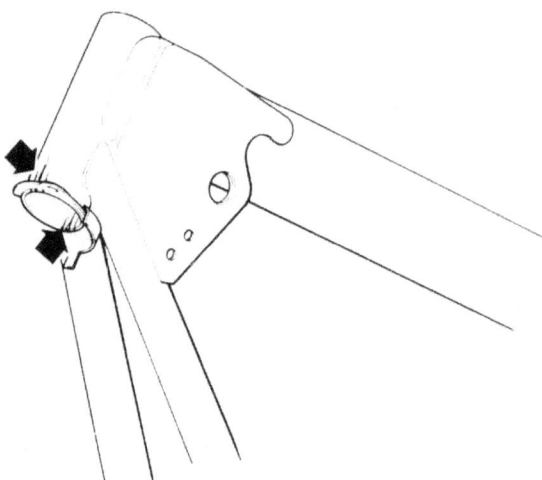

Fig. E14. Fracture at bottom bearing housing

FRAME E

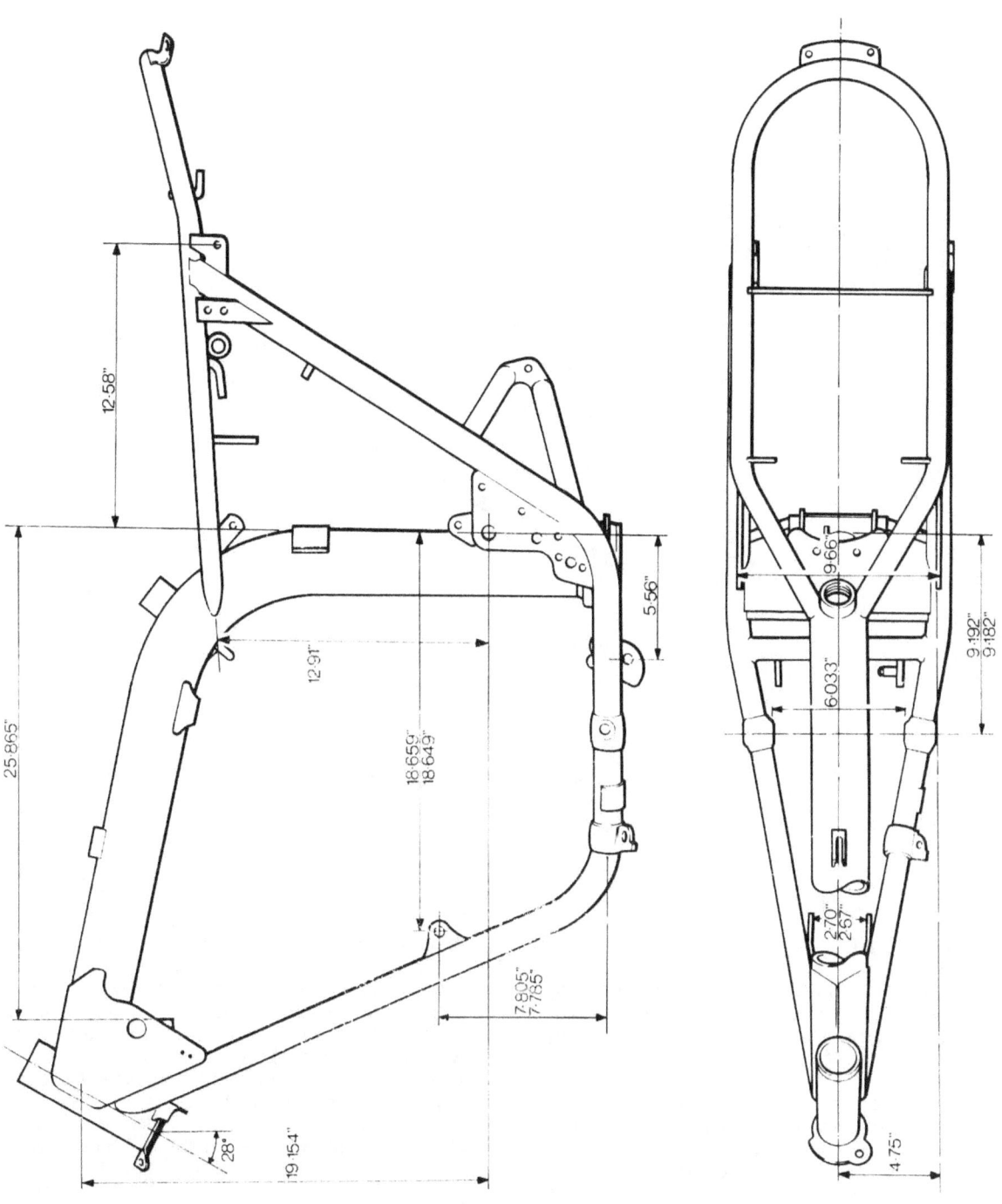

Fig. E15. Basic frame dimensions

E   FRAME

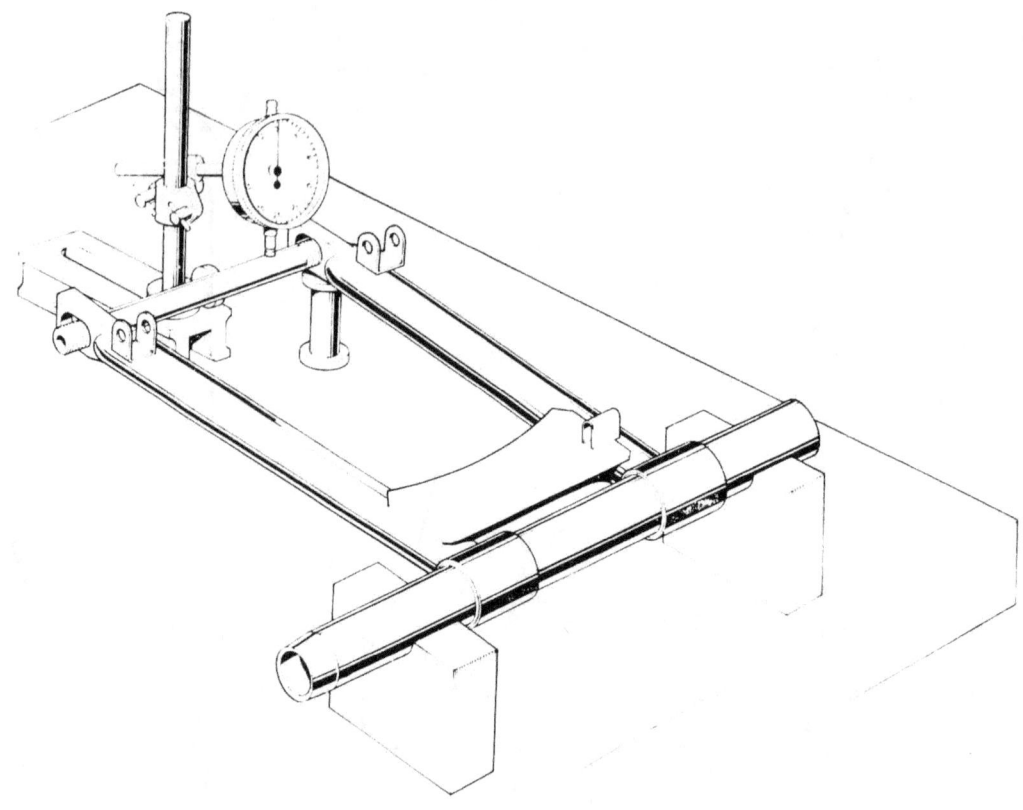

Fig. E16. Checking the swinging fork

Swinging Fork
It is required to check that the centre line of the pivot spindle is in the same plane as the centre line of the rear spindle. To do this, first place a tube or bar of suitable diameter into the swinging fork bearing bushes, then mount the swinging fork on two "V" blocks, one either side, and clamp it lightly as the edge of the checking table. Fit the rear wheel spindle into the fork end slots or, alternatively, use a straight bar of similar diameter, then support a fork end so that the swinging fork is approximately horizontal. Height readings should then be taken at both ends of the wheel spindle to establish any mis-alignment. (Fig. E16).

Next, check that the distance between the fork ends is as given in "Technical Data"

It is now necessary to lever the fork ends in the correcting direction until the wheel spindle can be inserted and found to be parallel with the pivot bush centre line. To do this, a bar of 4ft. length and suitable diameter is required. It is now that great care is required. Insert the bar at the end of the swinging fork adjacent to the suspension unit mounting brackets so that it is over the "high" fork leg and under the "low" fork leg. Exert gentle pressure at the end of the bar then insert the spindle and re-check the alignment. Repeat this procedure using increased loads until the spindle height readings shows that he swinging arm is now mis-aligned in the opposite sense. a small leverage now applied from the other side will bring the wheel back to parallel.

Note: Apply the leverage bar as near as possible to the suspension unit brackets, otherwise the tubes may become damaged. DO NOT USE THE FORK ENDS.

SECTION E22

PAINTWORK REFINISHING

PAINT STRIPPING
Except in cases where a "touch-up" is to be attempted, it is strongly recommended that the old finish is completely stripped and the refinish is carried out from the bare metal. A suitable paint stripper can be obtained from most paint stores and accessory dealers.

The stripper should be applied with a brush and allowed approximately 10 minutes to react. A suitable scraper should be used to remove the old finish, then the surface cleaned with water using a piece of wire woold. Ensure that all traces of paint stripper are removed. If possible, blow out crevices with compressed air.

It is advisable to strip a small area at a time to avoid the stripper drying and also to enable easier neutralizing of the stripper.

Finally, the surface should be rubbed with a grade 270 or 280 emery cloth to give a satisfactory finish then washed off with white spirits or a suitable cleaner solvent.

PRIMING
A thin coat of cellulose primer must be sprayed onto the surface prior to application of an undercoat or stopper. Undercoat and stopper will not adhere satisfactorily to bare metal. It is advisable to thin the primer by adding 1 part cellulose thinners to 1 part primer. Ensure that the primer is dry before advancing further.

APPLYING STOPPER
Imperfections and slight dents in the surface may be filled with stopper, but rubbing down with "wet and dry" should not be attempted until the undercoat or surfacer has been applied.

Apply the stopper with a glazing knife in thin layers, allowing approximately 20 minutes for drying between each layer. After the last layer, allow to dry. Heavy layers or insufficient drying time will result in risk of surface cracking.

UNDERCOAT (SURFACER)
Most cellulose undercoats also called surfacers, will suffice for a base for TRIUMPH finishes. About two or three coats are required and should be sprayed on in a thinned condigion using 1 part cellulose thinners to 1 part undercoat. Allow approximately 20 minutes between each coat.

If stopper has been applied the final layer of undercoat should be sprayed on after smoothing the surface with "wet and dry" abrasive as shown below.

WET AND DRY SANDING
After application of the undercoat, the surface should be rubbed down with 270 or 280 grade abrasive paper used wet. An ideal method is to have a rubber block around which to wrap the emery paper. However, this is only recommendable for flat surfaces; where rapid change of sections occur, a thin felt pad is more useful.

The abrasive paper should be allowed to soak in cold water for at least 15 minutes before use. A useful tip is to smear the abrasive surface of the paper with soap prior to rubbing down. This will prevent clogging and should at least treble the useful life of the paper if it is washed thoroughly after each rub-down.

When the surface is smooth enough, wash it thoroughly with water and dry off with a clean sponge.

If smoother surface than this is required it can be given another layer of undercoat and then the rubbing down procedure repeated using 320 or 400 grade of paper depending upon conditions.

FINISHING
Before spraying on the finishing coats the surface must be quite smooth, dry and clean. It is important that conditions are right when finish spraying is to be carried out otherwise complications may occur. Best conditions for outdoor spraying are those on a dry sunny day without wind. Moisture in the atmosphere is detrimental to paint spraying.

The first coat should be thinned in the ratio of 50% cellulose thinners to 50% lacquer. Subsequent coats should have a higher proportion of thinners as shown below.

	Cellulose Thinners	Lacquer
1st Coat	50%	50%
2nd Coat	60%	40%
3rd Coat	70%	30%
4th Coat	80%	20%

Between each coat the surface may be flatted by hand with 320 or 400 abrasive paper as required.

E FRAME

Allow at least 10 minutes between each coat and after the final coat leave overnight or 24 hours if possible. For most purposes the 2nd coat of finishing is more than adequate.

POLISHING

The final colour coat must be completely dry before cutting and polishing. Using a clean rag rub down with brass polish or fine cutting paste and burnish to a high gloss using a clean mop before applying a suitable wax polish for protection and shine.

SECTION E23

FITTING REPLACEMENT SEAT COVERS

'Quiltop' twinseats have a cover retained by sprags. Fitted along the bottom edge of the seat trim.

When fitting a replacement seat cover it is **very important** to first soak the complete cover assembly in hot water in order to soften the plastic as that it can easily be stretched into place. After soaking the cover in hot water, wring out the excess water and you will find that the cover can very easily be stretched into place to give a neat fit without any wrinkles. This job is very difficult if you do not follow this suggested method.

Ideally the seat should be allowed to dry out in a warm place before being put back into service.

SECTION F

BRAKES WHEELS AND TYRES

INDEX

DESCRIPTION	Section
BRAKE ADJUSTMENTS	F1
FRONT BRAKE MASTER CYLINDER	F2
FRONT BRAKE PIPES AND HOSES - REMOVAL AND REFITMENT	F3
REAR BRAKE PIPES AND HOSES, MASTER CYLINDER AND RESERVOIR	F4
"BLEEDING" THE HYDRAULIG SYSTEM - FRONT AND REAR	F5
FLUSHING THE HYDRAULIC SYSTEM	F6
BRAKE FLUID LEVEL	F7
BRAKE PAD LINING - FRONT AND REAR	F8
STRIPPING AND REASSEMBLING THE FRONT AND REAR CALIPERS	F9
BRAKE DISCS	F10
FAULT FINDING - FRONT AND REAR HYDRAULIC DISC BRAKES	F11
REMOVING AND REFITTING THE FRONT WHEEL	F12
REMOVING AND REFITTING THE FRONT WHEEL BEARINGS	F13
REMOVING AND REFITTING THE REAR WHEEL (DISC TYPE)	F14
REAR WHEEL REMOVAL AND REPLACEMENT (DRUM TYPE)	F15
REMOVING AND REPLACING THE REAR WHEEL BEARINGS	F16
STRIPPING AND REASSEMBLING REAR BRAKE (DRUM TYPE)	F17
WHEEL BUILDING	F18
WHEEL BALANCING	F19
FRONT AND REAR WHEEL ALIGNMENT	F20
REMOVING AND REFITTING TYRES	F21
SECURITY BOLTS	F22
TYRE MAINTENANCE	F23
TYRE PRESSURES	F24
REAR CHAIN ADJUSTMENT	F25

F BRAKES, WHEELS AND TYRES

DESCRIPTION

Certain machines are fitted with a Lockheed hydraulic disc brake on the front and rear wheels (some models are fitted with a rear drum brake). The disc brake assembly consists of a high quality cast iron disc attached to the wheel hubs and a brake caliper(s) attached to the fork leg(s) or the rear swinging fork. The brake caliper houses two co-axially aligned pistons (Fig. F1) and a pair of brake pads the latter being retained by two split pins.

The pistons and their bores are protected by dust seals fitted in the open ends of the bores. (See Fig. F1). Application of the brake lever generates hydraulic pressure within the system and brake lever generates hydraulic pressure within the system and brake caliper causing the pistons (Fig. F1) to apply equal and opposite pressure on the brake pads (Fig. F1) which in turn move into contact with the rotating brake disc. The operation of the master cylinder and hydraulic flow is detailed in Section F7.

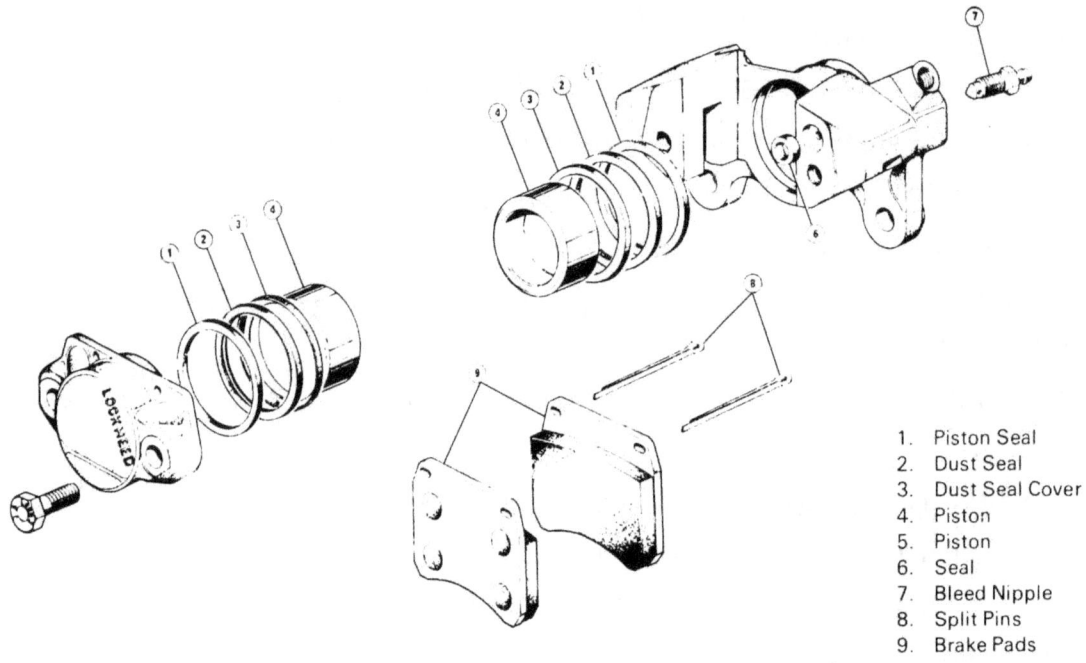

1. Piston Seal
2. Dust Seal
3. Dust Seal Cover
4. Piston
5. Piston
6. Seal
7. Bleed Nipple
8. Split Pins
9. Brake Pads

Fig. F1. Front and rear brake caliper-exploded

SECTION F1

BRAKE ADJUSTMENTS

FRONT BRAKE ADJUSTMENT-DISC
The brake pads of the disc brake will require no adjustment as the reducing thickness of the friction material is automatically cancelled out by the displacement of hydraulic fluid in the system.

REAR BRAKE ADJUSTMENT-DISC
The brake pads of the disc brake will require no adjustment as the reducing thickness of the friction material is automatically cancelled out by the displacement of hydraulic fluid in the system. However, the rear brake pedal must be positioned to prevent a foul condition against the R.H. footrest and consequently causing the rear brake to bind.

The adjuster nuts (see Fig. F2) should be set to give a MINIMUM clearance of $1/16$ in. (1.58mm.) between the brake pedal and the R.H. footrest. Ensure both the adjuster nuts are tight against the operating lever, after adjusting.

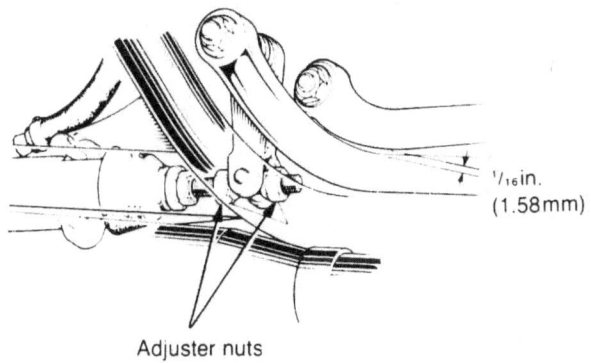

Adjuster nuts

Fig. F2. Rear brake pedal adjustment

REAR BRAKE ADJUSTMENT-DRUM
Certain models are fitted with a rear drum brake with internally expanding fully floating brake shoes. The L.H. rear brake pedal is connected to the brake shoe operating cam by means of an operating rod which in turn is adjustable.

The brake must be adjusted to give maximum efficiency at all times and for this to be maintained, the shoes should be just clear of the drum when the brake is off, and close enough for immediate contact when the brake is applied. The brakes must not be adjusted so closely, however, that they are in continual contact with the drum; excessive heat may be generated, resulting in deterioration of braking efficiency.

The rear brake is adjusted by turning the self-locking sleeve in a clockwise direction (view from the rear of the machine), to shorten the effective length of the brake rod and so open the shoes in the drum.

Note that if maximum efficiency is to be obtained the angle between the brake rod and the operating lever on the brake plate should not exceed 90° when the brake is fully applied.

The rear brake shoes are of the fully-floating type (i.e., they are not pivoted on a fulcrum) and are therefore self-centralizing.

The brake pedal is adjustable to suit individual requirement, care should be taken however to ensure that making this adjustment does not interfere with the foregoing instructions.

Ideally the pedal position stop should be set before carrying out other adjustments.

F BRAKES, WHEELS AND TYRES

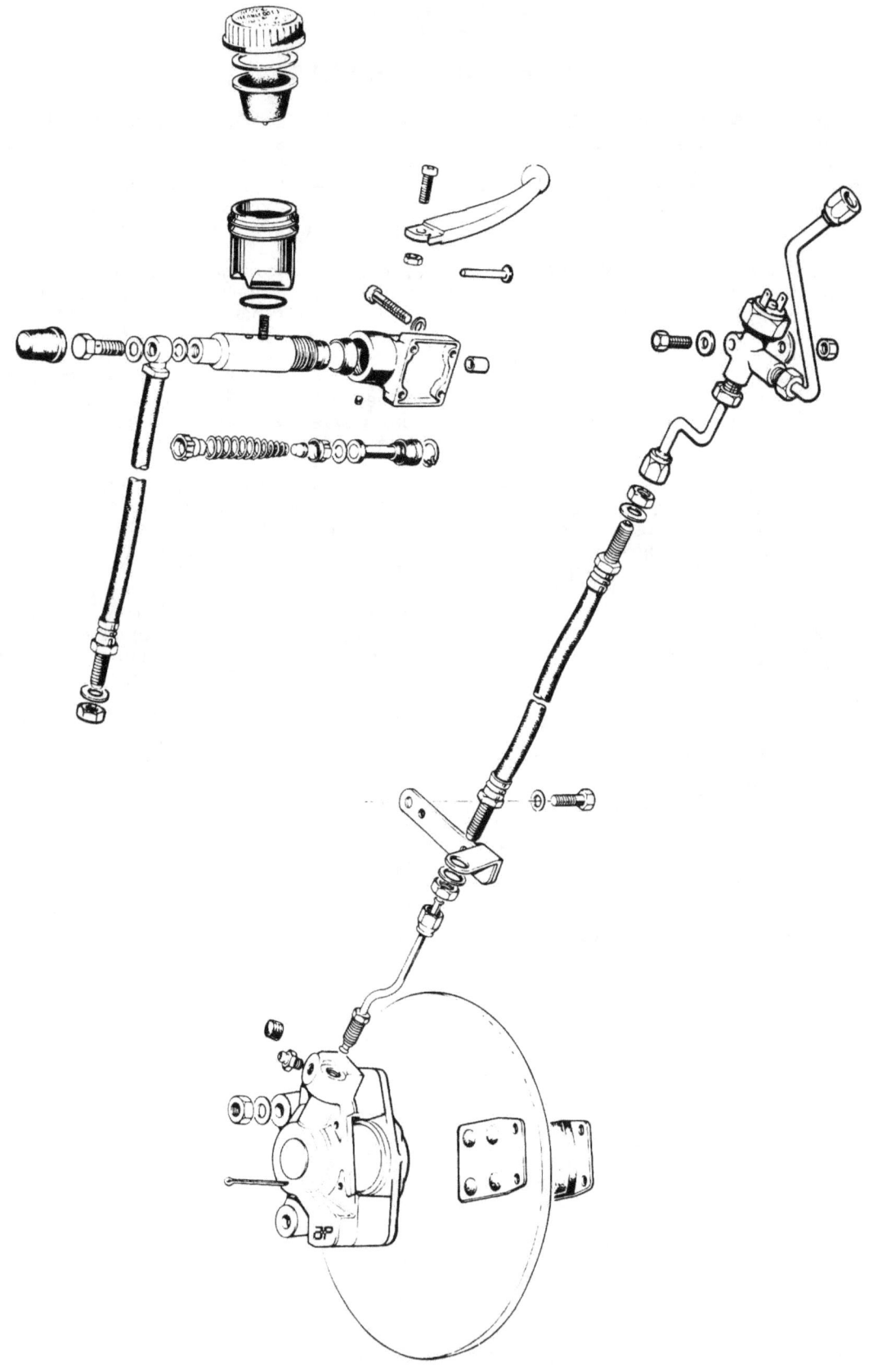

Fig. F3. Front brake components (U.S.A. model shown)

BRAKES, WHEELS AND TYRES

SECTION F2

FRONT BRAKE MASTER CYLINDER

The master cylinder is mounted onto the right hand handlebar electrical switch. It consists of a fluid reservoir bolted to a cylinder body containing a piston, seals and other parts as shown in Fig. F4.

1. Push Rod
2. Piston
3. Check Valve
4. Return Spring
5. Primary Seal
6. Circlip
7. Piston Washer
8. Secondary Seal
9. Spring Retainer
10. Dust Cover
11. Grub Screw
12. Reservoir Retaining Nut
13. 'O' Ring
14. Paper Washer
15. Rubber Diaphram
16. Cap
17. Distance Piece
18. Bush for Push Rod

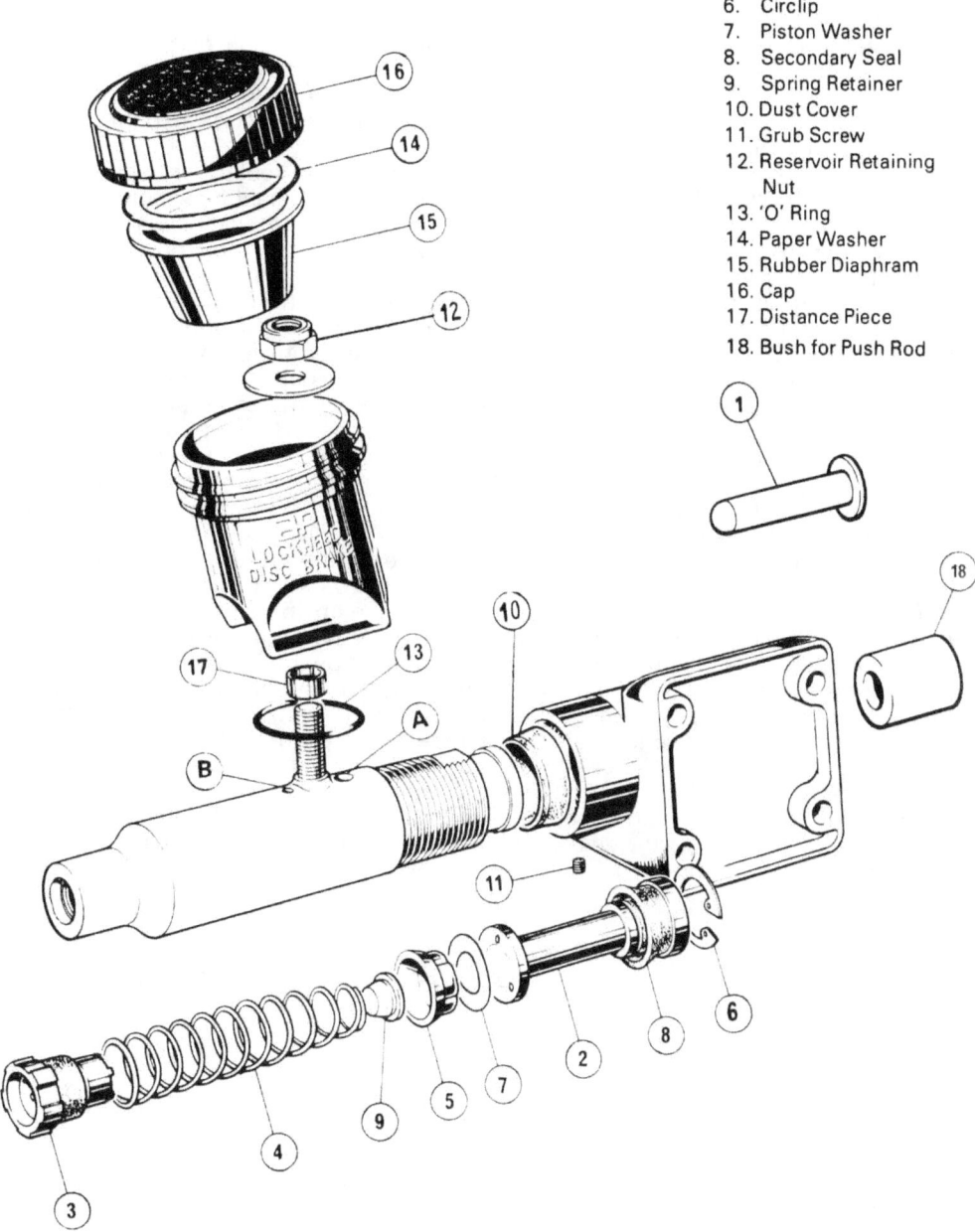

Fig. F4. Exploded view of master cylinder

F BRAKES, WHEELS AND TYRES

With reference to the hydraulic flow diagram (Fig. F5) and the exploded view. (Fig. F4) the operation of the cylinder is as follows:- When the front brake lever is pulled on the push rod (1) moves the piston (2) down the bore. The displaced fluid in front of the piston is forced through holes in the check valve (3) lifting the rubber seal clear of the holes to provide an unblocked passage to the wheel cylinders. On releasing the front brake lever the return spring (4) thrust the piston (2) back faster than the fluid is able to return from the wheel cylinders. This creates a partial vacuum in the cylinder which causes fluid to be drawn past the lip of th primary seal (5) from the main reservoir via the main feed port (A) and the small feed holes in the head of the piston (2).

Meanwhile fluid returning from the wheel cylinder lifts the check valve (3) away from its seat and re-enters the cylinder. When the piston has fully returned a small breather port (B) is uncovered which allows a release of excess fluid to the reservoir and also compensates for contraction and expansion of the fluid due to changes in temperature. The purpose of the check valve (3) is to prevent the re-entry into the master cylinder of fluid pumped into the line during the "bleeding" operation, thus ensuring a fresh charge of fluid at each stroke of the lever.

Removal and dismantling procedure of the cylinder is as floows:-Firstly drain the system of fluid. See Section F5. Remove the rubber hose from the wheel cylinder. Remove the brake lever and push rod by unscrewing the pivot bolt. Unscrew the four retaining screws that retain the right switch console and remove the master cylinder from the handlebar. Detach the reservoir bowl from the handlebar. Detach the reservoir bowl from the cylinder by removing the attachment nut from the inside (See Fig. F4). Note assembly of washer, spacer and 'O' ring. Remove the grub screw that locks the cylinder in position (See Fig. F4) and the unscrew the cylinder. Detach the rubber boot from the end of the cylinder. Using the push rod (1) depress the piston in the cylinder to relieve the load on the spring and remove the circlip (6). Remove the piston (2) piston washer (7), primary seal (5), return spring (4) and check valve (3). The removal of the primary seal (5) may be simplified by applying gentle air pressure to the pipe connection at the end of the cylinder.

Remove the secondary seal (8) by stretching it over the flange of the piston. Renew all seals and check the bore of the cylinder for deep score marks. If such damage is apparent a new cylinder should be fitted.

It is important that all parts are meticulously cleaned with brake fluid before assembly. Do not use petrol, trichlorethylene or any other similar cleaning agents to wash the parts.

Fit the secondary seal (8) onto the piston (2) so that the lip of the seal faces forwards the head (drilled end) of the piston. See Fig. F4. Gently work the seal around the groove with the fingers to ensure that it is properly seated. Fit the spring retainer (9) onto the small end of the spring (4) and the check valve (3) onto the large end. Insert the spring assembly onto the cylinder bore, large end first. Insert the primary seal (5) into the cylinder bore, large end first. Insert the primary seal (5) into the cylinder bore, lip foremost (See Fig. F4), taking care not to damage or turn back the lip. Insert the piston washer (7) into the barrel with the dished side towards the primary seal (5) (See Fig. F4) followed by the piston, head (drilled end) innermost, see Fig. F4. Push the piston inwards with the end of the push rod and refit the circlip (6). Make sure that the circlip beds evenly in its groove. Refit the boot (10) by stretching it over the barrel. Refit the reservoir bowl, (tighten the securing nut to a torque of 4 to 7lbs. ft. (6 to 7Nm.) not forgetting the 'O' ring and test the cylinder by filling the reservoir and pushing the push rod and piston inwards and allowing it to return unassisted. After a few applications fluid should flow from the outlet connection at the cylinder head.

BRAKES, WHEELS AND TYRES F

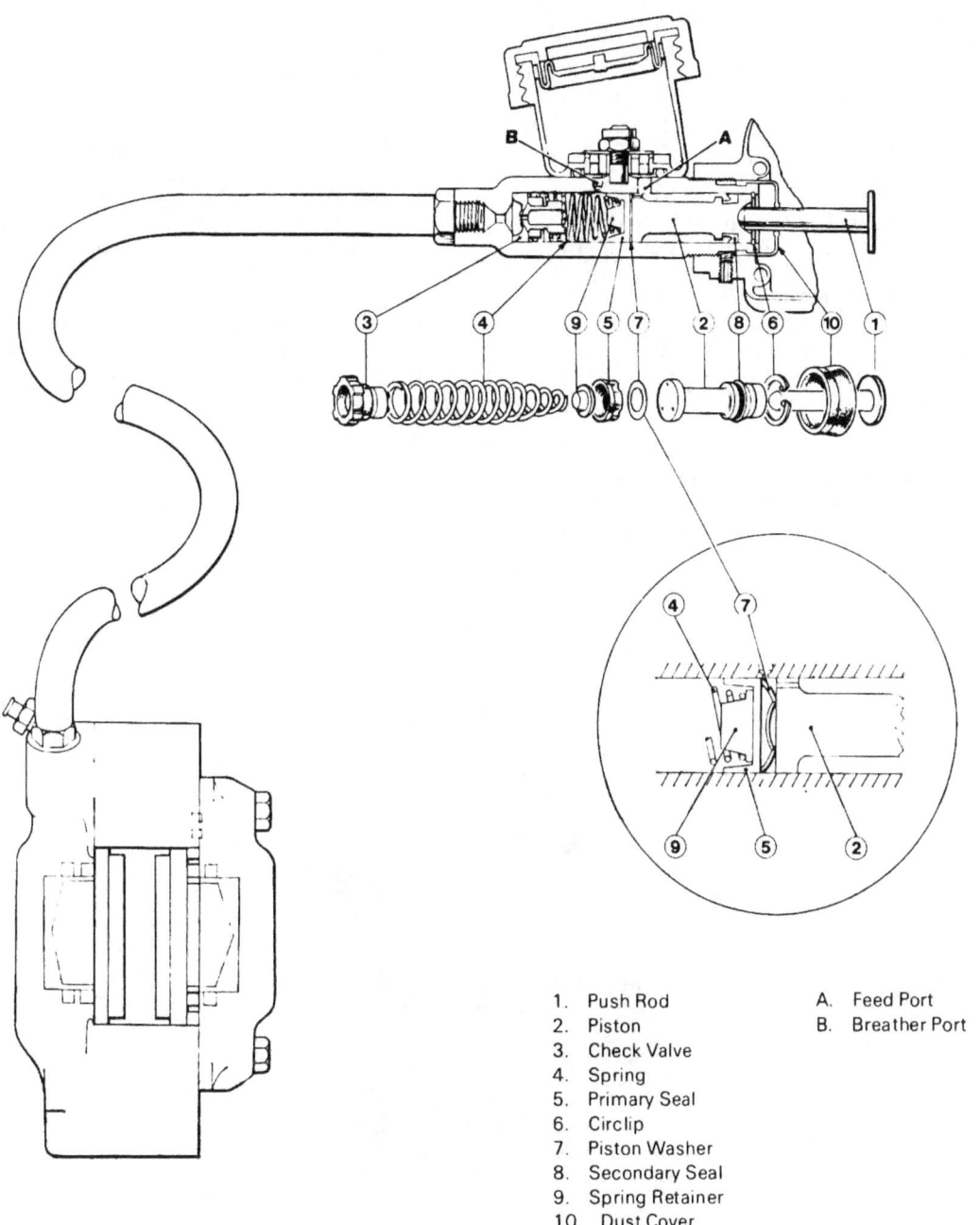

1. Push Rod
2. Piston
3. Check Valve
4. Spring
5. Primary Seal
6. Circlip
7. Piston Washer
8. Secondary Seal
9. Spring Retainer
10. Dust Cover

A. Feed Port
B. Breather Port

Fig. F5. Hydraulic flow diagram-front brake

BRAKES, WHEELS AND TYRES

If necessary refit the return spring. Empty the cylinder of fluid and proceed to re-assemble the cylinder barrel into the switch housing. At this stage the final position of the cylinder barrel in the housing must be determined. Here reference must be made to Fig. F5. It will be observed from Fig. F5 that the lip of the primary seal (5) must be $1/16$ of an inch behind the breather port and the reservoir set at an angle of 10° to the vertical. The milled flats on the threaded end of the cylinder are machined relative to the 10° position and the appropriate one must be used when assembly takes place.

The following method can be used to determine the correct linear position of the cylinder barrel.

(1) Remove the reservoir from the cylinder.

(2) Re-assemble the front brake lever and push rod to the switch housing. Tighten the nylon nut to a torque of 5 to 7 lb.ft. (7 to 9 Nm.).

(3) Screw the cylinder barrel into the switch housing whilst holding the brake lever in the closed position until it will screw no further.

(4) Place finger over the main port (A) Fig. F5 and by blowing through the outlet end of the cylinder it will be observed that no air will escape from the breather port (B) Fig. F5.

(5) Now unscrew the cylinder barrel until air is heard to escape from the breather port (B). At this point the port will have just become uncovered.

(6) Unscrew the barrel one complete turn and set the angle to 10° as shown in Fig. F6. The milled flat on the threaded end of the barrel must be located when the grub screw (Fig. F4) is being re-tightened and will set the angle automatically.

Re-assemble the master cylinder to the handlebar replenish the reservoir with fluid and "bleed" the system as described in Section F5.

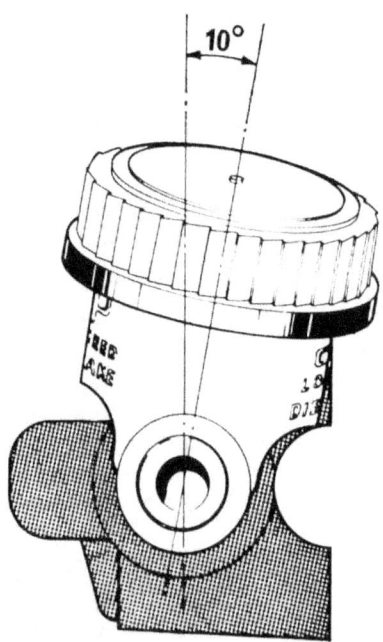

Fig. F6. Showing angle of brake reservoir

BRAKES, WHEELS AND TYRES

SECTION F3

FRONT BRAKE PIPES AND HOSES - REMOVAL AND REFITMENT

The hydraulic flow is taken from the master cylinder to the front brake caliper via a rubber pressure hose coupled to a steel brake pipe at the top head lug then to a second hose coupled at the middle lug. The first hose allows for adjustment of the handlebar position. DO NOT adjust the handlebars such that the hose becomes kinked or stretched. The second hose allows for the compression and extension of the front suspension. The position of the hose coupling at the middle lug is important, see Fig. F7.

The brake hoses and pipe should be checked at the intervals stated in "Routine Maintenance" for leakage, chafing or general deterioration. Do not attempt to clear the bore of a flexible hose by probing. If a hose is choked or perished, fit a replacement.

Hoses and pipe may be replaced as follows:-
Firstly drain the system of its fluid see Section F5. Unscrew the fixing bolt from the end of the master cylinder and detach the union (U.S.A. models only). Note the copper sealing washers at the front and back of the union. These sealing washers must be annealed if they are to be reused and this is effected by heating the washers to a cherry red colour and plunging them into cold water. (Other export models with low handlebars have a feed hose that screws directly into the master cylinder and this hose should be disconnected at the fork top lug first and then unscrewed from the master cylinder).

Unscrew the union at the top fork lug and disconnect the pipe.

See Fig. F2 for assembly details. Similarly disconnect the remaining pipe and hoses from the middle lug, left fork leg and caliper. Note that the pipe junction at the middle lug is mounted in such a fashion that the rubber hose that hence travels down to the left fork leg is splayed outwards and away from the wheel when the front forks are compressed. See Fig. F7 for detail drawing. **When installing the hose ensure that the coloured stripe travelling the length of the hose is arranged such that it is not twisted.** To reset the angle as shown simply loosen the bolt clamping nut and alter the position of the bolt accordingly.

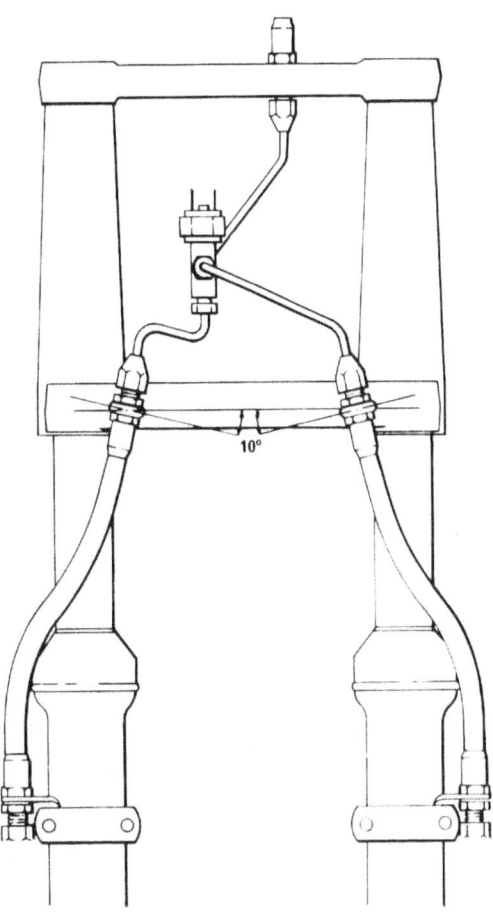

Fig. F7. Showing front brake pipe installation

Be careful not to overtighten the union nuts as their threads may be easily stripped. After refitting the hoses replenish the system as described in Section F5. Check that no chafing of the hoses or pipes occurs when the handlebars are turned from left lock to right lock and when the front forks are fully compressed.

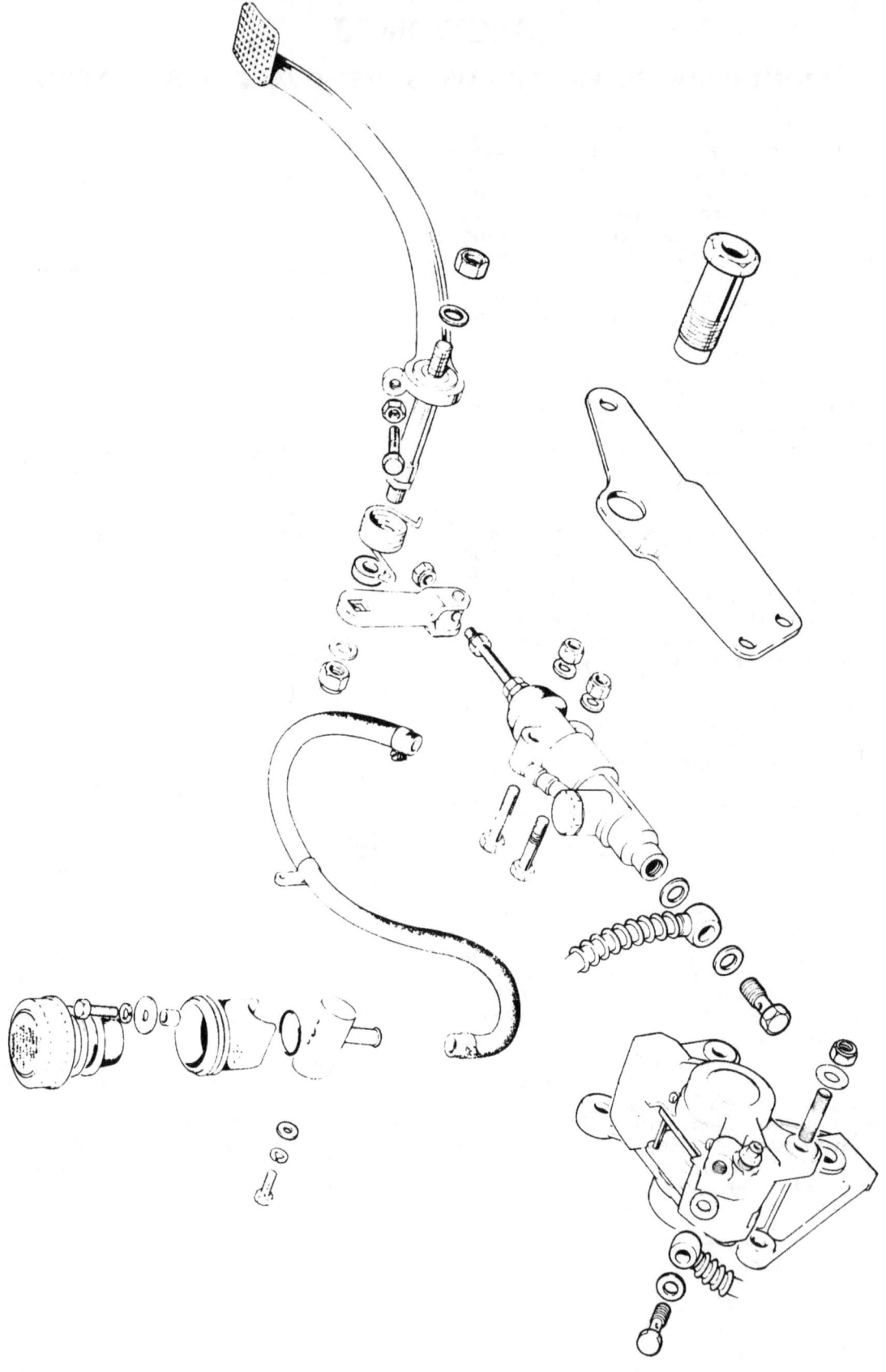

Fig. F8. Rear brake components

BRAKES, WHEELS AND TYRES

SECTION F4

REAR BRAKE PIPES AND HOSES, MASTER CYLINDER AND RESERVOIR

REAR BRAKE PIPES AND HOSES

Brake fluid is contained in a separate reservoir mounted beneath the twinseat. Fluid is supplied to the master cylinder by a rubber hose retained by two hose clips. Hydraulic flow is taken from the master cylinder via a rubber pressure hose to a coupling at the caliper.

The rubber hose allows for movement of the rear swinging fork.

The brake hose and pressure pipe should be checked at the intervals stated in "routine Maintenance" for leakage, chafting or general deterioration. Do not attempt to clear the bore of a flexible hose by probing. If a hose is choked or perished, fit a replacement.

The hose and pressure pipe may be replaced as follows: Firstly drain the system of its fluid.

Unscrew the bolt at the caliper and the master cylinder. The hose is then free to be removed.

When refitting the hose tighten the unions such that the hose is in the position shown in Fig. F9. See Fig. F8 for assembly details.

If the copper washer is to be re-used it should be annealed as described in the front brake section.

Be careful not to overtighten the union nuts as their threads may be easily stripped. After refitting the hose replenish and 'bleed' the system as described in Section F5. Check that no chafting of the hose occurs when the rear suspension is compressed or extended. Ensure that the rear metal brake pipe does not foul the caliper casting.

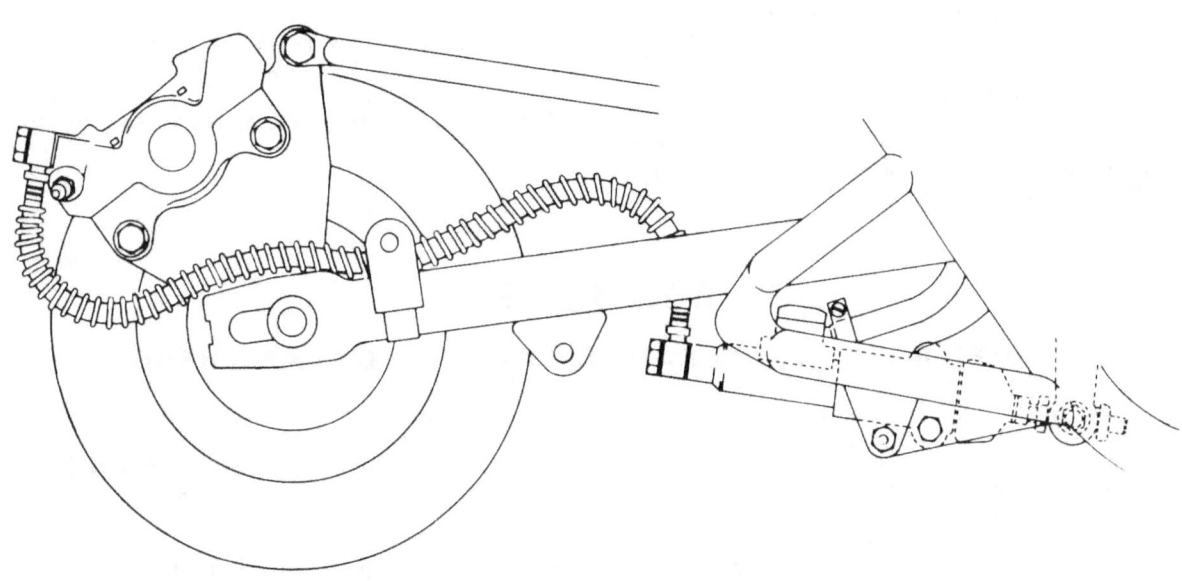

Fig. F9. Rear brake pipe installation

F

BRAKES, WHEELS AND TYRES

REAR BRAKE MASTER CYLINDER

The rear brake master cylinder is a sealed unit and is only serviced as such. The principle of operation is identical to that of the front master cylinder with the exception that he reservoir is mounted remotely.

To remove the master cylinder first remove the rear wheel, see Section F14.

Drain the system of its fluid see Section F5.

Disconnect the brake pedal return spring then remove the nut and washer and withdraw the master cylinder operating lever.

Disconnect the reservoir rubber hose from the master cylinder by slackening the clip.

Remove the two nuts and bolts and withdraw the master cylinder from the frame. Unscrew the master cylinder from the rubber hose. Note the copper sealing washer. (if the copper washer is to be renewed it must be annealed by heating the washer to a cherry red colour and plunging it into cold water).

Remove the operating lever by removing the adjuster nuts.

Prior to fitting a new master cylinder check the distance between the end of the cast mounting bracket and the face of the pushrod nut, see Fig. F10. This dimension should be 0.35in. to 0.37in. (8.9 to 9.4mm.) and should be adjusted as necessary.

Refitment of the master cylinder is a reversal of the above instructions, but see Section E5 for refitment of the rear brake pedal return spring; Section F5 for replenishing and bleeding the system with new brake fluid. See Section F1 for correct pedal rod setting.

Note the nut securing the master cylinder operating lever should be tightened to a torque of 20ft. lbs. (4.8kg.m.).

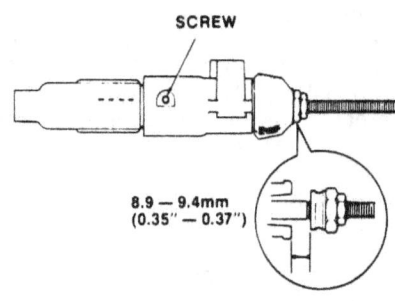

Fig. F10. Push rod adjustment

REAR BRAKE RESERVOIR

To remove the rear brake reservoir first drain the system of its fluid, see Section F6.

Disconnect the rubber hose from the reservoir at the master cylinder.

Lift the twinseat and remove the bolt and washer securing the reservoir assembly to the air box.

Remove the reservoir cap, sealing ring and the rubber diaphragm.

Remove the bolt, spring washer, plain washer, distance piece then remove the bowl from the mounting block. Detach the 'O' ring.

Reassembly is a reversal of the above instructions, but always fit a new 'O' ring.

Tighten the bowl retaining bolt to a torque of 4 to 5lb.ft. (6 to 7Nm.).

SECTION F5

"BLEEDING" THE HYDRAULIC SYSTEM-FRONT AND REAR

If at any time it has been found necessary to disconnect a part of the hydraulic system (for repair etc.) it will be necessary to replenish the master cylinder reservoir and "bleed" the system free of trapped air pockets. "Bleeding" (or expelling air from) the hydraulic system is not a routine maintenacne operation. Always keep a careful check on the fluid level in the rservoir during "bleeding". It is most important that it is kept at least half full, otherwise air may be drawn into the system necessitating a fresh start.

When bleeding the rear brake firstly.
Loosen wheel spindle "A".
Remove shock absorber bottom fixing bolt 'B' from swinging arm. Swing shock absorber out sideways.

Remove rear torque arm fixing bolt 'C' and move torque arm up away from caliper plate 'D' caliper plate 'D' can be pivoted forward. Until bleed nipple 'E' is at highest point.

BRAKES, WHEELS AND TYRES

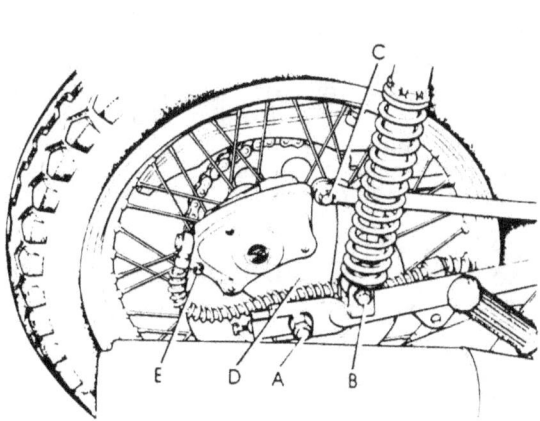

Fig. F11. Rear brake

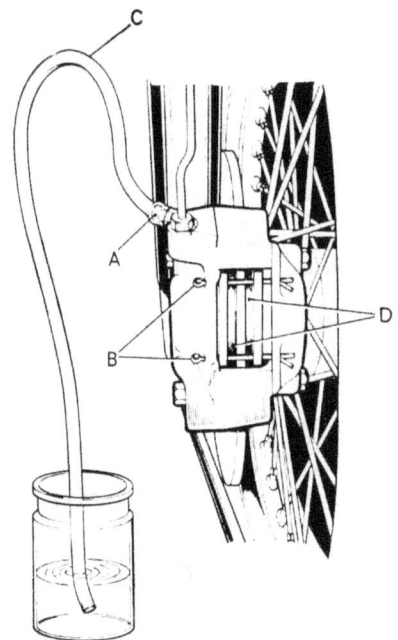

Fig. F12. Showing arrangement for bleeding the front brake.

The system may now be bled as follows:
Connect a suitable sized rubber "pipe" "C" Fig. F12 to the bleed nipple "A" Fig F12 and suspend the free end of the tube in a glass jar with the open end immersed in at least ½ in. (12.7mm.) of brake fluid. Remove the screwed cap from the master cylinder reservoir and take out the rubber diaphram "E" Fig. F15. Now slacken the bleed nipple ½ to ¾ of a turn, (with the bleed pipe still attached).

Ensure that the master cylinder is full of the correct fluid before commencing further. Now operate the brake lever firmly holding fully depressed position for a few seconds. Air in the system will now be expelled through the rubber tube and will be observed in the form of bubbles rising in the jar. Release the brake lever and repeat the operation until air bubbles are no longer seen to escape. As a safeguard to prevent any air being drawn back into the system when the lever and repeat the operation until air bubbles are no longer seen to escape. As a safeguard to prevent any air being drawn back into the system when the lever is released, loop the "bleed" pipe as shown in Fig. F12. This ensures that a "head" of fluid is maintained between the top of the loop and the "bleed" nipple.

When the flow of air bubbles ceases hold the brake lever in the fully "on" position and retighten the bleed nipple (with the "bleed" pipe still connected).

Fluid drained from the system should not be used again in a brake system or put back into the can containing the new fluid.

Also ensure that the brake fluid container cap is replaced securely to avoid moisture from the atmosphere contaminating the brake fluid.

Remember to maintain the level of hydraulic fluid in the master cylinder during the entire operation. The correct level for the fluid is shown in Fig. F15 at "F". This will be the correct level when the brake pads are NEW When replacing the rubber diaphragm (Fig. F15 "F") it will be easier to replace the cap with the diaphragm in a folded condition. See Fig F13.

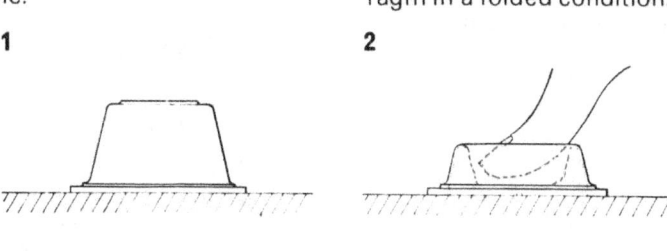

Fig. F13. Folded condition of rubber diaphragm

Hold the diaphragm upside down on a flat surface and push the middle section down until it touches the surface it is resting on. It will now remain in that position and the diaphragm can now be replaced into the reservoir and the cap refitted. Do not forget the paper washer that is fitted between the cap and the diaphragm. when fitting the cap make sure it is retightened firmly and make sure that the air vent is unobstructed.

If at any time it has been necessary to replenish the system with hydraulic brake fluid during the life of one set of brake pads, remember that when new pads are fitted the fluid level will arise appreciably in the cylinder and may spill onto the gas tank. Therefore the level will have to be corrected to that shown in Fig. F15 (Hydraulic fluid instantaneously corrodes cellulose paintwork and great care should be exercised when handling this fluid).

IMPORTANT:
Use only the specified type of hydraulic brake fluid.

SECTION F6

FLUSHING THE HYDRAULIC SYSTEM

If the hydraulic system has been contaminated by foreign matter or other fluids it should be flushed out and refilled with new fluid as described below. The system should be flushed out, in any case, at the interval stated in "Routine Maintenance".

Firstly, pump all the fluid out of the system by opening the bleed screw (connect a pipe to the bleed screw and safely collect in a container) and operating brake lever. Fill the master cylinder reservoir with methylated spirit and pump out through the bleed screw in a manner similar to that described above. Having ensured that all the methylated spirit has passed through the bleed screw replenish the master cylinder reservoir (see Section F7) with the specified grade of hydraulic brake fluid (see "Technical Data"). "Bleed" the brakes as described in Section F4.

IMPORTANT NOTE: If the system has been contaminated by a mineral oil, all rubber parts including flexible hoses must be replaced.

SECTION F7

BRAKE FLUID LEVEL

The brake fluid level in the master cylinder reservoir should be as shown in Fig. F15 (F). There is a mark running around the inside periphery of the reservoir about ¼ in. (6.35mm.) from the top. The level will drop slightly as the pads wear and when new pads are fitted the fluid will return to the original level provided no leakage has occurred.

It is necessary to 'top-up' the fluid level at the intervals stated in "Routine maintenance".

Always hold the handlebars against full RIGHT lock when 'topping-up' the front brake reservoir. Do not overfill.

NOTE: IMPORTANT
Use only hydraulic brake fluid conforming to SAE J1703 or D.O.T. 3 when replenishing or topping up.

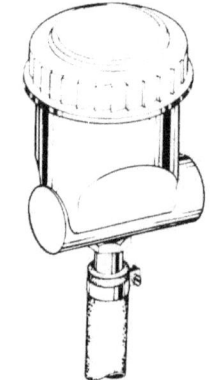

Fig. F14. Rear brake reservoir

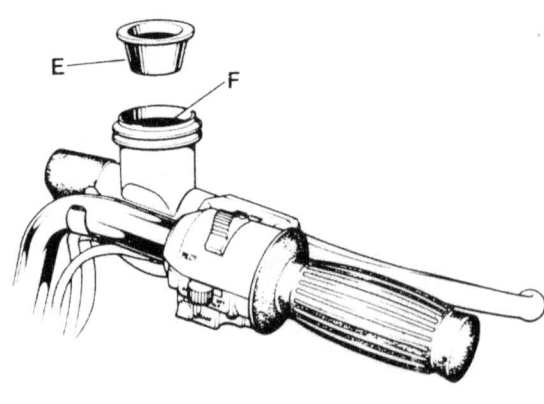

Fig. F15. Showing the front brake reservoir fluid level and cap

BRAKES, WHEELS AND TYRES

SECTION F8

BRAKE PAD LINING-FRONT AND REAR

DISC BRAKE, MODELS ONLY
The brake pads will require replacement when the lining thickness reaches a minimum of ⁵⁄₆₄ in. This can be easily determined by removing the pad from the caliper. Remove both the split pins "B" and pull out both the pads "D".

In certain cases it is necessary to remove the styling cover to enable the split pins to be extracted.

The brake pad friction material is bonded to the pressure plate of the brake pad and therefore can only be renewed by the fitting of complete brake pad assemblies. New split pins are advisable when fitting new or replacing used brake pads.

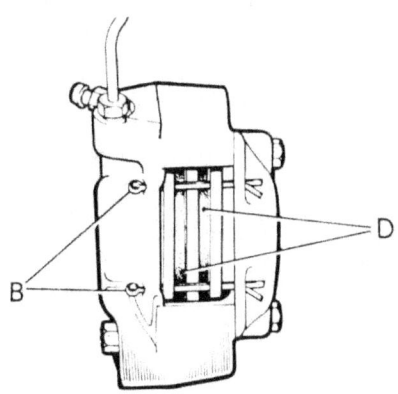

Fig. F16. Showing brake pads and split pins

SECTION F9

STRIPPING AND REASSEMBLING THE FRONT AND REAR BRAKE CALIPERS

FRONT BRAKE
Detach the styling cover from the caliper by removing the two crosshead screws. Drain the system of fluid. See Section F6. Detach the feed pipe from the caliper and remove the two securing nuts bolts at he fork leg and withdraw the caliper from its mounting studs. After firstly removing the front wheel see Section. F12.

REAR BRAKE
Drain the system of fluid by removing the banjo-bolt retaining the hydraulic feed pipe to the caliper. Remove the caliper to plate securing nuts. Remove the bolt securing the torque stay to the caliper. Undo and remove the wheel spindle.

NOTE: Take care when handling brake fluid as it is a powerful paint stripper.

Replacement is a reversal of the above but refer to Section F5 for 'bleeding' the system.

No attempt should be made to remove the caliper bridge bolts jointing the two halves of the caliper. There is no necessity to do so and all the servicing can be carried out without splitting the halves, and in addition the bolts are tightened to a critcal torque loading.

If in an emergency, the brake caliper has been split and in event of the fluid channel seal being undamaged, the caliper and bridge bolts should be thoroughly cleaned. dried and reassembled and the bridge bolts tightened to a torque loading of 35-40ft. lbs. (4.8 to 5.5Kg.m). After reassembling, the brake caliper should be chekked for fluid tightness under maximum brake lever pressure.

It should be understood that this procedure will only provide a temporary remedy and a caliper should be returned to the manufacturers for over-haul at the first opportunity. Service the rubber seals as follows:- (read in conjunction with Fig. F1).A rubber sealing ring (1) is fitted in a groove machined in each pistons bore to seal off the hydraulic fluid. A "U" shaped rubber dust seal (2) having two wiping edges and housed in a metal container (3) is pressed into the open end of the piston bore to prevent the ingress of dust from the brake pads.

The dust seal (2) together with its retainer (3) must be renewed each time they are removed from the piston bore. When the rubber seal (1) is worn or damaged it must be renewed. Before installation the seals should be lubricated with Lockheed disc brake lubricant. The movement of the pistons (4) and (5) withint their respective bore extrude the rectangular rubber seal (1) from its groove. On releasing the brake lever the hydraulic pressure collapses and the rubber seal (1) retracts the pistons (4) and (5) a pre-determined amount, thus maintaining a constant clearance between the brake pads and the brake disc when the brakes are not in use.

To remove rubber seals:- Prise out and discard the dust seal (2) and (3) from the open end of each piston bore by inserting a blade of blunt screwdriver between the seal and retainer. Eject

F   BRAKES, WHEELS AND TYRES

each piston from their bores by applying compressed air to the fluid inlet. Lift out and discard the sealing rings (1) from the grooves in the piston bores by inserting a blunt screwdriver under each ring taking care not to damge the grooves.

Dry the new seal rings (1) and smear them with Lockheed disc brake lubricant and refit them into the groom of each piston bore so that the large side is nearer the open end of the piston bore. Gently work the sealing rings into their respective grooves with the fingers to ensure correct seating. Dry the pistons and coat with Lockheed disc brake lubricant. Offer up the pistons, closed end first squarely to the bores in the caliper and press the pistons fully home. Dry the dust seals and coat with Lockhhed disc brake lubricant.

Fit a dust seal into a metal retainer and position both squarely into the mouth of one piston bore with the dust seal facing the bore. Press the dust seal into the mouth of the piston bore using a "G" clamp and support plate, until its outer edges are flush with the bore. Repeat with the second dust seal and retainer. Fit new brake pads (See Section F8). Refit the brake caliper. Reconnect the hydraulic feed pipe and "bleed" the system as in Section F5. Refit the protection cover (front brake only).

SECTION F10

BRAKE DISCS

The brake disc will require no maintenance other than when re-newal becomes necessary due to damage or becoming excessively scored. If this occurs the disc must be checked for run-out using a dial test indicator. The maximum reading should not exceed 0.0035ins. (0.89mm)

To replace the disc, firstly remove the front wheel. See Section F12. Unscrew the four securing nuts and detach the disc. Fit new disc and tighten the nuts diagonally opposite to each other to the torque figure given in Technical Data.

Replace the wheel into the forks and attach a dial test indicator to the fork leg and check the run-out to the figure previously quoted. If it is outside the limit the disc should be repositioned in an attempt to obtain a more satisfactory combination of machining limits.

Excessive run-out of the brake disc moves the pistons back into the bores and creates excessive lever travel when the brake is applied thus the run-out must be kept to the specified minimum.

NOTE: Machines subsequent to EDA 30,000 are fitted with plain untreated cast iron discs. If replacemnts are required the same type must be used.

BRAKES, WHEELS AND TYRES

SECTION F11

FAULT FINDING-FRONT AND REAR HYDRAULIC DISC BRAKES

PROBLEM	POSSIBLE CAUSE	ACTION
Excess travel of the front brake lever rear brake pedal or 'spongy' feel when applying either brake.	(a) Air trapped in the hydraulic system. (b) Incorrect positioning of master cylinder (c) Fluid leak past the main seal in the master cylinder.	Bleed the system, see Section F5. Reset position, see Section F2 & F4. Examine the seals, see Section F2 & F4.
Fluid level falls in either the front or rear brake fluid reservoirs.	(a) Friction pads wearing normally. (b) Brake fluid leaking	Top up the fluid, see Section F7. Check all the hoses, pipes and unions without applying the brakes and look for evidence of leaks. Repeat check with the brakes held on under pressure. If necessary tighten any unions or replace/service any components.
Brakes drag with subsequent over-heating of disc resulting in brake fade.	(a) Reservoir filler cap has a blocked vent hole. (b) Incorrect positioning of the cylinder. (c) The friction pads binding in their recess or the caliper piston is sticking. (d) The brake fluid contaminated with fuel, paraffin or oil.	Clean and inspect the filler cap vent hole. Clear the hole if necessary. Reset position, see Section F1 & F2. Remove the friction pads and clean out their recesses. Clean the exposed surface of the pistons with clean brake fluid. If a piston is found to be seized then a new caliper assembly must be fitted. If any high spots are found on the riction pad backing plates remove them with a file. If contamination is supected, first check by smlling the fluid in the reservoirs. If necessary dismantle the front brake master cylinder and check to see if the seals are considerably wollen. if so all rubber components must be replaced as a unit. Before fitting any new parts flush the system, see Section F6.

F   BRAKES, WHEELS AND TYRES

PROBLEM	POSSIBLE CAUSE	ACTION
Inefficient braking	(a) New friction pads, but are not "bedded-in".	Frequent use of brake will cure complaint.
	(b) Friction pads glazed on the brake disc has oxidised.	Remove the friction pads and remove any glazed areas with a fine abrasive. Inspect the contact area of the disc any minor imperfections can be removed with a fine carborundum paper but if in doubt replace the disc.
	(c) Friction pads contaminated by oil, grease or brake fluid.	Replace the friction pads
Friction pads wear raidly	(a) Friction pads fitted are the incorrect grade.	Replace pads with the correct type.
	(b) Brake disc has a scored contact area.	Minor imperfections may be removed with a fine grade carborundum paper, but otherwise replace the disc
	(c) Partly or completely seized caliper piston.	If the piston is found to be seized the whole caliper assembly must be replaced.
Squealing brakes	(a) Friction pads vibrate at a high frquency.	Remove the friction pads and lubricate the metal backing plate with high melting point copper based grease such as 'COPASLIP'. DO NOT allow the grease to contact the riction pad material.
	(b) Loose caliper mounting bolts.	Confirm and recitfy by tightening the bolts.

SECTION F12

REMOVING AND REFITTING THE FRONT WHEEL

To remove front wheel - twin disc
Unscrew and remove the two bolts which secure the brackets retaining the RH hydraulic pipe.
Detach the RH caliper by removing the two securing bolts. This will allow the caliper to swing away from the disc.
Unscrew the four cap nuts. Remove both caps. Withdraw the wheel.

Important: Do NOT apply the front brake whilst the wheel is out of the forks.

To replace front wheel - twin disc
Ensure the wheel is the correct way round, i.e. spindle locking nut must be positioned towards LH caliper. Engage the disc between the pads in the LH caliper.

Replace the end caps and nuts. **NOTE:** Tighten the four nuts of the LH fork leg before finally tightening the RH fork leg nuts. This enables the wheel spindle to align correctly. Replace the RH caliper and tighten the securing bolts. Refit and tighten the bracket retaining bolts.

Important: Operate the front brake lever BEFORE putting the motorcycle into operation.

BRAKES, WHEELS AND TYRES F

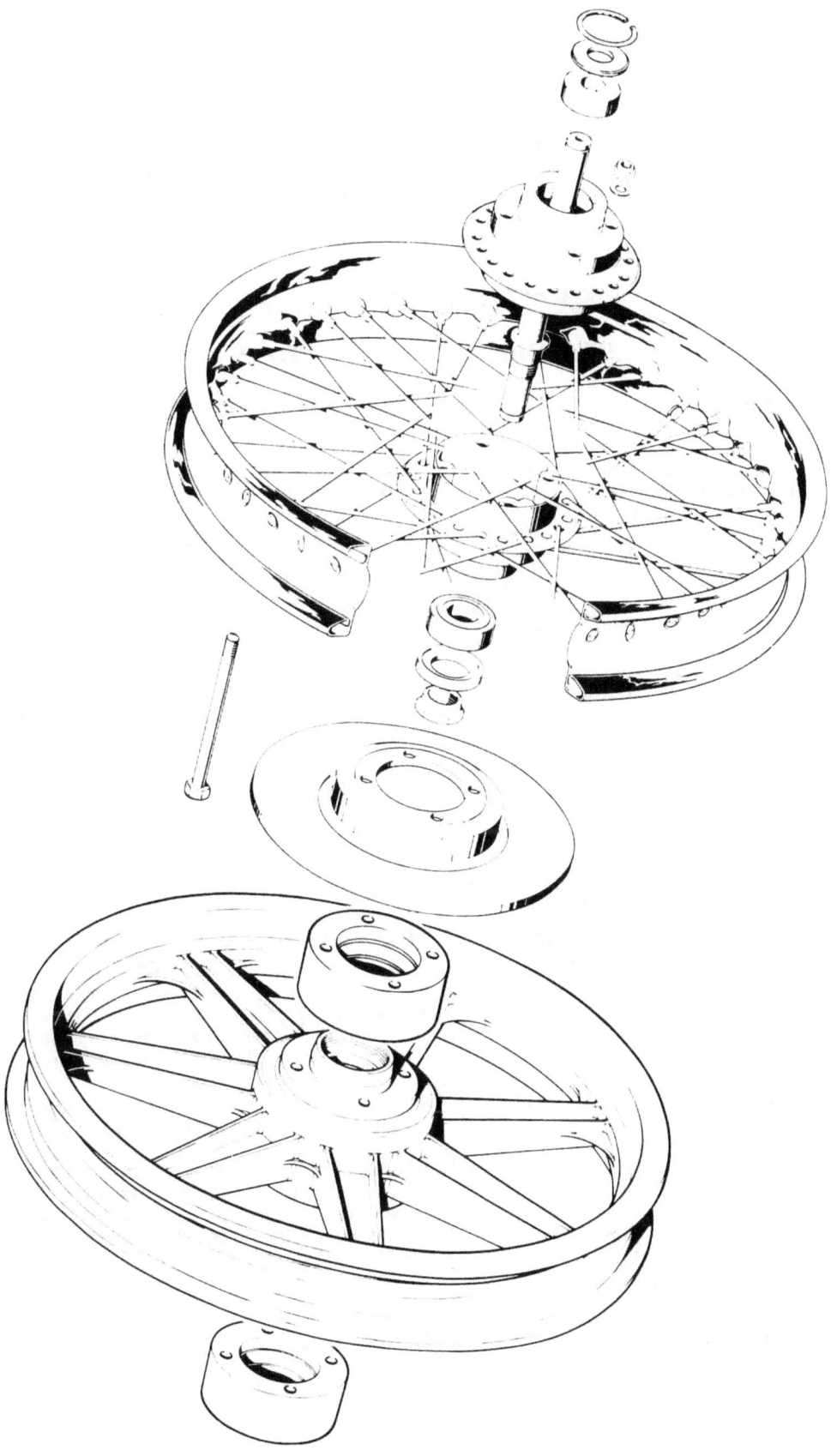

Fig. F17. Exploded view of front wheel bearing arrangement

F BRAKES, WHEELS AND TYRES

To remove the front wheel - single disc
Unscrew the eight fork cap nuts.
Remove both caps.
Withdraw the front wheel. **IMPORTANT** - Do not apply the front brake when the wheel is out of the forks.

To replace the front wheel - single disc
Engage the disc between the pads in the caliper.

Replace the end caps & nuts **Note:** Tighten the four nuts of the left hand fork leg before finally tightening the right hand fork leg nuts. This enables the wheel spindle to align correctly.

WARNING: Always actuate the front brake prior to moving off with the machine. This will re-charge the hydraulic circuit with fluid in readiness for the first braking application.

SECTION F13

REMOVING AND REFITTING THE FRONT WHEEL BEARINGS

Remove the front wheel (See Section F12). Unscrew the wheel spindle fixing nut from the left hand side and then unscrew the retaining ring with service tool 61-3694 (Right hand thread). The left hand bearing can now be removed by driving the wheel spindle through from the right hand side. Withdraw the inner grease retaining disc from the left hand side. To remove the right hand side bearing, spring out the circlip and insert the wheel spindle from the left hand side and drive the bearing out complete with inner and outer grease retaining plates.

NOTE: Always fit bearings of the latest sealed type when servicing. The sealed bearings can be easily recognised by the plastic covers fitted to each side of the ball race.

To refit the bearings first insert the right retainer, bearing and outer dust cap. Refit the spring circlip and insert the shouldered end of the wheel spindle from the left and using it as a drift drive the bearing and grease retainer until they come up to the circlip. re-insert the spindle the opposite way round and refit the left hand grease retainer disc. Drive the left bearing into position. Apply loctite 270 to the retaining ring (ensure the hub thread and retaining ring are grease free before doing so).

Then screw in the retainer ring (right hand thread) until tight. Using Service Tool No. 61-3694. Tap the spindle from the right to bring the spindle shoulder up against the left bearing. Replace the spindle fixing nut and re-tighten firmly. (Refer to Fig. F17 for layout and identification).

SECTION F14

REMOVING AND REFITTING THE REAR WHEEL (DISC TYPE)

Raise the machine on its centre stand then lift the machine an additional 3in. by placing a suitable block underneath the stand. Remove the L.H. muffler by removing the L.H. pillion footrest securing bolt and allow the muffler to drop down enough to clear the spindle. Disconnect the rear chain by removing the split link.

Using a tommy bar to secure the wheel spindle remove the spindle nut. Withdraw the wheel spindle and swing the caliper assembly away from the disc. Carefully allow the wheel to drop. Leaving speedo drive unit attached to the speedo cable.

NOTE: Take care not to operate the rear brake lever whilst the caliper is disconnected from the disc.

Replacement is the reversal of the above instructions but ensure that the closed end of the chain split link faces the direction of travel. And that the speedo drive arm is located properly in its slot.
Check the wheel alignment (Section F20) and rear chain adjustment (Section F27)

WARNING: Always actuate the rear brake prior to moving off with the machine. This will re-charge the hydraulic circuit with fluid in readiness for the first braking application.

BRAKES, WHEELS AND TYRES   F

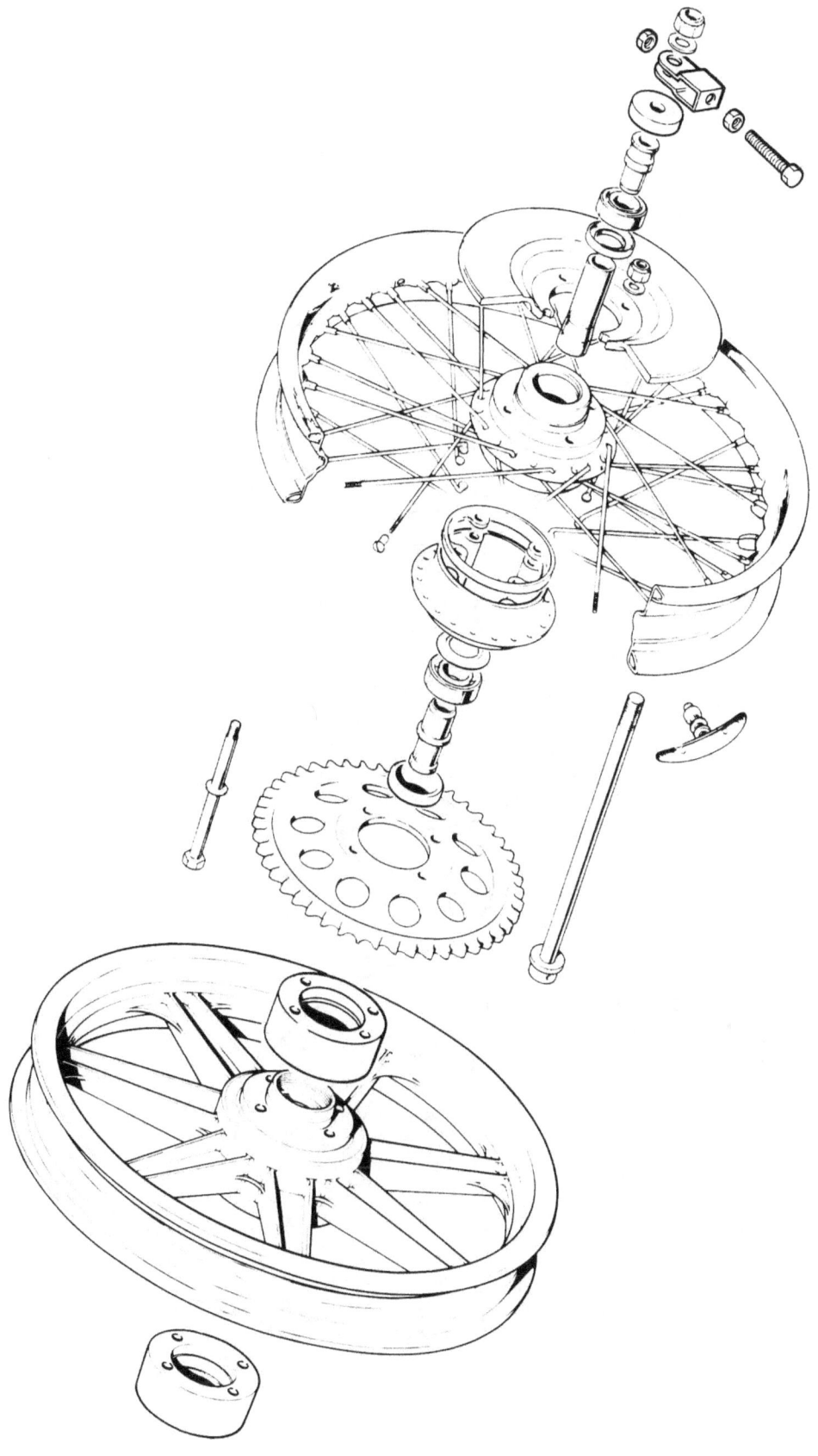

Fig. F18. Rear wheel arrangement - disc type

F21

F BRAKES, WHEELS AND TYRES

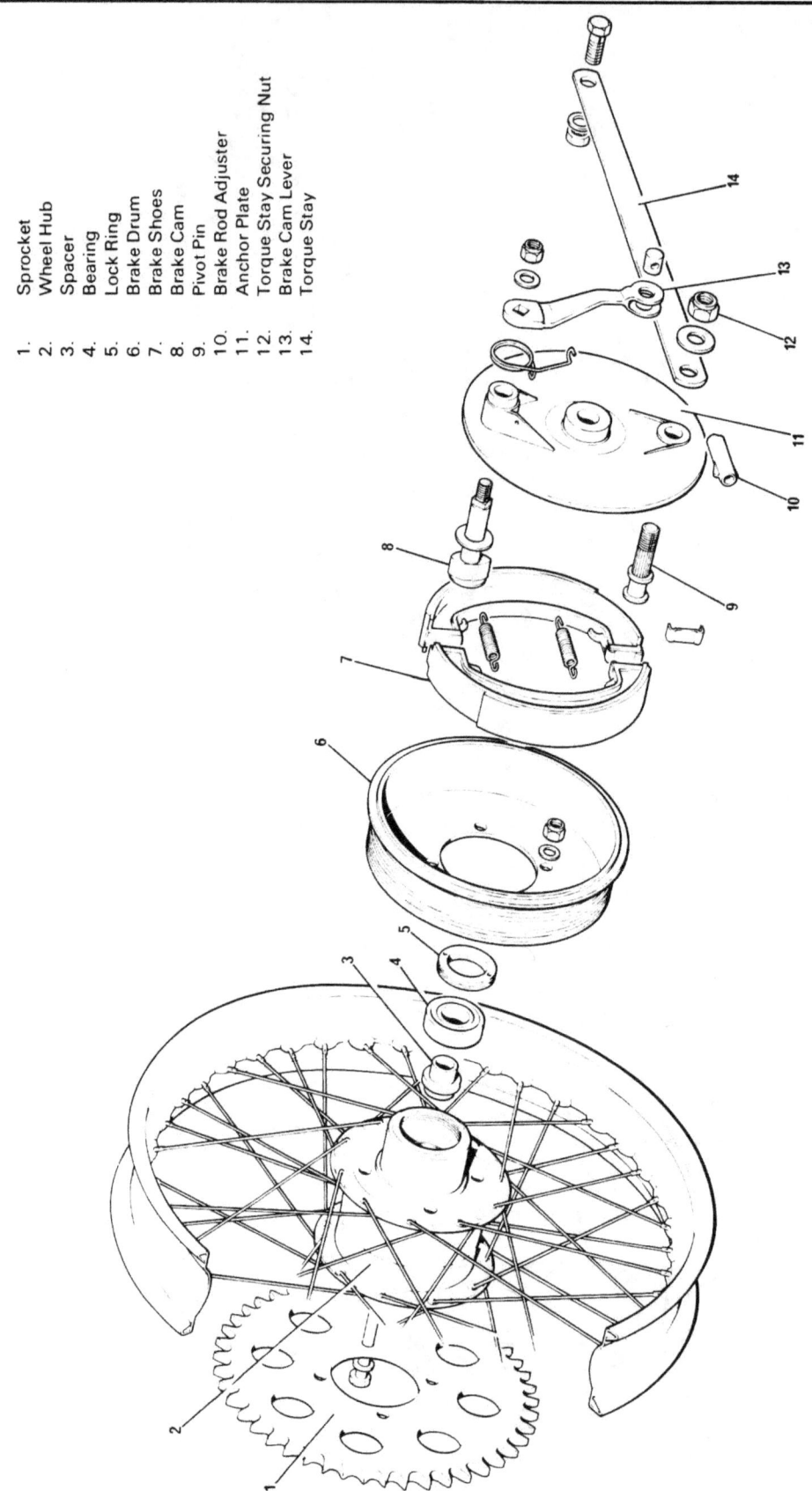

1. Sprocket
2. Wheel Hub
3. Spacer
4. Bearing
5. Lock Ring
6. Brake Drum
7. Brake Shoes
8. Brake Cam
9. Pivot Pin
10. Brake Rod Adjuster
11. Anchor Plate
12. Torque Stay Securing Nut
13. Brake Cam Lever
14. Torque Stay

Fig. F19. Rear wheel arrangement - drum type

BRAKES, WHEELS AND TYRES F

SECTION F15

REAR WHEEL REMOVAL AND REPLACEMENT (DRUM TYPE)

Place the machine on the centre stand. Uncouple the rear chain at its spring link leaving the chain in position on the gearbox sprocket.

Detach the torque arm by removing the fixing nut at the brake plate end.
Unscrew and remove the rear brake rod adjuster remove the wheel spindle nut and withdraw the spindle allow the speedo drive to hang on the cable, the wheel can now be removed.

Replacement is a reversal of the above paying particular attention to chain and brake adjustment.

SECTION F16

REMOVING AND REPLACING THE REAR WHEEL BEARINGS

Remove the rear wheel, see Section F14 & F15.

Unscrew the threaded retainer ring (L.H. Thread) from the R.H. side of the wheel and remove. Using a long punch drive out the spindle support spacer from each side.

The bearings can then be drifted out from each side using a long punch through the hub.

Replacement is a reversal of the preceding instructions but it is important to note that the threaded retainer ring must have loctite 270 applied before refitting.

NOTE: Always fit sealed type bearings when replacement is required,

SECTION F17

STRIPPING AND REASSEMBLING REAR BRAKE (DRUM TYPE)

Access to the rear brake shoes is gained by removing the rear wheel. (See Section F15). Remove the brake shoes by lifting one brake shoe away from the brake plate until the return spring becomes disconnected. (See Fig.20).

Check the linings for wear. If the lining has worn down to the surface of any of the rivets then the linings must be replaced. Check the surface of the brake drum; if heavy scoring or damage is evident the brake drum need replacing.

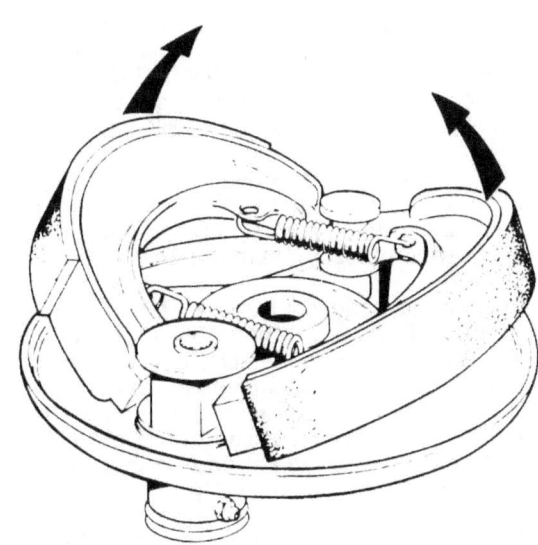

Fig. F20. Removing brake shoes

F

BRAKES, WHEELS AND TYRES

To reassemble the brake shoes to the brake anchor plate first place the two brake shoes on the bench on their relative positions. Fit the return springs to the retaining hooks, then taking a shoe in each hand (see Fig. F20) and at the same time holding the springs in tension, position the shoes as shown over the cam and fulcrum pin and snap down into position by pressing on the outer edges of the shoes.

Note. When replacing the brake shoes, note that the leading and trailing brake shoes are not interchangeable and ensure that they are in their correct relative positions as shown in Fig. F21.

Adjustment of the rear brake is achieved by the wing nut on the rear end of the brake operating rod. Turn the nut clockwise to reduce clearance. From the static position before the brake is applied there should be about ½ in. (1.2cm.) of free movement before the brake starts to operate.

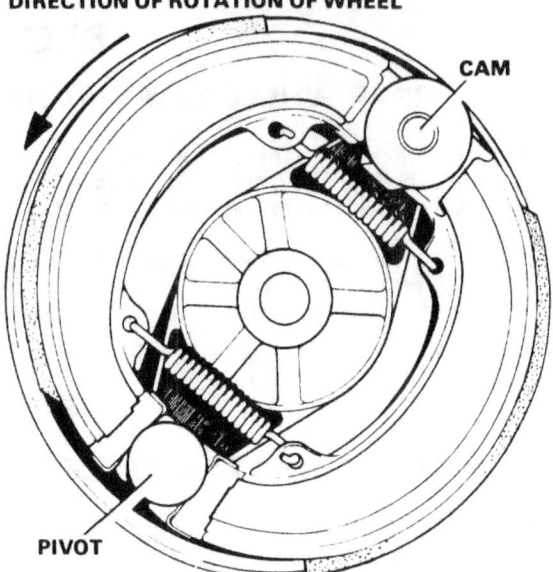

Fig. F21. Position of brake shoes

SECTION F18

WHEEL BUILDING

This is a job which is best left to the specialist as it is essential that the wheel is laced correctly and that when truing, the spokes are correctly tensioned.

It is however, possible for the less experienced to avoid troubel by periodically examining the wheels. As spokes and nipples bed down the tension will be lost and unless this is corrected the spokes will chafe and ultimately break.

Periodically test the tension either by "ringing", that is striking with a metal tool or by placing the fingers and thumb of one hand over two spokes at a time and pressing them together.

If tension has been lost there will be no ringing tone and the spokes will move freely across each other. When the spoke needs tensioning, the nipple through the rim must be screwed further on to the spoke but at the same time, the truth of the wheel must be checked and it may be necessary to ease the tention at another part of the wheel in order to maintain its truth.

Front wheel rim offset 1.875" measured from the disc abutment face (L.H side) to the centre of the rim.

It will therefore be obvious that spoke replacement, spoke tensioning or wheel truing are not operations to be treated lightly.

Carefully examination of the wheel will show that for every spoke there is another pulling in the opposite direction and that the adjacent spoke goes to the opposite side of the hub.

Increasing the tension tends to pull the rim so, to counteract this, it is sometimes necessary to increase the tension on the spoke or spokes either side to maintain the truth of the wheel.

With a little care and patience it is possible for the unskilled to at least re-tension the spokes but, turn each nipple only a little at a time as, once the spoke is under tension only a fraction of a turn is sometimes sufficient to throw the rim badly out of truth.

Rear wheel rim offset 2.920" measured from the sprocket abutment face to the centre of the rim.

BRAKES, WHEELS AND TYRES

SECTION F19

WHEEL BALANCING

When a wheel is out of balance it means that there is more weight in one part than in another. This is very often due to variation in the tyre and at moderate speeds will not be noticed but at high speeds it can be very serious, particularly if the front wheel is affected.

Wheel balancing can be achieved by fitting standard one ounce and half ounce weights which are readily available, as required. All front wheels are balanced complete with tyre and tube before leaving the factory and if for any reason the tyre is removed it should be replaced with the white balancing "spot" level with the valve. If a new tyre is fitted, existing weights should be removed and the wheel re-balanced, adding weights as necessary until it will remain in any position at rear. Make sure that the brake is not binding while the balancing operation is being carried out.

For normal road use it is not found necessary for the rear wheel to be balanced in this way.

SECTION F20

FRONT AND REAR WHEEL ALIGNMENT

When the rear wheel has been fitted into the frame it should be aligned correctly by using two straight edges or "battens" about 7 feet long. With the machine off the stand the battens should be placed alongside the wheel, one either side of the machine and each about four inches from the ground. When both ar touching the rear tyre on both sides of the wheel the front wheel should be mid way between and parallel to both battens. Turn the front wheel slightly until this can be seen. Any necessary adjustments must be made by first slackening the rear wheel spindle nut, then turning the spindle adjuster nuts as required ensuring that the rear chain adjustment is maintained. Refer to Fig. 22 for illustration of correct alignment. Note that the arrows indicate the adjustment required.

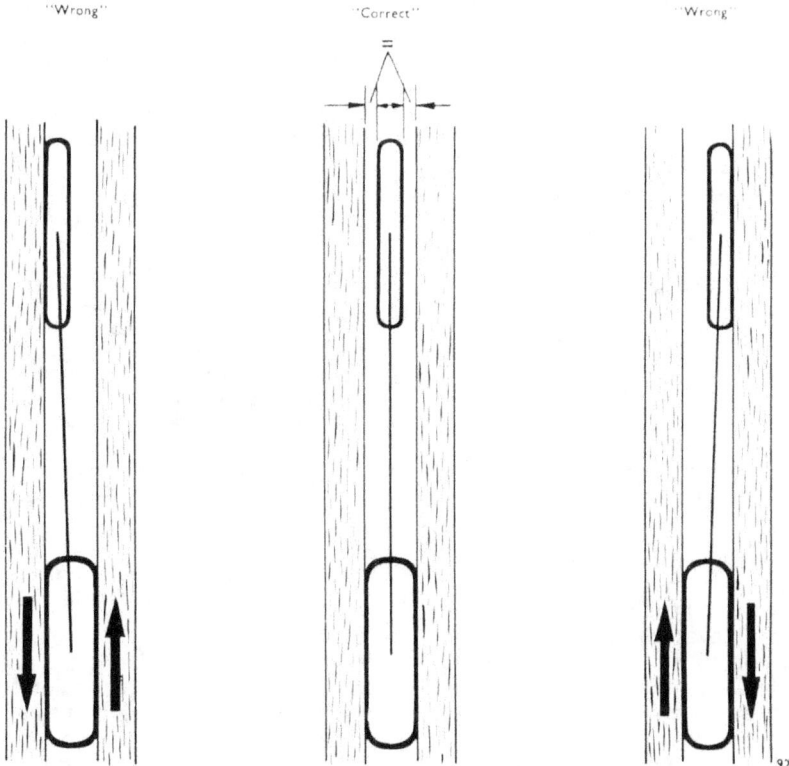

Fig. F22. Aligning the front and rear wheels

F BRAKES, WHEELS AND TYRES

SECTION F21

REMOVING AND REFITTING TYRES

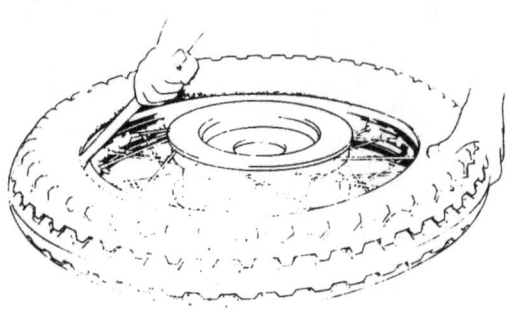

Fig. F23. Removing the first bead of the tyre - lever inserted close to valve whilst head is pressed into well on opposite side of wheel

To remove the tyre first remove the valve cap and valve core, using the valve cap itself to unscrew the core. Unscrew the knurled valve securing nut and then place all parts where they will be free from dirt and grit. It is recommended that the cover beads are lubricated with a little soapy water before attempting to remove the tyre. The tyre lever should be dipped in this solution before each application. First, insert a lever at the valve position and whilst carefully pulling on this lever, press the tyre bead into the well of the rim diametrally opposite the valve position (see Fig.

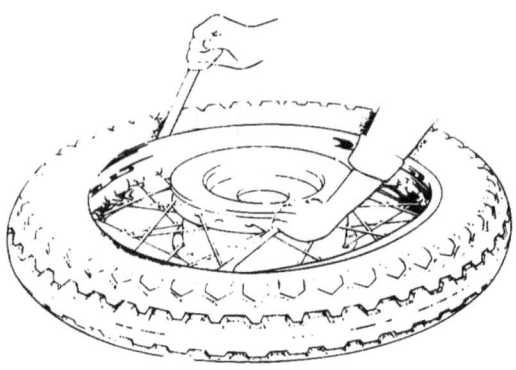

Fig. F24. Removing the first bead of the tyre, using two tyre levers

F23). Insert a second lever close to the first and prise the bead over the rim flange. Remove the first lever and reinsert a little further round the rim from the second lever. Continue round the bead in steps of two to three inches until the bead is completely away from the rim. Push the valve out of the rim and then withdraw the inner tube. To completely remove the tyre first stand the wheel upright and then insert a lever between the remaining bead and the rim. The tyre should be easily removed from the rim as shown in Fig. F24.

REFITTING THE TYRE

First place the rubber rim band into the well of the rim and make sure that the rough side of the rubber band is fitted against the rim and that the band is central in the well. Replace the valve core and inflate the inner tube sufficiently to round it out without stretch, dust it with french chalk and insert it into the cover with the valve located at the white "balancing spot" leaving it protruding outside the beads for about four inches either side of the valve. At this stage it is advisable to lubricate the beads and levers with soapy water (see Fig. 25)

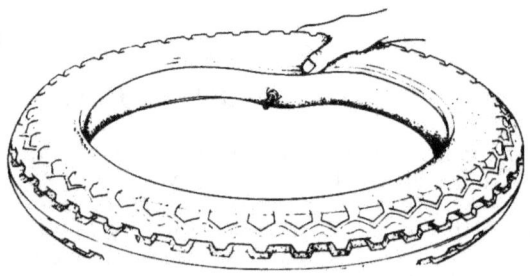

Fig. F25. Cover and tube assembled ready for refitting to the wheel

Squeeze the beads together at the valve position to prevent the tube from slipping back inside the tyre and offer the cover to the rim, as shown in Fig. F26, at the same time threading the valve through the valve holes in the rim band and rim. Allow the first bead to go into the well of the rim and the other bead to lie above the level of the rim flange.

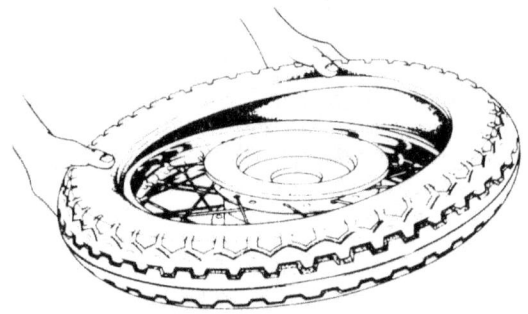

Fig. F26. Refitting the tyre to the wheel. Note valve engaged in rim hole.

Working from the valve, press the first bead over the rim flange by hand, moving forward in small steps and making sure that the part of the bead already dealt with, lies in the well of the rim. If necessary use a tyre lever for the last few inches, as shown in Fig. F27. During this operation continually check that the inner tube is not trapped by the cover bead.

BRAKES, WHEELS AND TYRES   F

Press the second bead into the well of the rim diametrally opposite the valve. Insert the lever as close as possible to the point where the bead passes over the flange and lever the bead into the flange, at the same time pressing the fitted part of the bead into the well of the rim. Repeat until the bead is completely over the flange, finishing at the valve position (see Fig. F28).

Fig. F28. Refitting the second bead over the wheel rim. Care should be taken not to trap inner tube.

Push the valve inwards to ensure that the tube near the valve is not trapped under the bead. Pull the valve back and inflate the tyre. Check that the fitting line on the cover is concentric with the top of the rim flange and that the valve protrudes squarely through the valve hole. Fit the knurled rim nut and valve cap. The tyre pressure should then be set to the figure given in Technical Data.

Fig. F27. Levering the first bead onto the rim

SECTION F22

SECURITY BOLTS

Security bolts are fitted to the rear wheel to prevent the tyre "creeping" on the rim when it is subjected to excessive acceleration or braking. Such movement would ultimately result in the valve being torn from the inner tube. There are two security bolts fitted to the rear wheel, which are equally spaced either side of the valve and thereby do not affect the balance of the wheel.

Note. The security bolt nuts must not be overtightened, otherwise excessive distortion may occur.

Where a security bolt is fitted the basic procedure for fitting and removing the tyre is the same, but the following instruction should be followed:-

(1) Remove the valve cap and core as described.
(2) Unscrew the security bolt nut and push the bolt inside the cover.
(3) Remove the first bead as described.
(4) Remove the security bolt from the rim.
(5) Remove the inner tube as described.
(6) Remove the second bead and tyre.

For refitting the tyre and inner tube:-
(1) Fit the rim band.
(2) Fit the first bead to the rim without the inner tube inside.
(3) Assemble the security bolt into the rim, putting the nut onto the first few threads (see Fig. F29).
(4) Partly inflate the inner tube and fit it into the tyre.
(5) Fit the second bead but keep the security bolt pressed well into the tyre, as shown in Fig. F30, and ensure that the inner tube does not become trapped at the edges.
(6) Fit the valve stem nut and inflate the tyre.
(7) Bounce the wheel several times at the point where the security bolt is fitted and then tighten the security bolt nut.

Fig. F29. Placing security bolt in position

Fig. F30. Refitting the second bead with the security bolt in position.

F BRAKES, WHEELS AND TYRES

SECTION F23

TYRE MAINTENANCE

To obtain optimum tyre mileage and to eliminate irregular wear on the tyres it is essential that the recommendations governing tyre pressures and general maintenance are followed. The following points are laid out with this in mind.

(1) Maintain the correct inflation pressure as shown in Technical Data. Use a pressure gauge frequently. it is advisable to check and restore tyre pressures at least once per week. Pressures should always be checked when tyres are cold and not when they have reached normal running temperatures.

(2) When the pillion passenger or additional load is carried, the rear tyre pressure should be increased appropriately to cater for the extra load.

(3) Unnecessary rapid acceleration and fierce braking should always be avoided. This treatment invariably results in rapid tyre wear.

(4) Regular checks should be made for flints, nails, small stones etc, which should be removed from the tread or they may ultimately penetrate and damage the casing and puncture the tube.

(5) Tyres and spokes should be kept free of oil, grease and paraffin. Regular cleaning should be carried out with a cloth and a little petrol (gasoline).

(6) If tyres develop irregular wear, this may be corrected by reversing the tyre to reverse its direction of rotation.

Before inflating, check that the fitting line on the tyre wall just above the bead on each side is concentric with the rim.

If necessary bounce the wheel to help seat the tyre but, see that there is adequate pressure to prevent damaging the tyre or tube and only use moderate force. If the tyre will not seat, it is better to release the pressure, apply soap solution to lubricate and re-inflate.

Inflate to the required pressure and check fitting lines again. Inflation should not be too rapid, particularly at the commencement, to allow the beads to seat correctly on the rim.

See that the valve protrudes squarely through the valve hole before screwing down the knurled nut and finally, replace the dust cap.

SECTION F24

TYRE PRESSURES

The recommended inflation pressure as shown in "Technical Data", are based on a riders weight of 140lb. If the riders' weight exceeds 140lb. the tyre pressure should be increased as follows:-

Front Tyre
Add 1lb. per square inch for every 28lb. in excess of 140lb.

Rear Tyre
Add 1lb. per square inch for every 14lb. in excess of 140lb.

SECTION F25

REAR CHAIN ADJUSTMENT

The adjustment of the rear chain is controlled by draw bolts fitted to each end of the rear wheel spindle. The correct adjustment for the rear chain is $\frac{3}{4}$ in. free movement with the machine on its wheels and the chain at its tightest point or $1\frac{3}{4}$ in. with the machine on the stand and the chain at its slackest point. If the adjustment of the chain is outside these limits it should be corrected by loosening the wheel spindle nuts (and the brake torque stay nut on the anchor plate on drum brake models) and then adjusting the draw bolts an equal number of turns. Always apply the brake pedal to centralise the brake plate and keep it applied while you tighten the spindle nut. Recheck the chain adjustment. If the wheel alignment was correct originally the adjustment of the nuts by an equal number of turns should preserve the alignment but if you are doubtful whether the rear wheel is in line then you should use a straight edge or piece of

BRAKES, WHEELS AND TYRES

string along side the rear wheel; making allowance for the difference in section between the rear tyre and the front tyre and then tighten or loosen the draw bolt adjuster on the right side so that the rear wheel lines up with the front wheel. If the rear wheel is not in line the road holding of the machine will be adversely affected and the effect on the rear chain and rear wheel sprocket will cause rapid wear. When the adjustment is satisfactory check the tightness of the wheel spindle nut, adjuster draw bolts (and brake torque stay nuts. Finally check the adjuster draw bolts (and brake torque stay nuts. Finally check the adjuster of the brake operating rod. On drum brake models. There is no automatic oil feed to the rear chain which should be lubricated manually with an oil gun weekly.

WARNING: For machines with a rear disc brake always actuate the rear brake prior to moving off with the machine. This will re-charge the hydraulic circuit with fluid in readiness for the first braking application.

SECTION G

TELESCOPIC FORKS

INDEX

	Section
DESCRIPTION	-
STEERING HEAD ADJUSTMENT	G1
RENEWING HEAD RACES	G2
STRIPPING AND REASSEMBLING THE FORK LEGS	G3
FORK ALIGNMENT	G4

TELESCOPIC FORKS

DESCRIPTION

The front fork is of the telescopic type using high grade steel tube stanchions. They are ground to a micro finish and hard chromium plated over their entire length.

The alloy bottom members are precision bored and provide the bearing for the stanchion. Internal main springs are fitted and locate on the damper tube.

An oil seal is contained in the top lip of each bottom member and is protected by a rubber dust cover.

Oil is contained in each bottom member and serves the dual purpose of damping and lubrication. Oil is added by removal of the fork cap nuts and drained at the plugs provided.

Damping of the fork action is achieved by the use of a damper valve in conjunction with a series of bleed holes in a fixed valve.

SECTION G1

STEERING HEAD ADJUSTMENT

It is most important that the steering head bearings are always correctly adjusted.

Place a strong support underneath the engine so that the front wheel is raised clear of the ground then, standing in front of the wheel, attempt to push the lower fork legs backwards and forwards. Should any play be detected, the steering head must be adjusted.

If possible, ask a friend to place the fingers of one hand lightly round the head lug, whilst the forks are being pulled back and forth. Any play will be felt quite easily by the fingers.

It should be possible to turn the forks from side to side quite smoothly and without any "lumpy" movement. If the movement is "lumpy", the rollers are indented into the races or broken. In either case the complete bearing should be renewed.

To adjust the steering head assembly, slacken the clamp nut B, Fig. G1 and the top yoke adjuster nut A then tighten down the adjuster nut until adjustment is correct. There should be no play evident in the races but great care must be taken not to overtighten, or the rollers will become indented into the races, making steering extremely difficult and dangerous.

Having carried out the adjustment, tighten the clamp nuts and the top yoke pinch bolt securely. Re-check the adjustment, by seeing that the steering goes from lock to lock quite freely.

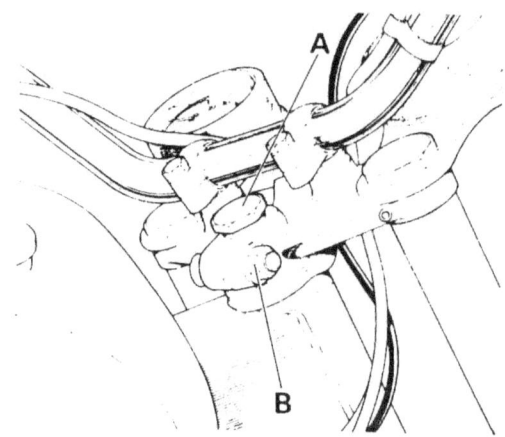

Fig. G1. Steering head adjustment

SECTION G2

RENEWING HEAD RACES

Place a strong support underneath the engine so that the front wheel is raised clear of the ground. Remove the front wheel (see Section F12). Remove the front mudguard (See Section E15).

The steering head can be dismantled without stripping the forks. First, disconnect the hydraulic brake pipe from the top and middle lug. See section F3. Remove the headlamp. See section H15. Detach the handle bar complete by unscrewing the two self locking nuts which secure the two eye bolts in the top lug. See fig. G2. Remove fork cap nuts. Place the speedometer and tachometer to one side after first disconnecting the drive cables and illuminating lights.

TELESCOPIC FORKS

Slacken the top lug pinch bolt (B) fig. G1 and remove adjuster and middle nut (A) Loosen both the top lug stanchion pinch bolts with an allen key.

Using a raw-hide mallet strike the undersides of the top lug alternately to release it from the stanchions. Slide fork leg and stanchion from the lugs. Place the yolk to one side and withdraw the steering stem out of the head lug. The taper roller bearings can now be removed from the stem and the top lug for cleaning and inspection. Check for pitting and fracture of the roller surface. The bearing must be replaced if any of these faults are in evidence.

The steering head outer races have a very long serviceable life and should not need replacement for a very considerable mileage. If however their replacement is deemed necessary the races can be removed using a suitable drift from inside the head lug. Replacement of the new race is effected by using service tool 61-6121. Do not forget to refit the bearing abutment rings behind the outer races. Reassembly is the reverse of the above procedure. Grease the bearings prior to replacement, see Section A1 for correct grade. Note that head of both the top lug and stanchion must be flush leaving the head of the inner retaining plug standing proud. Care must be taken to ensure that the headlamp shrouds are located correctly in the prespective recesses in the top lug. Note that when refitting the plastic dust cover ensure that it sits square to allow the adjuster nut, Fig. G1 (A) to locate on the bearing. Readjust the steering head bearing as in Section G1. Reassemble the hydraulic system as described in Section F3.

SECTION G3

STRIPPING AND REASSEMBLING THE FORK LEGS

Before-commencing work on the forks it is advisable to have the following service tools and replacements available:

(a) Oil seal for fork leg (2)

(b) Oil seal for damper valve (2)

(c) Service tool (61-6113)

Remove small drain plug at the bottom of each fork adjacent to the wheel spindle and drain out the oil by pumping the forks up and down. Support the machine on a box with the front wheel clear of the ground. Remove front wheel as described in Section F12. Remove front mudguard as described in Section E15.

Detach the handlebar complete by unscrewing the two self locking nuts which secure the two eye bolts in the top lug.

Disconnect the hydraulic brake pipe at middle lug and fork leg to stanchion. (See Section F3.) Remove caliper and place carefully to one side. Unscrew the two allen pinch bolts at the back of the top head lug. Remove alluminium cap screws with $7/16$" A/F Allen key.

Remove the stanchion top nuts then remove the internal fork springs. Using service tool 61-6113 placed down into the stanchion; hold the valve assembly while the retaining allen screw is being unscrewed at the base of the fork leg.
At this stage it will be possible to remove the fork leg by sliding it from the stanchion. Remove the stanchions by slackening the pinch bolts on the bottom yoke and withdrawing the stanchions.

The dust cover on the fork leg can easily be prised off by hand.

The damper valve assembly is retained in the bottom of the stanchion by an nut which should be carefully removed with a ring spanner or similar.

The valve assembly consists of a fixed bleed valve which has its own oil seal, a clapper valve, a spring support nut and a rebound spring. It should not be necessary to strip this assembly unless the fixed bleed valve has contracted damage in any way.

The oil seal on the bleed valve can easily be replaced by hand. If using a screwdriver to prise the seal away from the valve be careful not to damage the bearing surface as the material is a soft alloy. (Refer to Fig. G3 for details of the assembly).

Care must be taken not to lose the sealing washer contained in the bottom of the fork leg. The base of the valve stem rests on this seal and the allen screw is replaced from the outside of the leg. Refer to the exploded drawing on page G5 for assembly details.

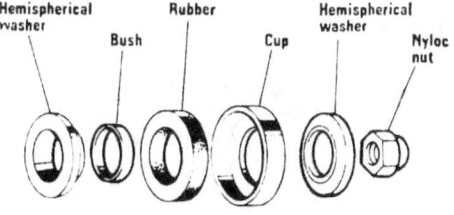

Fig. G2. Handlebar mountings

G TELESCOPIC FORKS

Remove the circlip and washer then pull out the oil seal from the top of the fork leg.

Place the stanchion into the fork leg and place a small polythene bag over the top lip of the stanchion. Push the oil seal over the stanchion and down into position on the fork leg. It is important that the polythene is used because the lip of stanchion has a sharp edge that may easily scratch or damage the precision edge of the seal. Even a scratch that may not be readily visible to the eye will cause leakage at the seal.

Push a new seal into position then fit the washer and circlip

Check all components for cleanliness and wash in fuel if necessary. Examine the bore of the stanchion and clean with a cloth pushed into the bore.

Reassembly of the fork leg is a reversal of the dismantling procedure.

Check that the small "Dowty" sealing washer is located in the well in the base of the fork leg. (If this washer shows signs of damage or wear it must be replaced).

Push the rubber dust cover onto its location groove on the fork leg and then replace the leg on the stanchion.

As the leg is refitted onto the stanchion the stem of the damper valve assembly must be located on top of the "Dowty" sealing washer. If difficulty is encountered during this operation, service tool 61-6113 which is used to retain the valve assembly while it is being removed may be used to navigate the damper valve onto its location.

The allen screw can then be replaced into the bottom of the fork leg and fully tightened, see Technical Data for correct torque.

Replace fork leg and stanchion by sliding it up through the rubber, middle lug, headlamp bracket and top lug until the top of the stanchion and the surface of the top lug lie exactly flush. Re-tighten top lug and middle lug pinch bolts to a torque setting of 25ft/lbs.

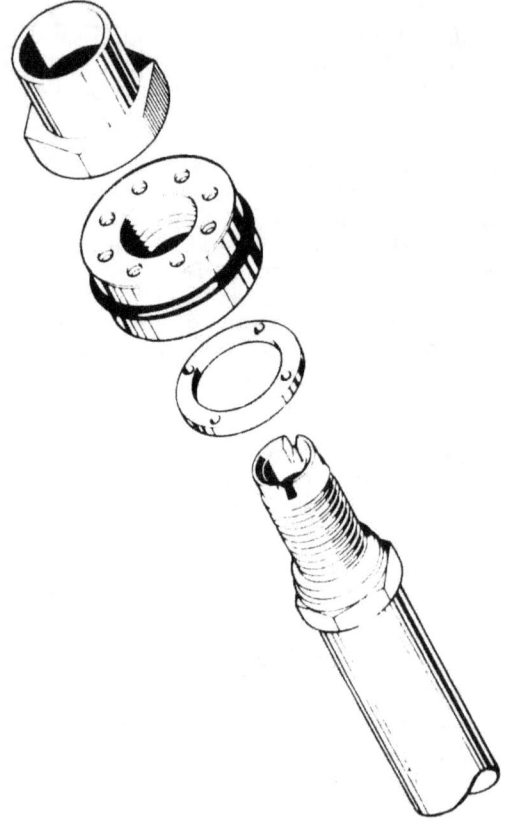

Fig. G3. Damper valve assembly

Replace the fork springs and refill the fork legs with the correct quantity of oil. See Section A15.

Coat the threads of the stanchion top nuts with jointing compound and refit, tightening to a torque of 30ft/lbs. speedometer drive cable and illuminating lights.

Refit the caliper on fork leg and reassemble the hydraulic brake system as described in Section Replace the handlebars (see Section G3).

Replace the front mudguard. Refit the front wheel (see Section E15 & F12).

SECTION G4

FORK ALIGNMENT

After replacing the fork legs, mudguard and wheel, it may be found that the fork is incorrectly aligned.

To rectify this, the fork wheel spindle cap nuts must first be screwed up tight on the right-hand leg and the spindle cap on the left-hand leg slac- kened off. Also loosen the top caps and the pinch bolts in both the bottom and top yokes. The forks should now be pumped up and down several times to line them up and then tighten up from bottom to top, that is, wheel spindle, bottom yoke pinch bolts, top caps and finally, the steering stem pinch bolt in the top yoke.

TELESCOPIC FORKS G

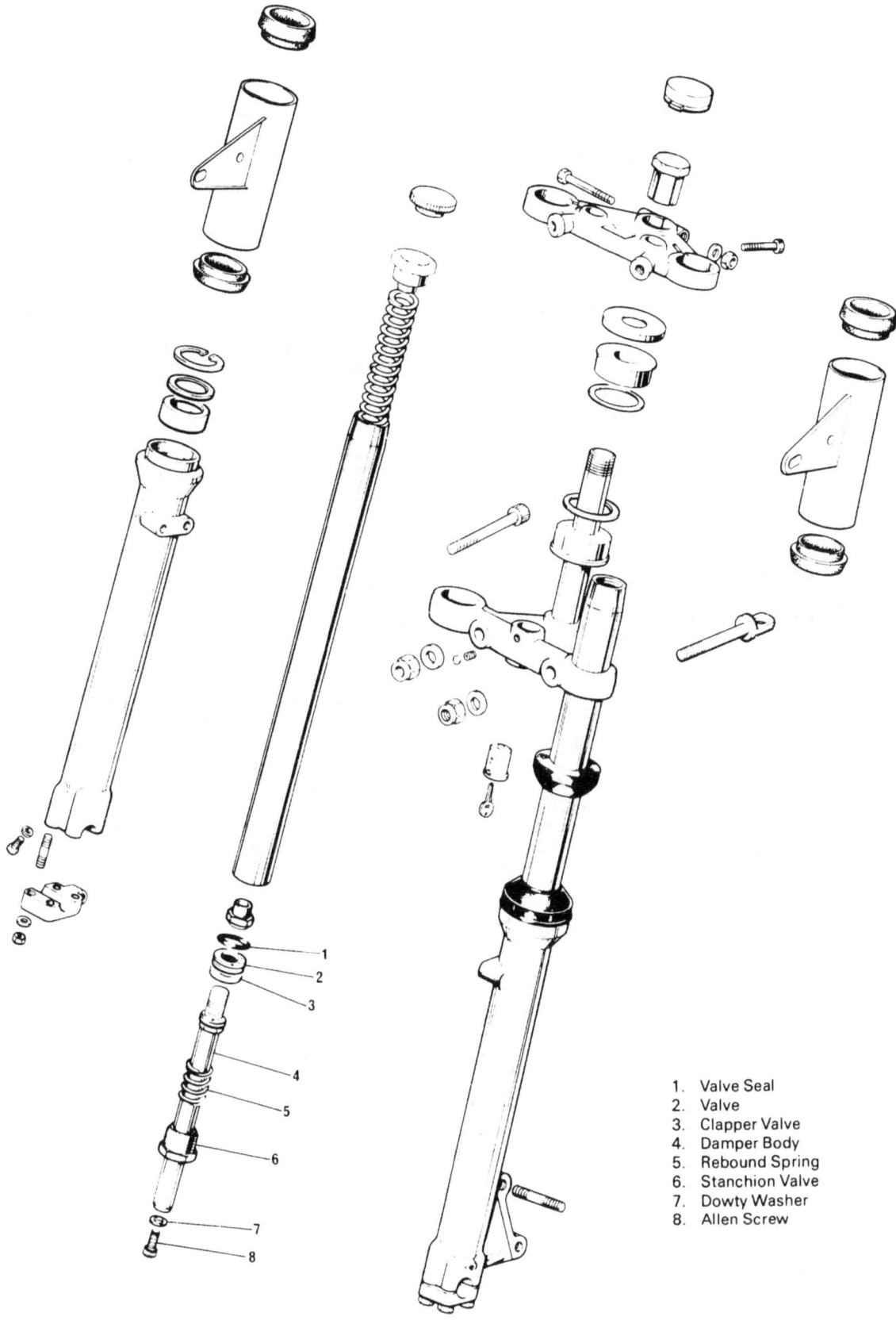

1. Valve Seal
2. Valve
3. Clapper Valve
4. Damper Body
5. Rebound Spring
6. Stanchion Valve
7. Dowty Washer
8. Allen Screw

Fig. G4. Fork assembly details

G TELESCOPIC FORKS

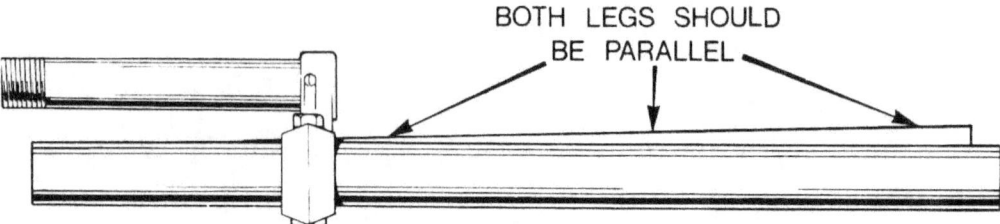

Fig. G5. Fork leg alignment

If, after this treatment, the forks still do not function satisfactorily then either the fork stanchions are bent or one of the yokes is twisted.

The stanchions can only be accurately checked for straightness with special equipment such as a surface plate. Special gauges are also required to check the yokes. It is possible, however, to make a reasonable check of the stanchions by rolling them on a surface plate or flat surface such as a piece of plate glass, but it is not a simple operation so straighten a bent tube, and a new part may be necessary.

Check the stanchions for truth by rolling them slowly on a flat checking table. A bent stanchion may be realigned if the bow does not exceed $5/32$ in. maximum. To realign the stanchion, a hand press is required. Place the stanchion on two swage "V" blocks at either end and apply pressure to the raised portion of the stanchion. By means of alternately pressing in this way and checking the stanchion on a flat table the amount of bow can be reduced until it is finally removed.

Having checked the stanchions for straightness and reset as necessary, the top and bottom yokes can now be checked. First, assembly the two stanchions into the bottom yoke so that a straight edge across the lower ends is touching all four edges of the tubes, then tighten the pinch bolts. Now view them from the side; the two stanchions should be quite parallel. Alternatively, the lower 12in. of the stanchions can be placed on a surface plate, when there should be no rocking.

To reset, hold one stanchion in a vice (using soft clamps) and reposition the other stanchion, using a longer and larger diameter tube to obtain sufficient leverage. Having checked the this way, check the gap between them on the ground portion.

The next step is to place the top yoke in position over the stanchions, when the steering stem should be quite central.

The final step is to check if the tubes are parallel when assembled into the top yoke only. In this case the bottom yoke can be fitted loosely on the tubes, acting as a pilot only.

Though it is permissible to rectify slight errors in alignment by resetting, it is much safer to replace the part affected especially when there is excessive misalignment. Works reconditioned units are available to owners in the United Kingdom through the dealer network.

SECTION H
ELECTRICAL SYSTEM
INDEX

Description	Section
INTRODUCTION	H1
LOCATION OF ELECTRICAL COMPONENTS	H2
CHARGING SYSTEM TECHNICAL DATA	H3
CHARGING SYSTEM FAULT DIAGNOSIS AND TESTING	H4
STATIC TEST-ZENER DIODE	H5
IGNITION SYSTEM TECHNICAL DATA-ELECTRONIC	H6
IGNITION SYSTEM FAULT DIAGNOSIS AND TESTING	H7
FAULT FINDING CHART	H8
ELECTRONIC IGNITION FAULT DIAGNOSIS	H9
STARTER SYSTEM	H10
ZENER DIODE LOCATION	H11
BATTERY INSPECTION AND MAINTENANCE	H12
ELECTRIC HORN	H13
HEADLAMP	H14
REMOVING AND REFITTING THE HEADLAMP	H15
TAIL AND STOP LAMP UNIT	H16
FUSES	H17
IGNITION SWITCH	H18
FLASHER LAMPS	H19
WARNING LAMPS	H20
STOP LAMP SWITCHES	H21
OIL PRESSURE SWITCH	H22
SPARKING PLUGS	H23

H   ELECTRICAL SYSTEM

SECTION H1

INTRODUCTION

CHARGING
The electrical system is supplied by an alternating current alternator contained in the primary chaincase and driven the crankshaft. The generator output is then fed as A.C. current to a triple pack Zener control unit which controls output in accordance with the electrical demands placed upon it. The current is then fed through a six diode rectifier pack and thence to the battery as D.C.

IGNITION - ELECTRONIC
The battery supplies current to the amplifier via the ignition switch when the key operated switch is turned to the right. The amplifier switching is controlled by a magnetic pick up situated in the timing cover and driven by the exhaust camshaft.

IGNITION - CONTACT BREAKER
The battery supplies current to the ignition coils via the ignition switch when the key operated switch is turned to the right. The firing of the plugs is controlled by a automatic advance and retard unit and contact breaker points situated in the timing cover and driven by the exhaust camshaft.

LIGHTING
The battery supplies current for all lighting requirements via the ignition switch.

SECTION H2

LOCATION OF ELECTRICAL COMPONENTS

Parts not immediately visible can be discovered as follows:

ALTERNATOR:-
Behind left hand side crankcase cover, at forward end of crankcase.
Access:- Release foot rest bolts and allow footrest to swing down. Release pinch bolt in gearchange lever and slide lever from splines. Remove Allen Head bolts from periphery of crank case cover and lift cover clear. to remove stator remove three securing nuts and release bullet connections from main harness. Lift stator clear and withdraw lead through grommet. To remove rotor, undo the central nut. N.B. it may be necessary to put the motorcycle in gear and apply the rear brake. When reassembling pass an 0.008 feeler gauge round the gap between rotor and stator. Ensure this clearance does not take-up when the rotor revolves.

AB11 AMPLIFER:-
Behind panel on left hand side below seat.
Access:- Release springs above and below carburettor inlets. Swing left hand model name panel out and to rear. Lift out sideways the "L" shaped rear edge which is hooked around the frame. Remove the single nut in the plastic air filter cover (Forward Panel) and lift out. Amplifier is secured top and bottom by nuts and bolts. A short earth lead is also secured by the topmost of these bolts.

BATTERY IGNITION COILS H.T. LEADS INDICATOR FLASHER UNIT:-
Beneath seat.
Access:- Unlock seat on right hand side with ignition key. Pull out seat catch knob, lift saddle to left. To remove battery, unhook strap remove leads and lift out. To remove coils, remove leads and slide upwards from rubber rings. To remove flasher can, remove leads and pull can out of retaining clip.

5PU PICK-UP:-
Behind ribbed cover at front of right hand crank case cover.
Access:- Remove two Philips head bolts and lift off cover and gasket. To remove the base plate and windings, release the two small hexagon barrel nuts at top and bottom. Release the pick-up cable connections from the main harness and the cable from the securing straps. Lift the base plate out and carefully withdraw the lead through the grommet in the crank case. To remove the reluctor. Remove single centre bolt, insert puller (Triumph part number 61-7023) and ease reluctor out of tapered hole in camshaft, taking care not to allow the reluctor to twist as this will damage the keyway. When replacing the reluctor, the securing bolt should be tightened to a torque of 5lb ft. See also "TIMING".

RECTIFIER:-
On the front of the rear mudguard behind air filters.
Access:- Remove springs above and below carbs swing out and lift off the right hand model name panel. Rectifier can be reached beneath the battery.

TIMING:-
When either the baseplate and winding or the amplifier is replaced, the ignition must be reset. Set the baseplate to the centre of the adjustment slot, secure lightly and start engine. Using

ELECTRICAL SYSTEM   H

a stroboscope, adjust the baseplate until the timing mark on the rotor appears stationary beneath the fixed timing mark, with the engine at 3500 rev/min. See also "Timing Marks".
Tighten base plate nuts

TIMING MARKS:-
Behind forward Philips head cover in left hand side crankcase cover. (Above the word "TRIUMPH").

3 ZENER PACK:-
On rear of right hand air filter box in front of battery.
Removal:- Lift out battery, remove 2 self tapping screws and single bolt. Disconnect from main harness at alternator connections below carburators and lift out through battery compartment.

STARTER:-
Beneath carburators behind cylinders.

Removal:- Disconnect battery, disconnect lead on rear of starter body. Remove 3 socket head pins holding small cover at top rear of right hand engine/gear box cover. Lift off cover. Remove 3 socket head pins from within the cover, between the gears. Lift starter clear.

STARTER SOLENOID:-
Below right hand model name panel. Behind small spray cover.
Access:- Disconnect battery. Release spring above and below carburators and swing out right hand model name plate and lift clear. Remove single nut securing spray cover and lift out cover, disconnect leads from 4ST. Remove single engine plate fixing bolt below 4ST which secures 4ST mounting bracket and engine earth lead. Lift out 4ST and mounting bracket complete. Retain mounting bracket for new 4ST.

SECTION H3

CHARGING SYSTEM TECHNICAL DATA

The alternator produces 3 phase AC, rectified to DC by a 3DS5 rectifier and voltage controlled by a 2CDP zener diode pack. The rectifier is surge and polarity conscious. DC circuits must not be disconnected while the engine is running.

A.C. Output
4.5V Min at 1000 REV/MIN
(Measured between any two stator leads)
6.5V Min at 5000 REV/MIN

DC Output.......................13.0V (Min) 15V (Max) at 5000 rev/min (measured between rectifier large terminal and earth across 1 ohm (100W) Load Resistor

Stator resistance...........0.49 - 0.54 ohm (Measured between any two stator leads)

Stator insulation.............100 megohms (min.) at 500VDC (Measured between any one of the stator leads and laminations)

ZENER DIODE PACK VOLTAGE REGULATOR 2CDP
Negative earth type Regulating A/C voltage at........ 14.7-16.2 Volts.

SECTION H4

CHARGING SYSTEM FAULT DIAGNOSIS AND TESTING

NOTE 1
If the battery is incapable of starting the engine, it must be recharged or a slave battery utilised for testing purposes (observe polarity. Reverse connections will damage the rectifier).

NOTE 2
Test requirements:
  Centre zero 25A moving-coil ammeter
  AC Voltmeter
  DC Voltmeter
  1 ohm (100 W) load resistor

FLAT OR DISCHARGED BATTERY
SUSPECT:
The battery, the alternator and rectifier, and the voltage control zener diode pack (proceed to test 1).

OVERCHARGED BATTERY
SUSPECT:
Voltage control zener diode pack (proceed direct to Test 5).

H

ELECTRICAL SYSTEM

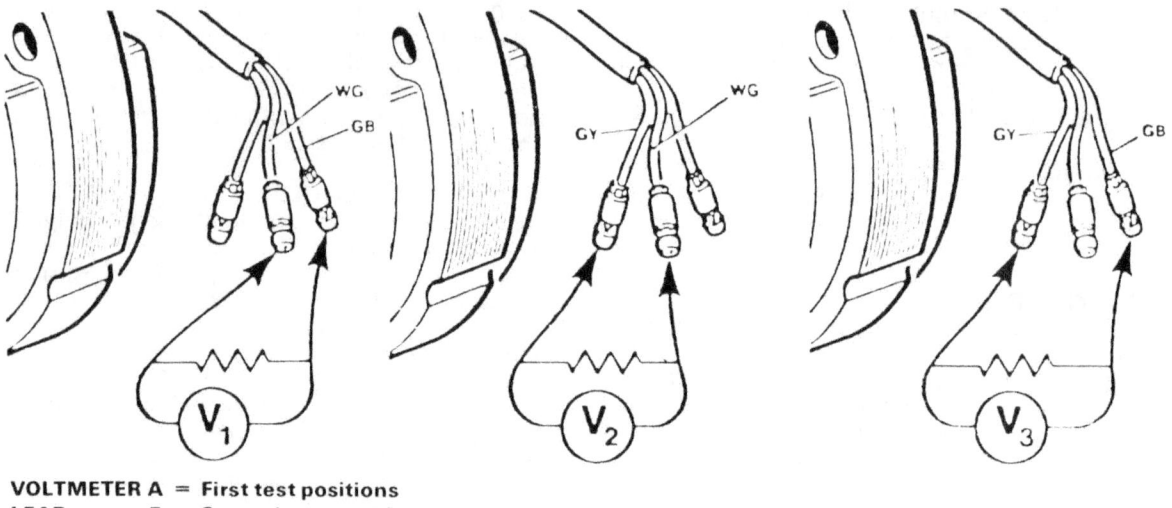

VOLTMETER A = First test positions
LEAD   B = Second test positions

Fig. H1. Alternator AC output test

TEST 1
Alternator charging current

Connect ammeter in series with the battery positive cables. It is convenient to do this at the battery feed main fuse, in which case connect BLACK lead to battery and RED lead to harness.

Run the engine at approximately 2000 rev/min and switch the headlamp to main beam. The ammeter should show a small amount of charge, indicating the alternator is exceeding the maximum continuous electrical load.

If the test is satisfactory, stop engine, restore original connections and proceed direct to TEST 5.

If the test is unsatisfactory, proceed to TEST 2.

TEST 2
Alternator AC output

Disconnect the three snap connectors between alternator and rectifier. Connect AC voltmeter, with a 1 ohm (100W) load resistor across its terminals, for six tests as shown. Run the engine at approximately 2000 rev/min for each test.

The voltmeter should show 6V minimum for all three pairs of cables, and zero for each earth test, in which case the alternator AC output is satisfactory. Stop engine, restore original connections and proceed to TEST 3.

If zero or a low voltage is obtained in any tests of pairs of cables, the alternator stator is faulty. If zero is not obtained on any earth test the stator is faulty.

If zero or a low voltage is obtained in all three tests either the alternator stator is faulty or the rotor is demagnetised. Determine whether the stator can be eliminated, by checking the resistance and insulation of its windings.

Refer to page 1 for resistance values. Use proprietary test equipment which complies with the Health and Safety at Work (HSW) Act 1974, to check the stator insulation.

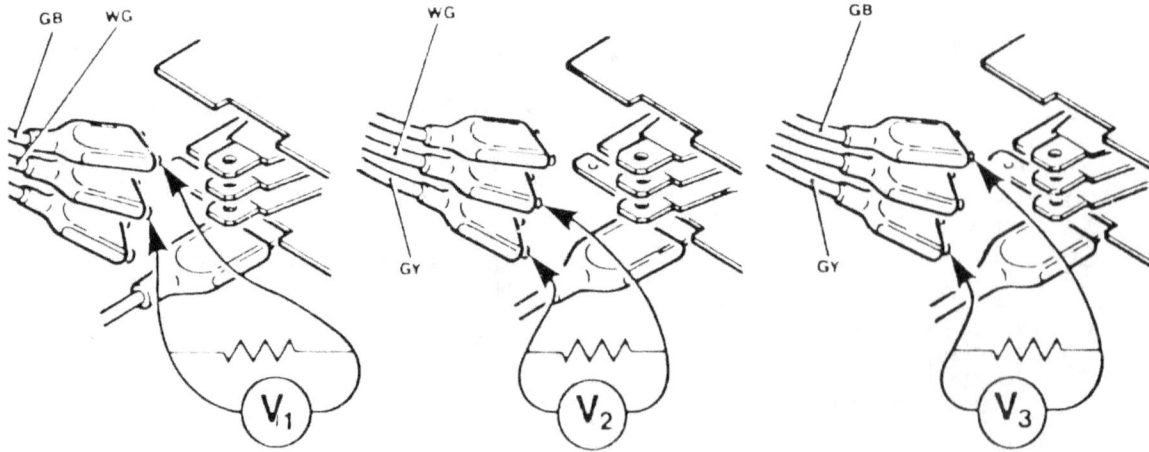

Fig. H2. Alternator AC continuity test

ELECTRICAL SYSTEM H

TEST 3
Alternator AC continuity
Remove the side panels, for access to the rectifier.

Disconnect the three alternator connections to the rectifier (see below) and repeat TEST 2 (V A, V A and V A) at the ends of the disconnected rectifier leads. The test results should be the same as TEST 2, in which case stop the engine, restore original connections and proceed to TEST 4.

If test unsatisfactory, check snap connectors and leads to alternator.

TEST 4
Rectifier DC Output
Disconnect the large (DC output) terminal of the rectifier. Connect DC voltmeter with a 1 ohm (100 W) load resistor across its terminals, as shown. Run the engine at approximately 2000 rev/min.

The voltmeter should show 10V min., in which case stop the engine, restore original connections and refit the side panels and proceed to TEST 5.

If zero or a low voltage is obtained, the rectifier is faulty.

TEST 5
Zener diode pack voltage regulator
Switch on ignition, ensure no other electrical loads are on start the engine. Disconnect the battery + ve. It is convenient to remove the fuse. Connect a DC voltmeter at the disconnected fu-

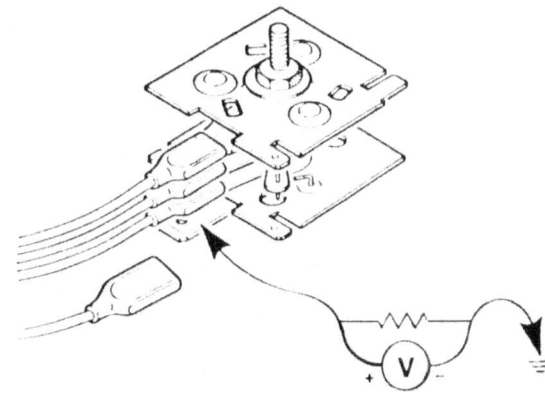

Fig. H3. Rectifier DC output test

se lead (engine harness side) and a good earth point. Increase engine speed to approximately 2,000 rev/min whilst observing voltmeter reading.

The regulator is working correctly if a reading of approximately 15 volts is obtained.

A reading above 16.2 volts indicates either a faulty connection or a zener which is open circuit. A reading below 13 volts indicates a short circuited zener. If a faulty reading is obtained, recheck with a substitute diode pack after checking harness connections carefully.

Warning Note: Never run the engine with both the battery and diode pack disconnected as the excessively high voltage obtained is liable to destroy the AB11 electronic ignition amplifier.

SECTION H5

STATIC TEST - ZENER DIODE

A static test of the individual diodes in the pack can be carried out with the zener in site on the motorcycle with the aid of a test lamp or continuity meter.

Firstly disconnect the diode leads located under the carburettor with test lamp or meter check each lead in turn noting result first test must be with battery + To Earth.
Second test must be with battery − To Earth

Any deviations from the advised results indicate a faulty unit

TEST 1
Test lamp should light as each diode is checked in turn.

TEST 2
Test lamp should not light as each diode is chekked in turn.

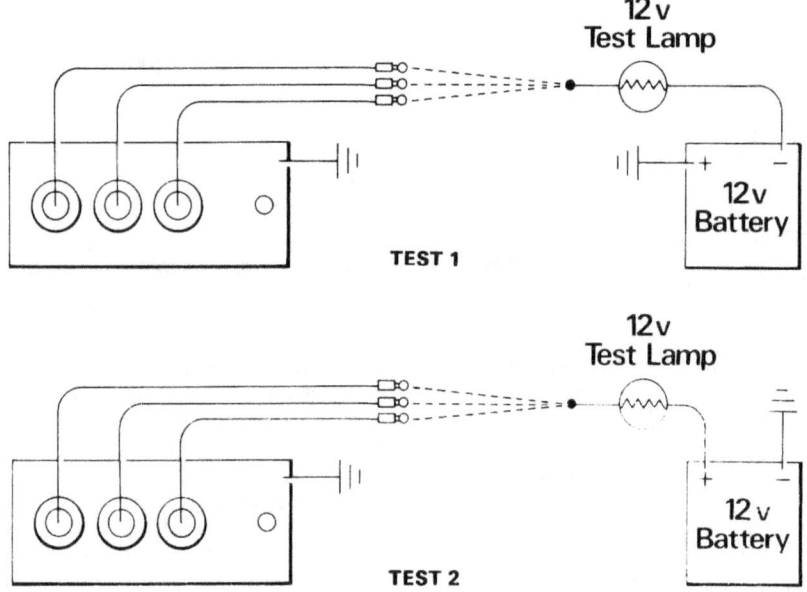

Fig. H4. Static test - zener diode

SECTION H6

IGNITION SYSTEM TECHNICAL DATA - ELECTRONIC

The two 6V ignition coils are connected in series to provide simultaneous HT sparking. The engine still fires in the correct sequence with the spurious sparks having no effect.

The primary circuit of the ignition coils is electronically switched by the remotely mounted amplifier unit which is triggered by pulses from the pick-up and reluctor working in conjunction with each other.

17M6 Ignition Coil
Primary winding resistance: 1·7-1·9ohms.

AB11 Amplifier
A remotely mounted electronics switching system contained in a cast aluminum box.

5PU Pick-up
A rivetted assembly comprising encapsulated winding, a fixing plate with pole-studs, and a permanent magnet sandwiched between the fixing plate and a base plate. The assembly is a stationary component mounted in the engine crankcase, around the reluctor. Two fixing screws tighten on slots in the fixing plate, the slots providing adjustments for ignition timing.

5 PU Reluctor
A specially shaped steel timing device, mounted on the end of the camshaft. Its position relative to the camshaft is determined by a keyway. Fixing is by means of a hexagon-headed bolt.

ELECTRICAL SYSTEM   H

Working Principles

When the ignition is switched ON, the amplifier unit is conductive and current flows through the primary windings of the two series-connected ignition coils and through the amplifer unit to earth.

A permanent magnetic field surrounds the pick-up base plate, the encapsulated winding and the pole-studs. When the engine is cranked the arms of the rotating reluctor approach these poles, causing the field strength to change which produces a pulse in the pick-up winding. This pulse is transmitted to the amplifier unit, causing it to switch off and break the primary circuit of the ignition coils. The HT spark is then produced in the conventional manner.

OPERATING CHARACTERISTICS

Electronic advance curve

The advance curve is automatically determined by the amplifier unit.

ENGINE REV/MIN	DEGREES ADVANCE
100	0
500	8
1000	19
2000	30
3000	36
3500	38
5000	40

Voltage operating range

Limits: 8-16V. Within this voltage range:

(a) A maximum timing tolerance of 1.5 is permissible at 2000 reluctor rev/min.

(b) Consistent sparking, without missing, must occur at reluctor speed range of 90 4000 rev/min.

The ignition system comprises an electronic amplifier unit, a pick-up assembly, a reluctor and two (twin) ignition coils. These components and a circuit diagram are illustrated in FIGS. H5 & H6.

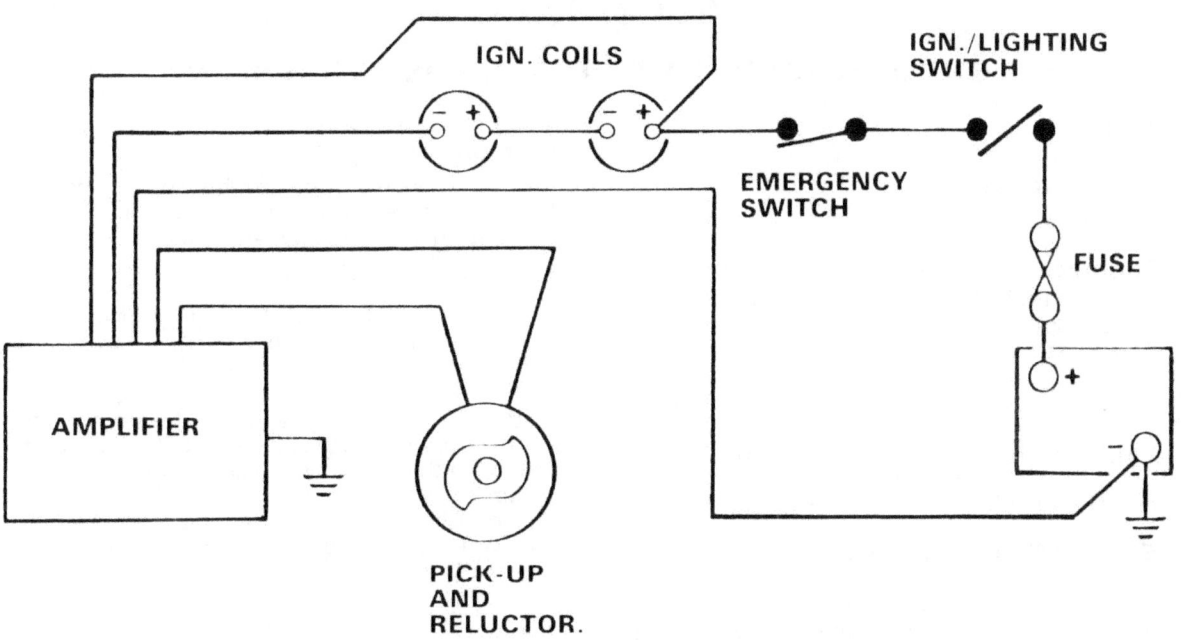

Fig. H5. Circuit diagram - ignition

H ELECTRICAL SYSTEM

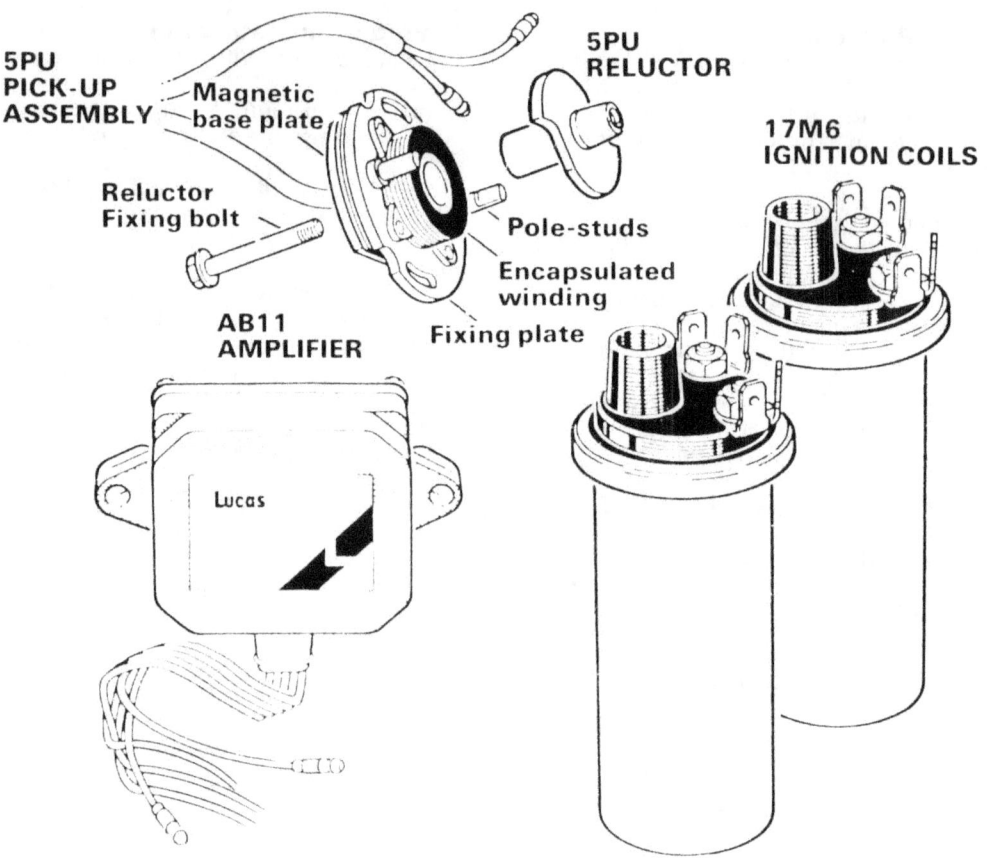

Fig. H6. Ignition system components

SECTION H7

IGNITION SYSTEM FAULT DIAGNOSIS AND TESTING

NOTE:
Test requirements:
    DC voltmeter
    Ohmmeter

Engine fails to start
Suspect: Discharged battery or no spark at one or both spark plugs.
Check battery and if satisfactory proceed to TEST 1.

Engine Runs on One Cylinder Only
Suspect: Spark plug, HT lead, or ignition coil.
Proceed to TEST 1, then if necessary TEST 2.

Engine Misfires or Runs Erratic
Suspect:
Spark plugs, HT leads, ignition timing, ignition coil, electronic amplifier and associated pick-up.

Clean spark plugs and check gaps.
Check timing. Finally, prove all items by substitution.

TEST 1:
HT Spark at Plugs.
Remove spark plugs and lay them on engine, HT leads connected and spark gaps visible. Switch on ignition, crank engine and check for regular sparking at both plugs.

If the test is satisfactory, check ignition timing. If this is also satisfactory, then the ignition system is not the cause of the engine failing to start.

If sparking occurs at one plug only interchange the two plugs and repeat the test. If fault is now transferred from one HT lead to the other, replace the non-sparking plug. If fault is not transferred, either the HT lead or ignition coil associated with the non-sparking plug is faulty (proceed to TEST 2).

Leave spark plugs removed from engine.

If there is no sparking at both plugs, check primary circuit of ignition coils (proceed directly to TEST 3).

ELECTRICAL SYSTEM H

TEST 2
HT Spark at Ignition Coils
Remove HT leads from one of the ignition coils and fit substitute lead. Position free end of lead 6mm or 1/4" from a good earth point (e.g. coil fixing bracket). Switch on ignition, crank engine and check for regular sparking at end of lead. Repeat test with other coil.

Sparking from both coils, replace faulty HT lead (Reference TEST 1).

Sparking from one coil only, replace non-sparking coil.

No sparking from either coil, check primary circuit of ignition coils (proceed to TEST 3). Leave spark plugs removed from engine.

TEST 3
Ignition Coil Primary Circuit
With reference to FIG.H7, disconnect the WB (WHITE/BLACK) lead from ignition coil No.2, switch on the ignition and connect DC voltmeter in four tests A,B,C, & D as shown.

Voltmeter should show battery voltage (12V) for each test, in which case leave ignition switched on and volt meter connected as for Test D and proceed directly to (v).

(i) No voltage in Test A: Ascertain reason for lack of supply voltage between coil, ignition switch and battery.

(ii) No voltage in Test B: Coil primary winding open-circuit. Replace coil.

(iii) No voltage in Test C: Coil-to-coil WP (WHITE/PINK) lead open-circuit.

(iv) No voltage in Test D: Coil primary winding open-circuit. Replace coil.

(v) Reconnect WB (WHITE/BLACK) lead to coil No. 2 Volt-meter needle should now show zero volts, indicating true coil primary circuit is satisfactory.

TEST 4
Pick-up Winding Resistance Continuity
Disconnect the white/orange and the white purple leads which connect the pulse sensor to the main harness. Check the resistance and continuity of the pulse sensor by connecting an OHM meter between the two leads. The OHM meter should show between 1100 - 1200 ohms.

If the test is unsatisfactory replace the pulse sensor.

NOTE:
The pick-up fixing screws also determine the rotary position in which the pick-up is fixed relative to ignition timing. The screws locate in slots which provide adjustment for ignition timing when the pick-up is fitted. Before disturbing the fixing screws of the original pick-up, choose a datum point on the pick-up (e.g. a shoulder of the magnetic base plate) and scribe a mark on the engine as a timing reference otherwise when fitting the new pick-up the timing will need to be reset and this will necessitate the use of a strobe light.

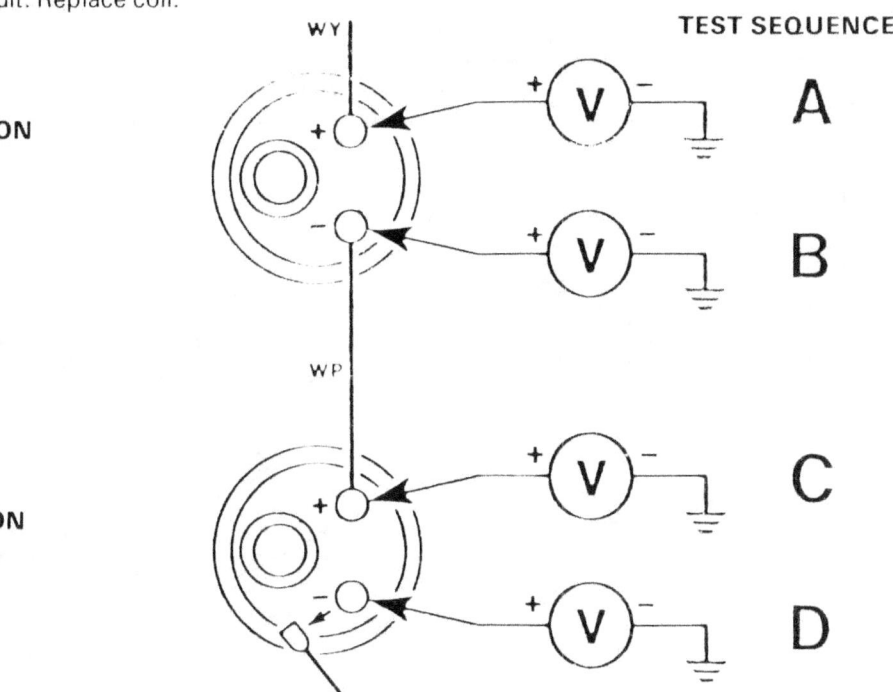

Fig. H7. Ignition coil primary circuit test

H ELECTRICAL SYSTEM

SECTION H8
FAULT FINDING CHART
ELECTRONIC IGNITION SYSTEM

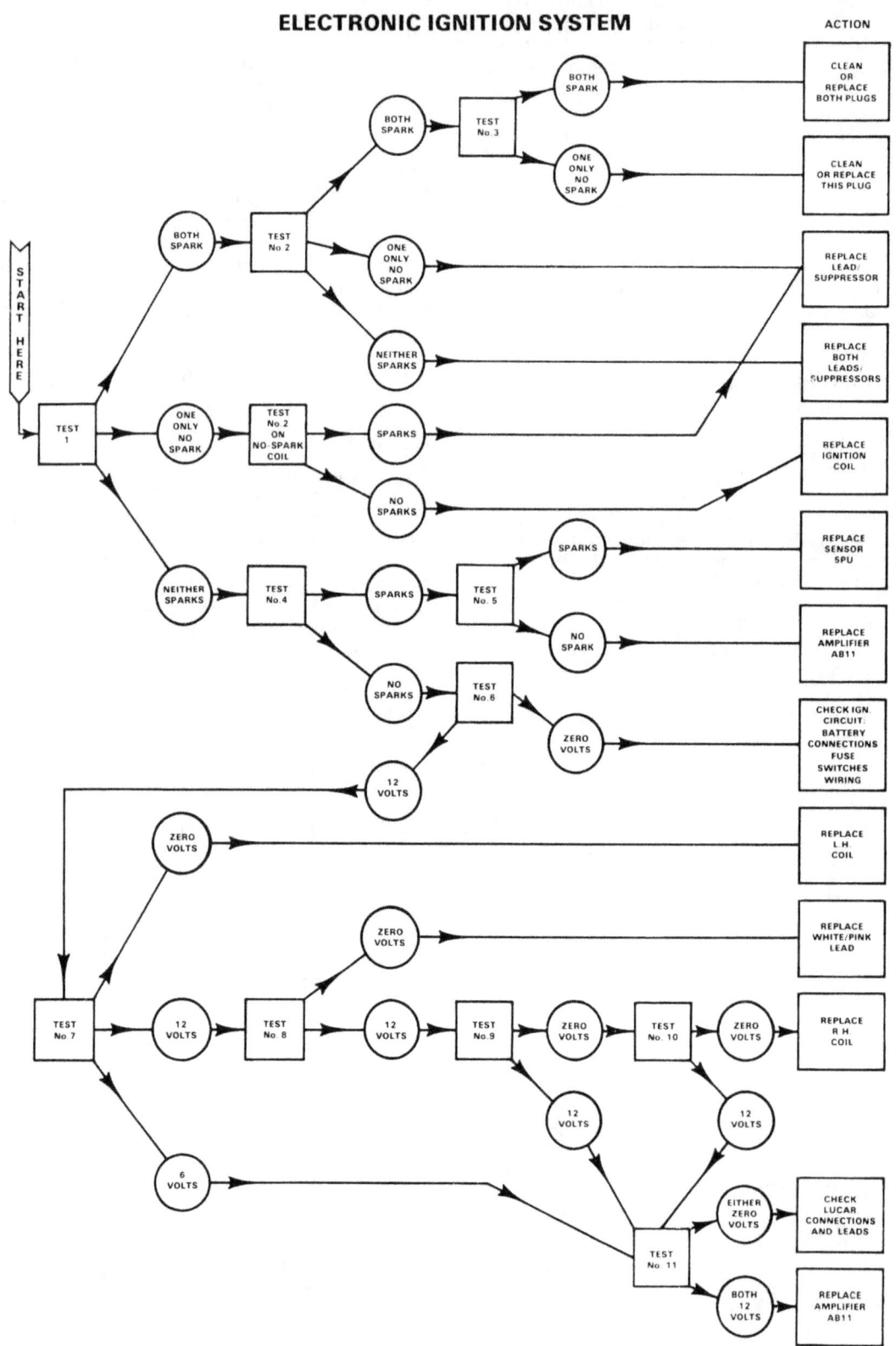

H10

ELECTRICAL SYSTEM H

SECTION H9

ELECTRONIC IGNITION FAULT DIAGNOSIS

The procedure detailed here and on the opposite page is recommended to locate any fault in the ignition system.

Follow the tests as shown on the chart and depending on the observed results (detailed in the circles) take the action specified. This will result in the fault being identified. Should this not be so repeat the procedure as a recheck.

TEST 1
Remove one H.T, lead from coil, hold the H.T, lead approx 3/16" from the coil H.T. chimmeny and operate the kickstart lever with the ignition switched on. Repeat with other coil.

TEST 2
Disconnect H.T. lead at spark plug, repeat as test 1 using a length of wire inserted in plug cap to approx 1/4" from cylinder head. Repeat on other plug after reconnecting the first one.

TEST 3
Remove both spark plugs, reconnect to plug caps, lay on top of cylinder head and check for spark at electrodes when kickstarter is operated and the ignition switched on.

TEST 4
Operate ignition switch key several times. Check for spark when coil lead is held as in test 1.

TEST 5
Check white/orange and white/purple connections to pulse sensor and ABII if O.K. test substitute pulse sensor. This may be provisionally tried before installing by connecting up to harness and turning the reluctor by hand inside the pulse sensor windings. Observe for spark as in test 3.

TEST 6
Check L.T. circuit with D.C. voltmeter or a 12 volt 3 watt lamp bulb connect one lamp terminal (voltmeter-VE) to frame. Connect other terminal to + terminal of left hand coil
Note Voltages stated are only approximate: Lamp will be bright, dim, or off.

TEST 7
As test 6 but connect to − Terminal of left hand coil.

TEST 8
Ditto but connect to + terminal of right hand coil.

TEST 9
Ditto but connect to − Terminal of right hand coil.

TEST 10
Disconnect leads white/Black and white yellow at coils which come from the amplifier box and repeat test 9.

TEST 11
With leads disconnected as test 10 connect voltmeter or 12 volt 3 watt lamp bulb terminal to earth - and other terminal firstly to white/yellow amplifier lucar terminal and secondly to white/black lucar terminal.

SECTION H10
STARTER SYSTEM

Ensure battery is at least 80% charged. If not, charge or substitute a good charged battery. Remove HT leads from spark plugs. Remove the solenoid cover (see workshop information). Ensure all connections are clean and tight.

TEST 1. Battery voltage on load
Connect voltmeter across battery terminals and crank engine. Note voltage reading.

TEST 2. Voltage at solenoid operating terminal
Connect voltmeter between solenoid winding feed terminal (from start push button) and earth, crank engine. If voltage is below that noted in test 1, check ignition switch, start button, cables and connections.

TEST 3. Voltage at starter on load
Connect voltmeter between starter feed terminal (from solenoid) and earth, crank engine. Voltage reading should be within 0.5 volt of reading in Test 1. If more than 0.5V below proceed to next test.

TEST 4. Voltage drop, insulated line
Connect voltmeter between battery positive post and starter feed terminal, crank engine, voltage reading should be almost zero, if so proceed to Test 6. If reading exceeds 0.5V, proceed to Test 5.

TEST 5. Voltage drop, solenoid contacts
Connect voltmeter between main terminals of the solenoid, crank engine. Voltage reading should be almost zero. If it is, the solenoid is satisfactory and the volt drop is occuring in the circuit. Check all insulated line cables and connectors. Retest as 4.

TEST 6. Voltage drop, earth line
Connect voltmeter between battery negative post and earth, crank engine. Voltage reading should be almost zero. If above 0.25V check earth connections and earth lead between solenoid mounting bracket and battery negative post.

If non of the above test reveal the cause of failure to crank correctly, the starter motor should be suspected and a substitue starter motor fitted.

SECTION H11
ZENER DIODE LOCATION

The Zener Diode is mounted in the wall of the right hand side half of the air cleaner body. The aluminium construction of the air cleaner body serves as a heatsink and dissipates excess charge current in the form of heat.

To remove the diode pack firstly lift out battery, remove two self tap screws and single bolt. Disconnect from main harness at alternator connections below carburettors, lift out through battery compartment.

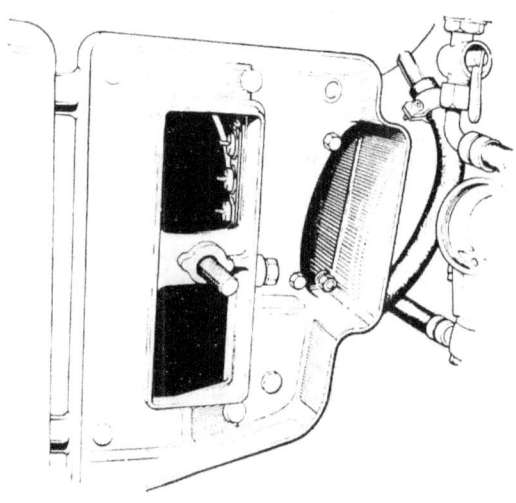

Fig. H8. Location of zener diode

SECTION H12

BATTERY INSPECTION AND MAINTENANCE

The battery containers are moulded in translucent polystyrene through which the acid level can be seen. The battery top is so designed that when the cover is in position, the special anti-spill filler plugs are sealed in a common venting chamber. Gas from the filler plugs leaves this chamber through a vent pipe union at the side of the top. The vent at the other side of the top is sealed off. Polythene tubing is attached to the vent pipe union to lead corrosive fumes away from parts of the machine which may otherwise suffer damage.

To prepare a dry-charged battery for service, first discard the vent hole sealing tape and then pour into each cell pure dilute sulphuric acid of appropriate specific gravity to THE COLOURED LINE. (See table (a)). Allow the battery to stand for at least one hour for the electrolyte to settle down, thereafter maintain the acid level at the coloured line by adding distilled water.

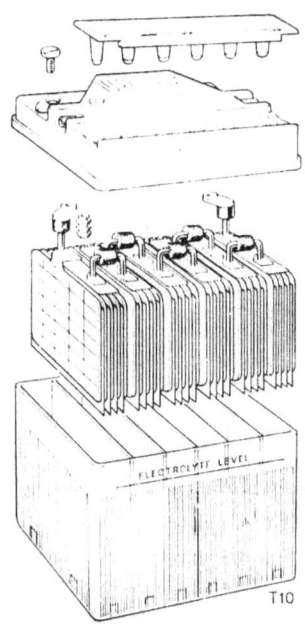

Fig. H9. Exploded view of battery

SECTION H13

ELECTRIC HORN

DESCRIPTION
The horn is of a high frequency single note type and is operated by direct current from the battery. The method of operation is that of a magnetically operated armature, which impacts on the cone face, and causes the tone disc of the horn to vibrate. The magnetic circuit is made self interrupting by contacts which can be adjusted externally.

If the horn fails to work, check the horn connection wiring. Check the battery for state of charge. A low supply voltage at the horn will adversely effect horn performance. If the above checks are made and the fault is not remedied, then adjust the horn as follows.

HORN ADJUSTMENT
A small hexagon head adjustment screw situated near the terminals is provided for adjustment. To adjust, turn this screw anticlockwise until the horn just fails to sound, and then turn it back (clockwise) about one quarter to half a turn.

NOTE - When adjusting and testing the horn, do not depress the horn push for more than a fraction of a second or the circuit wiring may be overloaded.

SECTION H14

HEADLAMP

DESCRIPTION

The headlamp is of the sealed beam unit type and access is gained to the light unit by withdrawing the rim and light unit assembly. To do so, slacken the screw at the top of the headlamp and prise off the rim and light unit assembly. Together the light unit can then be removed by disconnecting the feed plug and pilot light.

To remove the light unit from the rim prise out the retaining clips the light unit will then be free. When reassembling note that the light unit will then be free. When reassembling note that the light unit has a specific location arrangement with the rim, failure to observe this will result in incorrect beam spread.

Check the replacement for voltage and wattage specification and type before fitting. Focusing with this type of beam unit is unnecessary and there is no such provision.

BEAM ADJUSTMENTS

The beam must in all cases be adjusted as specified by local lighting regulations. In the united Kingdom the Transport Lighting Regulations reads as follows:-

A lighting system must be arranged so that it can give a light which is incapable of dazzling any person standing on the same horizontal plane as the vehicle at a greater distance than twenty five feet from the lamp, whose eye level is not less than three feet six inches above that plane.

The headlamp must therefore be set so that the main beam is directed straight ahead and parallel with the road when the motorcycle is fully loaded.

To achieve this, place the machine on a level road pointing towards a wall at a distance of 25 feet away, with a rider and passenger, on the machine, slacken the two pivot bolts at either side of the headlamp and tilt the headlamp until the beam is focused at approximately two feet six inches from the base of the wall. Do not forget that the headlamp should be on "full beam" lighting during this operation.

SECTION H15

REMOVING AND REFITTING THE HEADLAMP

Disconnect the leads from the battery terminals. Then slacken the light unit securing screws at the top of the headlamp. Prise the rim of the light unit free.

Remove light unit from lamp shell. Disconnect L.H. and R.H. switch plugs. Disconnect all earth wires unscrew the two bolts fixing the lamp shell to the forks.

Withdraw the lamp shell feeding the harness through the rubber grommets.

Reassembly is the reversal of the above procedure, but reference should be made to the wiring diagram. See section H24. Finally set the headlamp main beam. As described in Section H14.

SECTION H16

TAIL AND STOP LAMP UNIT

Access to the bulbs in the tail and stop lamp unit is achieved by unscrewing the two slotted screws which secure the lens. The bulb is of the doublefilament offset pin type and when a replacement is carried out, ensure that the bulb is fitted correctly.

Check that the two supply leads are connected correctly and check the earth (ground) lead to the bulb holder is in satisfactory condition.
When refitting the lens, do not overtighten the fixing screws or the lens may fracture as a result.

ELECTRICAL SYSTEM

SECTION H17

FUSES

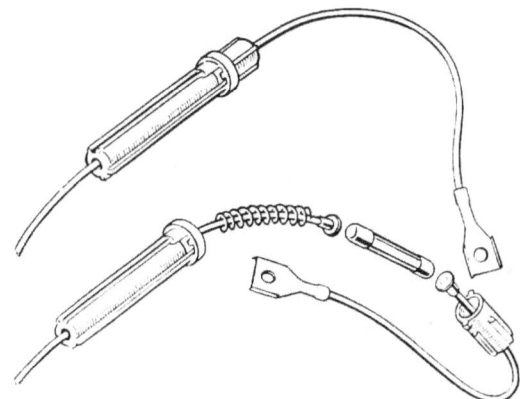

Fig. H10. Exploded view of fuseholder assembly

The fuse is to be found on the brown/blue live lead from the battery positive terminal. It is housed in a quickly detachable shell and is of 35 amp fuse rating.

Before following any fault location procedure always check that the fuse is not the source of the fault. A new fuse-cartridge should be fitted if there is any doubt about the old one.

SECTION H18

IGNITION SWITCH

All models are fitted with an ignition switch incorporating a "barrel" type lock. These locks use individual "Yale" type keys and render the ignition circuit inoperative when the switch is turned off and the key removed. It is advisable for the owner to note the number stamped on the key to ensure a correct replacement in the event of the key being lost.

Lucar connectors are incorporated in the switch and these should be checked from time to time to ensure good electrical contact.

To remove the switch take off the switch panel by removing the three Philips head screws.

Unscrew the single retaining nut on the switch body. Push the switch out of the panel location and remove the wiring Lucars.

The battery leads should be removed before attempting to remove the switch to avoid a short circuit.

The lock is retained in the body of the switch by a spring loaded plunger. This can be depressed with a pointed instrument through a small hole in the side of the switch body and the lock assembly withdrawn after the lock and switch together have been detached from the machine.

SECTION H19

FLASHER LAMPS

Access to the bulb in the flasher lamp unit can be obtained by unscrewing the two Phillips head screws. To remove the bulb, depress inwards and turn anti-clockwise. When replacing the bulb make sure it is securely fitted.

REMOVING AND REFITTING FRONT FLASHER LAMPS

Disconnect the green wires at the snap connectors. Remove the flasher lamp by loosening the locking nut and turning the lamp unit anti-clockwise.

Finally pull the green wire through the flasher stalk and grommet.

REMOVING AND REFITTING REAR FLASHER LAMPS

Disconnect the battery terminals and green wires at the snap connectors, found under the seat and repeat as in the removal of front flasher unit.

H ELECTRICAL SYSTEM

SECTION H20
WARNING LAMPS

Warning lamps are fitted on all models. The blue light indicates high beam. The orange warning light serves the flasher lamps and becomes illuminated in conjunction with the flasher lamps when they are operational. The red warning light is connected into the ignition circuit and also to an electrically controlled oil pressure switch situated at the timing cover. This results in the warning light operating as soon as the ignition is turned on with the engine stopped but extinguishes as oil pressure develops beyond a predetermined minimum critical pressure when the motor is running. The green light indicates when the gearbox is in the neutral position.

SECTION H21
STOP LAMP SWITCHES

A rear stop light light switch is fitted to both front and rear braking systems and operate independantly.

The rear brake switch is fitted to the frame behind the rear brake pedal and is controlled by adjusting the short bolt and locknut mounted at the pedal pivot. Adjustment should be such that the rear brake light becomes illuminated immediately the brake is applied. Other than checking the terminals for cleanliness and security the unit will require no further maintainence.

The front brake stop switch is operated by pressure from the hydraulic system. No adjustment or maintainence is required.

SECTION H22
OIL PRESSURE SWITCH

The oil pressure switch is a sealed unit fitted into the front of the timing cover on all models.

The oil switch is designed to operate at 3-5lb./in. (0.2 to 0.35kg./cm.) pressure at which stage the oil warning light will be extinguished. There is no simple method of checking the function of the switch except by substitution.

SECTION H23
SPARKING PLUGS

It is recommended that the sparking plugs be inspected, cleaned and tested every 3,000 miles (4,800km.) and new ones fitted every 12,000 miles (20,000km.).

To remove the sparking plugs a box spanner (13/16in. (19.5mm.) across flats) should be used and if any difficulty is encountered a small amount of penetrating oil (see lubricatiom chart Section A1) should be placed at the base of the sparking plug and time allowed for penetration. When removing the sparking plugs identify each plug with the cylinder from which it was removed so that any faults revealed on examination can be traced back to the cylinder concerned.

Due to certain features of engine design the sparking plugs will probably show slightly differing deposits and colouring characteristics. For this purpose it is recommended that any adjustments to carburation etc., which may be carried out to gain the required colour characteristics should always be referred to the left cylinder.

Examine both plugs for signs of oil fouling. This will be indicated by a wet, shiny, black deposit on the central insulator. This is caused by excessive oil in the combustion chamber during combustion and indicates that the piston rings or cylinder bores are worn.

Next examine the plugs for signs of petrol (gasoline) fouling. This is indicated by a dry, sooty, black deposit which is usually caused by overrich carburation, although ignition system defects such as a discharged battery, faulty contact breaker, coil or capacitor defects, or a broken or worn out cable may be additional causes. To rectify this type of fault the above mentioned

ELECTRICAL SYSTEM H

items should be checked with spcial attention given to carburation system. Again, the left plug should be used as the indicator. The right plug will almost always have a darker characteristic.

Over-heating of the sparking plug electrodes is indicated by severely eroded electrodes and a white, burned or blistered insulator. This type of fault is usually caused by weak carburation, although plugs which have been operating whilst not being screwed down sufficiently can easily become overheated due to heat that is normally dissipated through to the cylinder head not having an adequate conducting path. Over-heating is normally symptomised by pre-ignition, short plug life, and "pinking" which can ultimately result in piston crown failure. Unecessary damage can result from over-tightening the plugs and to achieve a good seal between the plug and cylinder head a torque wrench should be used to tighten the plugs to the figure quoted in "General Data".

A plug of the correct grade will bear a light flaky deposit on the outer rim and earth electrode, and these and the base of the insulator will be light chocolate brown in colour. A correct choice of plug is marked A. B shows a plug which appears bleached, with a deposit like cigarette ashe; this is too 'hot-running' for the performance of the engine and a cooler-running type should be substituted. A plug which has been running too 'cold' and has not reached the self-cleaning temperature is shown at C. This has oil on the base of the insulator and electrodes, and should be replaced by a plug that will burn off deposits and remove the possibility of a short-circuit. The plug marked D is heavily sooted, indicating that the mixture has been too rich, and a further carburation check should be made. At illustration E is seen a plug which is completely worn out and badly in need of replacement.

To clean the plugs it is preferable to make use of a properly designed proprietary plug cleaner. The maker's instructions for using the cleaner should be followed carefully.

When the plugs have been carefully cleaned, examine the central insulators for cracking and the centre electrode for excessive wear. In such cases the plugs have completed their useful life and new ones should be fitted.

Finally, before re-fitting the sparking plugs the electrodes should adjusted to the correct gap setting of .020in. (.5mm.). Before refitting sparking plugs the threads should be cleaned by means of a wire brush and a minute amount of graphite grease smeared onto the threads. This will prevent any possibility of thread seizure occuring.

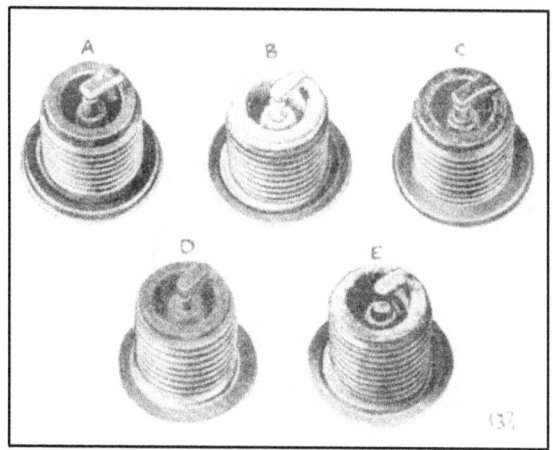

Fig. H11. Sparking plug diagnosis

If the ignition timing and carburation settings are correct and the plugs have been correctly fitted, but over-heating still occurs then it is possible that carburation is being adversely affected by an air leak between the carburetter, manifold and the cylinder head. This possibility must be checked thoroughly before taking any further action. when it is certain that none of the above mentioned faults are the cause of over-heating then the plug type and grade should be considered.

Normally the type of plugs quoted in "General Data" are satisfactory for general use of the machine, but in special isolated cases, conditions may demand a plug of a different head range. Advice is readily available to solve these problems from the plug manufacturer who should be consulted.

Note. All models are fitted with an air filter or cleaner and if this has been removed it will affect the carburation of the machine and hence may adversely affect the grade of sparking plugs fitted.

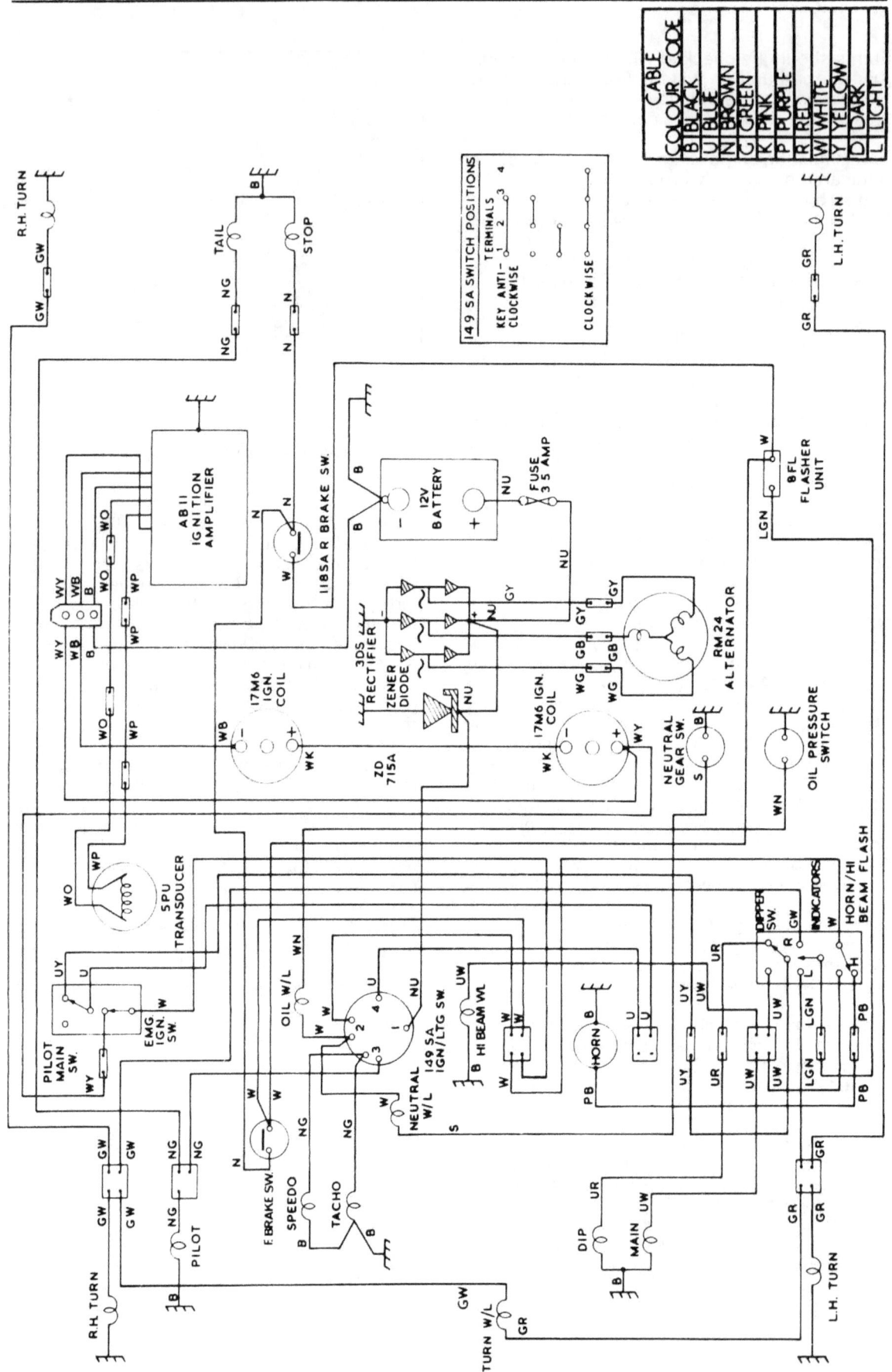

Fig. H12. Wiring diagram — 1979 standard model

ELECTRICAL SYSTEM H

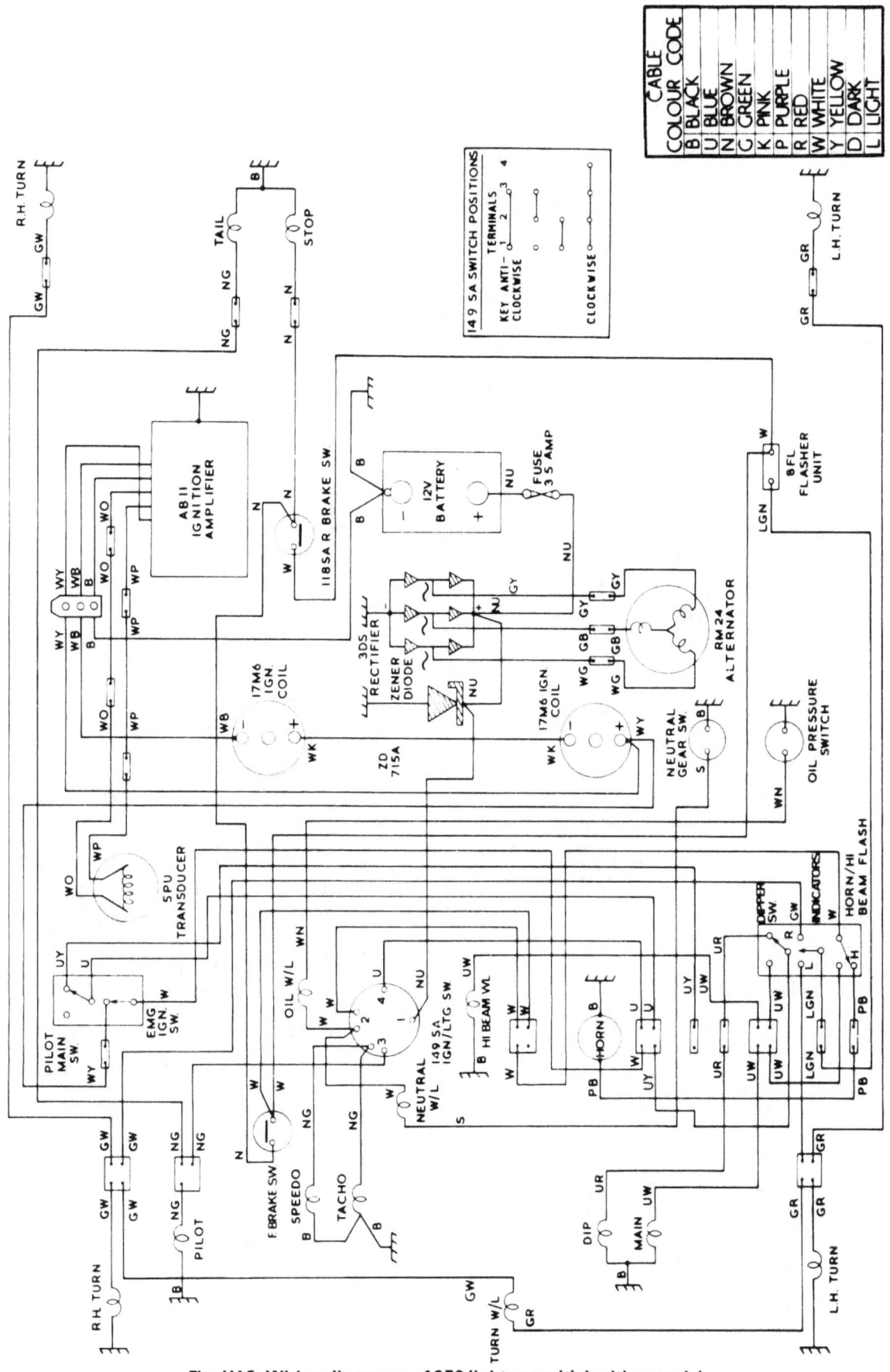

Fig. H13. Wiring diagram — 1979 lights on with ignition model

ELECTRICAL SYSTEM

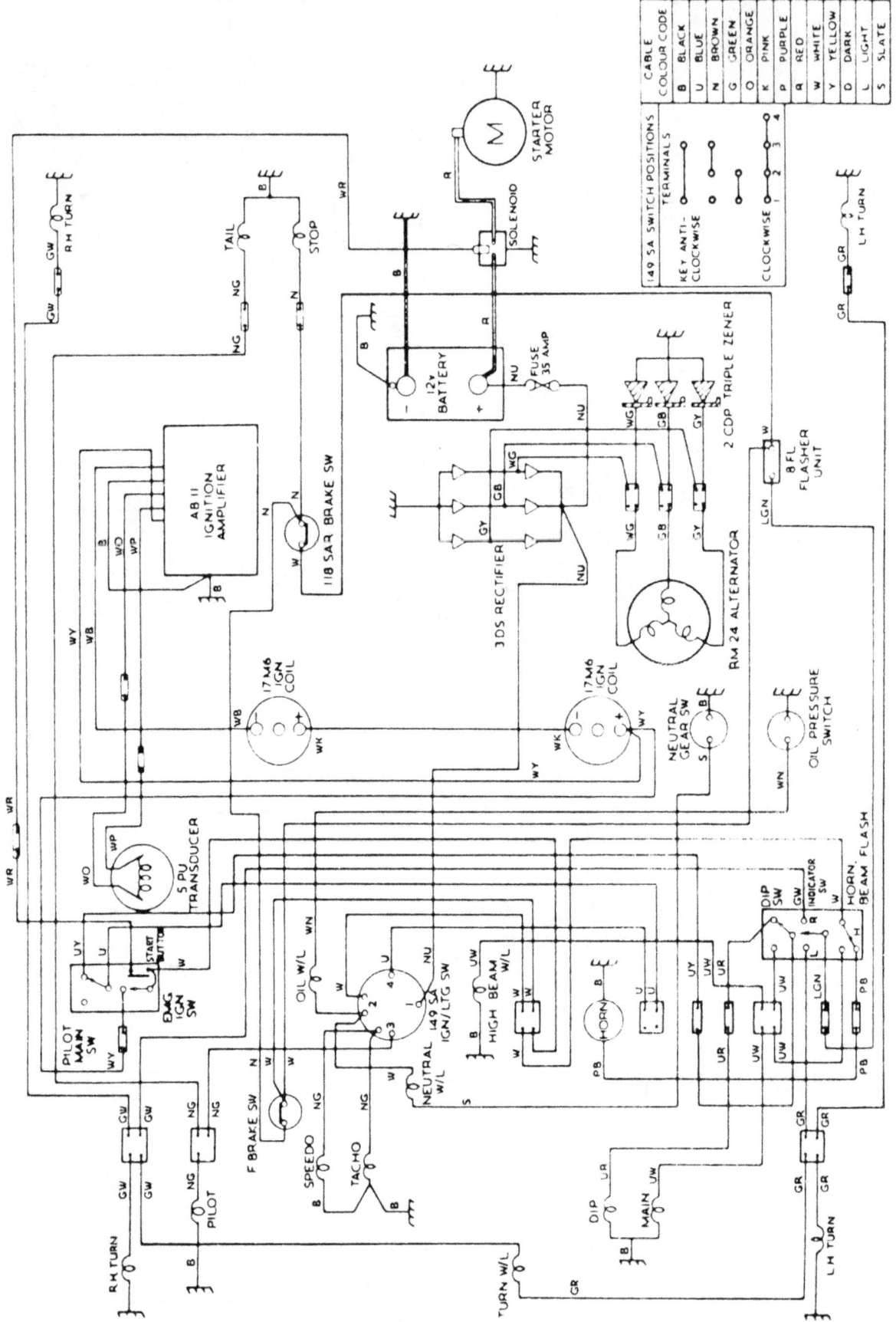

Fig. H14. Wiring diagram — standard model with electric start

ELECTRICAL SYSTEM H

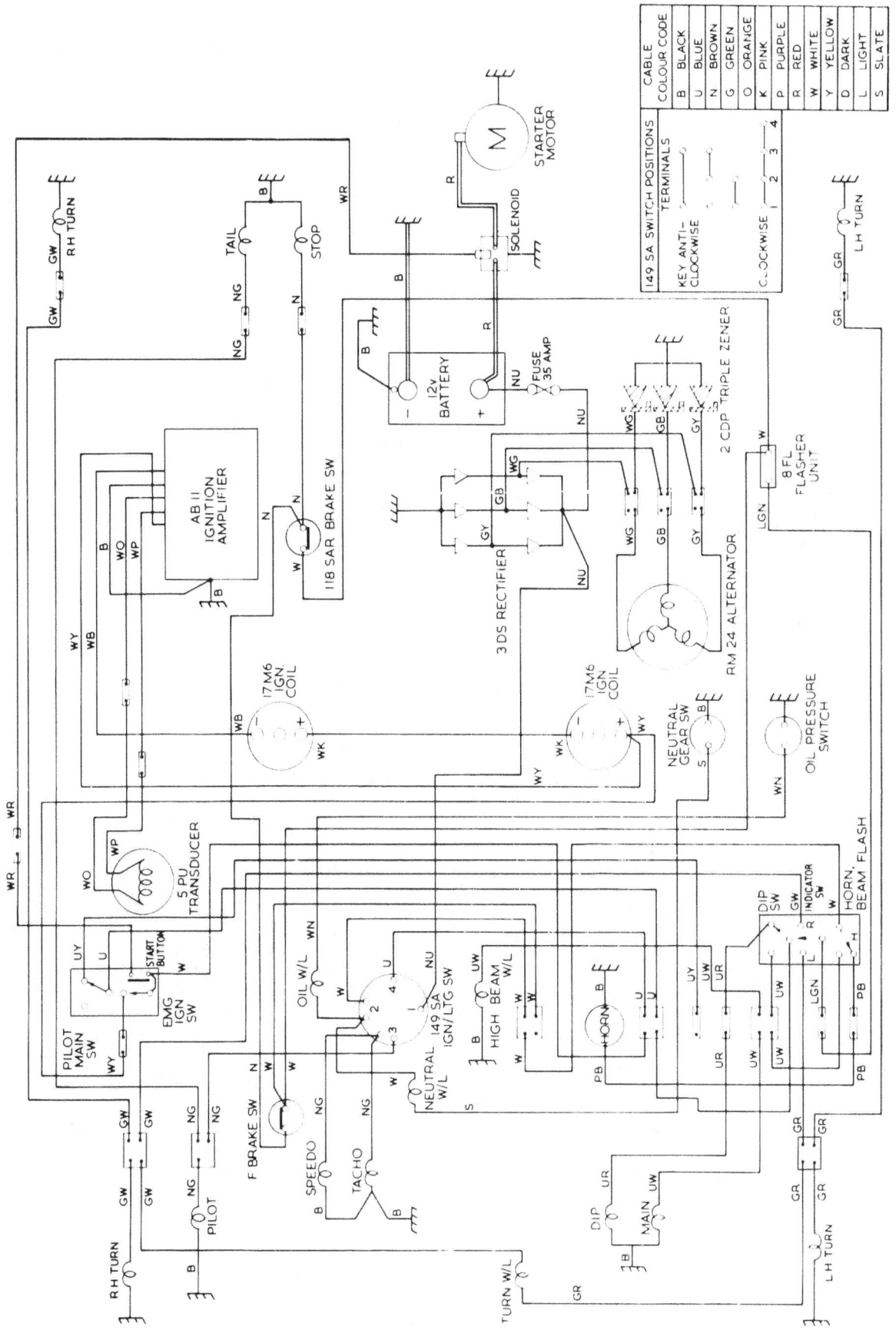

Fig. H15. Wiring diagram — electric start model - lights on with ignition

ELECTRICAL SYSTEM

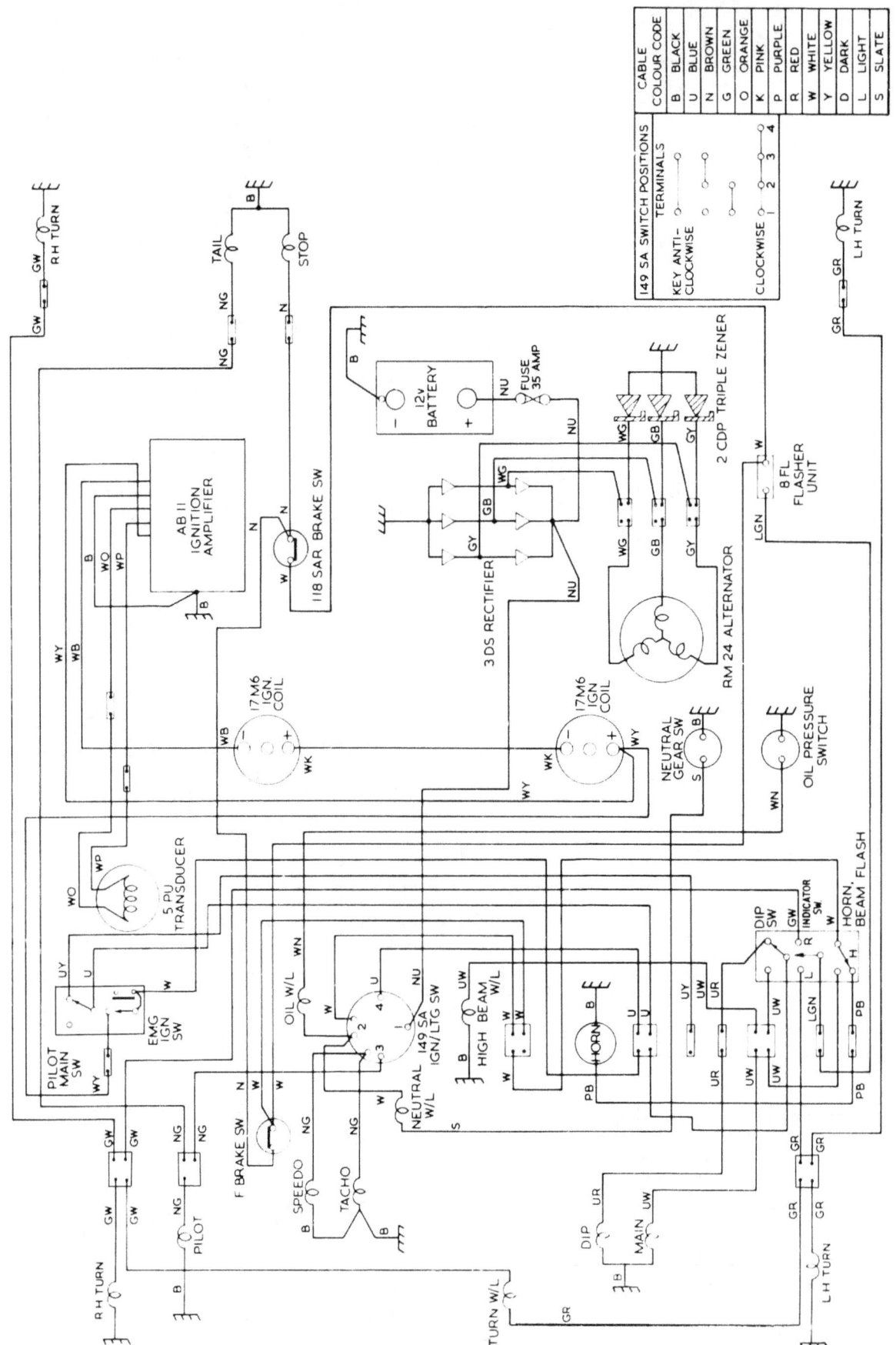

Fig. H16. Wiring diagram - standard model (kick start)

ELECTRICAL SYSTEM H

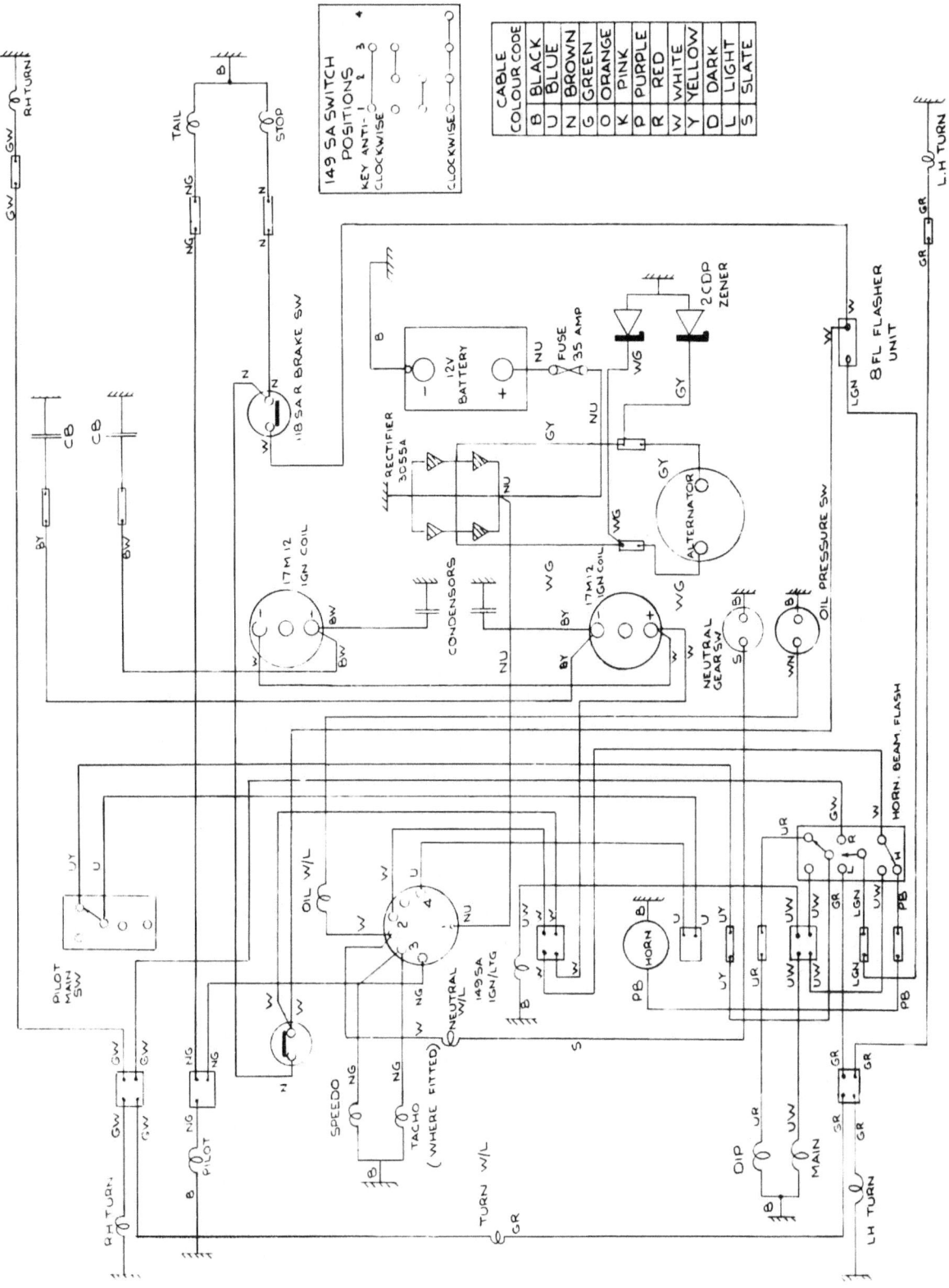

Fig. H17. Wiring diagram — TR65 only

H23

SECTION J

WORKSHOP SERVICE TOOLS

INTRODUCTION

This section of the Workshop Manual illustrates pictorially the workshop service tools that are available for carrying out the major dismantling and re-assembly operations on the UNIT CONSTRUCTION 750 c.c. Triumph Motorcycle.

The section is divided into sub-sections relating to the main section headings in this manual, illustrating those tools mentioned and used in the appropriate section text.

	Section
ENGINE	J1
TRANSMISSION	J2
GEARBOX	J3
FRAME/WHEELS	J4
FRONT FORKS	J5

SECTION J1
ENGINE

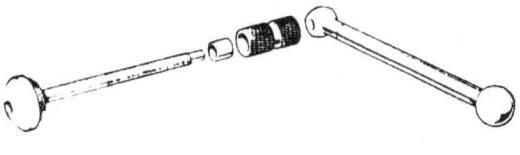

61-6063. Valve guide removal and replacement tool

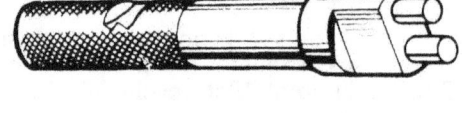

61-6008. Tappet guide block punch

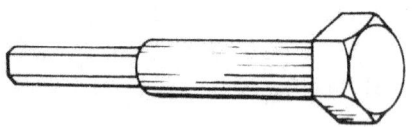

61-7010. Sleeve nut adaptor tool-cylinder head

61-7019. Oil seal compressor for replacing the rocker spindle

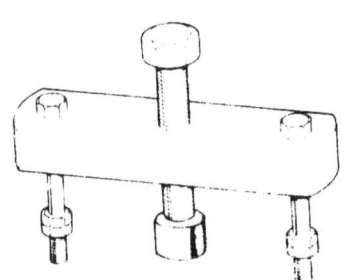

61-6132. Camwheel extractor.

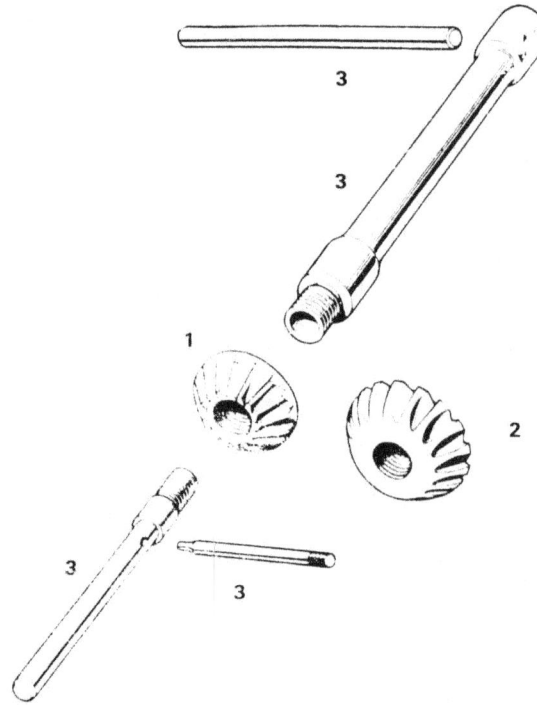

1. 61-7025 Valve seat cutter inlet and exhaust
2. 61-7027 Blending cutter inlet and exhaust
3. 61-7029 Arbor, pilot and tommy bars

SERVICE TOOLS   J

ENGINE (CONTINUED) J1

61-7023. Contact breaker cam extractor

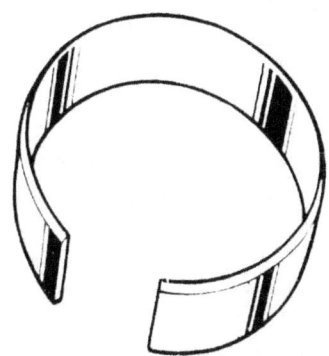

61-7013. Pilot for contact breaker oil seal when replacing timing cover

61-6135. Piston ring collar

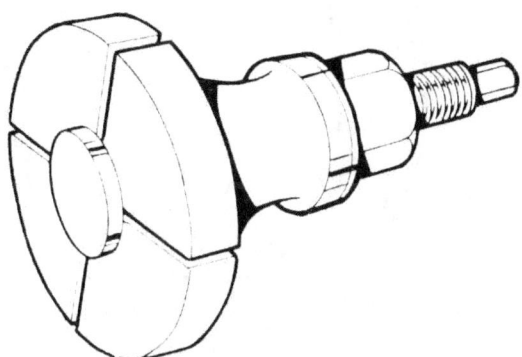

61-7017. Roller bearing outer race removal tool

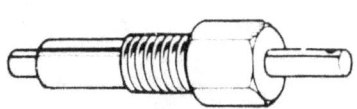

61-7022 Flywheel locating body and plunger

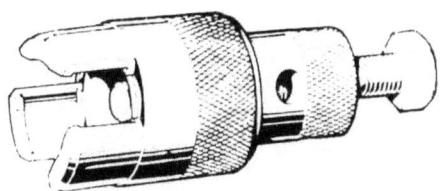

61-6019. Crankshaft pinion extractor

SECTION J2
TRANSMISSION

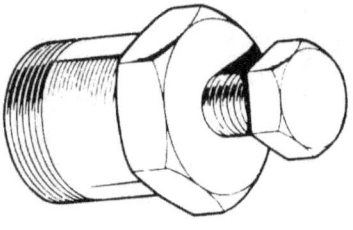

61-7014. Clutch hub extractor

61-7012. Chain tensioner adjuster plug

Pre Eng No PB25000

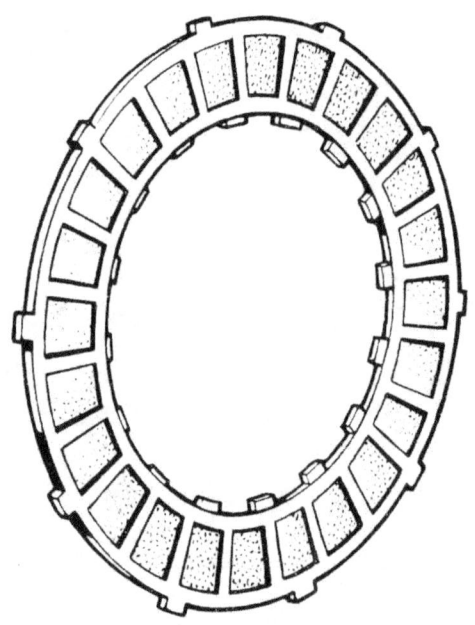

61-7018. Clutch locking plate

SECTION J3
GEARBOX

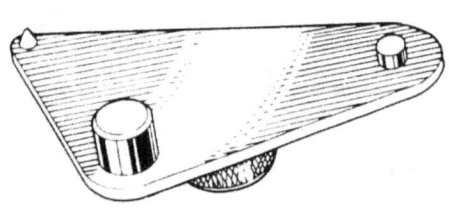

61-7011. Gear box assembly tool-quadrant locator

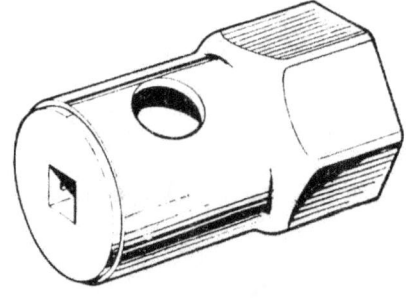

61-6125. Gearbox nut spanner

SECTION J4
FRAME/WHEELS

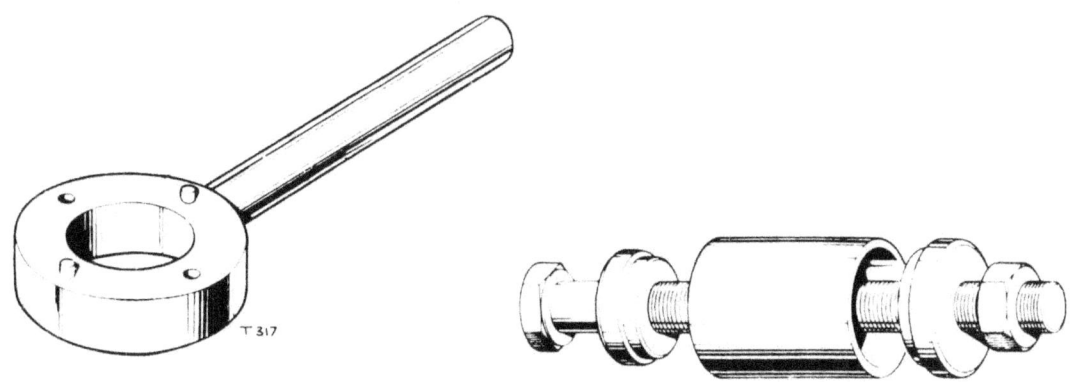

61-7024. Front wheel bearing locking ring spanner

61-6117 Swinging arm bush remover and replacer

SECTION J5
FRONT FORKS

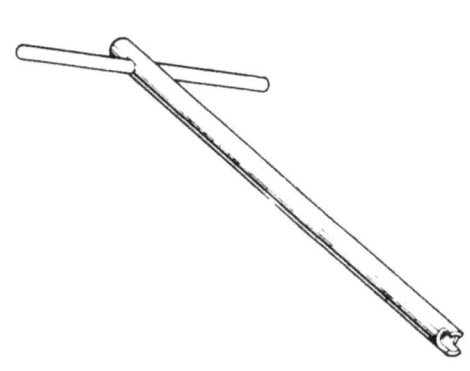

61-6113 Fork damper valve removal tool

61-6121 Head race bearing drift

CONVERSION

TABLES

INCHES TO MILLIMETRES—UNITS

Inches	0	10	20	30	40
0		254·0	508·0	762·0	1016·0
1	25·4	279·4	533·4	787·4	1041·4
2	50·8	304·8	558·8	812·8	1066·8
3	76·2	330·2	584·2	838·2	1092·2
4	101·6	355·6	609·6	863·6	1117·6
5	127·0	381·0	635·0	889·0	1143·0
6	152·4	406·4	660·4	914·4	1168·4
7	177·8	431·8	685·8	939·8	1193·8
8	203·2	457·2	711·2	965·2	1219·2
9	228·6	482·6	736·6	990·6	1244·6

One Inch—25·399978 millimetres
One Metre—39·370113 inches
One Mile—1·6093 kilos
One Kilo—·62138 miles

DECIMALS TO MILLIMETRES—FRACTIONS

1/1000	
inches	mm.
·001	·0254
·002	·0508
·003	·0762
·004	·1016
·005	·1270
·006	·1524
·007	·1778
·008	·2032
·009	·2286

1/100	
inches	mm.
·01	·254
·02	·508
·03	·726
·04	1·016
·05	1·270
·06	1·524
·07	1·778
·08	2·032
·09	2·286

1/10	
inches	mm.
·1	2·54
·2	5·08
·3	7·62
·4	10·16
·5	12·70
·6	15·24
·7	17·79
·8	20·32
·9	22·86

CONVERSION TABLES

FRACTIONS TO DECIMALS AND MILLIMETRES

Fractions			Decimals	mm.
		1/64	·015625	·3969
	1/32		·03125	·7937
		3/64	·046875	1·1906
1/16			·0625	1·5875
		5/64	·078125	1·9844
	3/32		·09375	2·3812
		7/64	·109375	2·7781
1/8			·125	3·1750
		9/64	·140625	3·5719
	5/32		·15625	3·9687
		11/64	·171875	4·3656
3/16			·1875	4·7625
		13/64	·203125	5·1594
	7/32		·21875	5·5562
		15/64	·234375	5·9531
1/4			·25	6·3500
		17/64	·265625	6·7469
	9/32		·28125	7·1437
		19/64	·296875	7·5406
5/16			·3125	7·9375
		21/64	·328125	8·3344
	11/32		·34375	8·7312
		23/64	·359375	9·1281
3/8			·375	9·5250
		25/64	·390625	9·9219
	13/32		·40625	10·3187
		27/64	·421875	10·7156
7/16			·4375	11·1125
		29/64	·453125	11·5094
	15/32		·46875	11·9062
		31/64	·484375	12·3031
1/2			·5	12·7000

Fractions			Decimals	mm.
		33/64	·515625	13·0969
	17/32		·53125	13·4937
		35/64	·546675	13·8906
9/16			·5625	14·2875
		37/64	·578125	14·6844
	19/32		·59375	15·0812
		39/64	·609375	15·4781
5/8			·625	15·8750
		41/64	·640625	16·2719
	21/32		·65685	16·6687
		43/64	·671875	17·0656
11/16			·6875	17·4625
		45/64	·703125	17·8594
	23/32		·71875	18·2562
		47/64	·734375	18·6531
3/4			·75	19·0500
		49/64	·765625	19·4469
	25/32		·78125	19·8437
		51/64	·796875	20·2406
13/16			·8125	20·6375
		53/64	·828125	21·0344
	27/32		·84375	21·4312
		55/64	·859375	21·8281
7/8			·875	22·2250
		57/64	·890625	22·6219
	29/32		·90625	23·0187
		59/64	·921875	23·4156
15/16			·9375	23·8125
		61/64	·953125	24·2094
	31/32		·96875	24·6062
		63/64	·984375	25·0031
1				25·4000

CONVERSION TABLES

MILLIMETRES TO INCHES—UNITS

mm.	0	10	20	30	40
0		·39370	·78740	1·18110	1·57480
1	·03937	·43307	·82677	1·22047	1·61417
2	·07874	·47244	·86614	1·25984	1·65354
3	·11811	·51181	·90551	1·29921	1·69291
4	·15748	·55118	·94488	1·33858	1·73228
5	·19685	·59055	·98425	1·37795	1·77165
6	·23622	·62992	1·02362	1·41732	1·81103
7	·27559	·66929	1·06299	1·45669	1·85040
8	·31496	·70866	1·10236	1·49606	1·88977
9	·35433	·74803	1·14173	1·53543	1·92914

mm.	50	60	70	80	90
0	1·96851	2·36221	2·75591	3·14961	3·54331
1	2·00788	2·40158	2·79528	3·18891	3·58268
2	2·04725	2·44095	2·83465	3·22835	3·62205
3	2·08662	2·48032	2·87402	3·26772	3·66142
4	2·12599	2·51969	2·91339	3·30709	3·70079
5	2·16536	2·55906	2·95276	3·34646	3·74016
6	2·20473	2·59843	2·99213	3·38583	3·77953
7	2·24410	2·63780	3·03150	3·42520	3·81890
8	2·28347	2·67717	3·07087	3·46457	3·85827
9	2·32284	2·71654	3·11024	3·50394	3·89764

MILLIMETRES TO INCHES—FRACTIONS

1/1000	
mm.	inches
0·001	·000039
0·002	·000079
0·003	·000118
0·004	·000157
0·005	·000197
0·006	·000236
0·007	·000276
0·008	·000315
0·009	·000354

1/100	
mm.	inches
0·01	·00039
0·02	·00079
0·03	·00118
0·04	·00157
0·05	·00197
0·06	·00236
0·07	·00276
0·08	·00315
0·09	·00354

1/10	
mm.	inches
0·1	·00394
0·2	·00787
0·3	·01181
0·4	·01575
0·5	·01969
0·6	·02362
0·7	·02756
0·8	·03150
0·9	·03543

CONVERSION TABLES

DRILL SIZES

Letter	Size	Letter	Size
A	·234	N	·302
B	·238	O	·316
C	·242	P	·323
D	·246	Q	·332
E	·250	R	·339
F	·257	S	·348
G	·261	T	·358
H	·266	U	·368
I	·272	V	·377
J	·277	W	·386
K	·281	X	·397
L	·290	Y	·404
M	·295	Z	·413

Number	Size	Number	Size	Number	Size	Number	Size
1	·2280	14	·1820	27	·1440	40	·0980
2	·2210	15	·1800	28	·1405	41	·0960
3	·2130	16	·1770	29	·1360	42	·0935
4	·2090	17	·1730	30	·1285	43	·0890
5	·2055	18	·1695	31	·1200	44	·0860
6	·2040	19	·1660	32	·1160	45	·0820
7	·2010	20	·1610	33	·1130	46	·0810
8	·1990	21	·1590	34	·1110	47	·0785
9	·1960	22	·1570	35	·1100	48	·0760
10	·1935	23	·1540	36	·1065	49	·0730
11	·1910	24	·1520	37	·1040	50	·0700
12	·1890	25	·1495	38	·1015	51	·0670
13	·1850	26	·1470	39	·0995	52	·0635

WIRE GAUGES

No. of Gauge	Imperial Standard Wire Gauge		Brown and Sharpe's American Wire Gauge	
	Inches	Millimetres	Inches	Millimetres
0000	·400	10·160	·460	11·684
000	·372	9·448	·410	10·404
00	·348	8·839	·365	9·265
0	·324	8·299	·325	8·251
1	·300	7·620	·289	7·348
2	·276	7·010	·258	6·543
3	·252	6·400	·229	5·827
4	·232	5·892	·204	5·189
5	·212	5·384	·182	4·621
6	·192	4·676	·162	4·115
7	·176	4·470	·144	3·664
8	·160	4·064	·128	3·263
9	·144	3·657	·114	2·906
10	·128	3·251	·102	2·588
11	·116	2·946	·091	2·304
12	·104	2·641	·081	2·052
13	·092	2·336	·072	1·827
14	·080	2·032	·064	1·627
15	·072	1·828	·057	1·449
16	·064	1·625	·051	1·290
17	·056	1·422	·045	1·149
18	·048	1·219	·040	1·009
19	·040	1·016	·035	·911
20	·036	·914	·032	·811
21	·032	·812	·028	·722
22	·028	·711	·025	·643
23	·024	·609	·023	·573
24	·022	·558	·020	·511
25	·020	·508	·018	·454
26	·018	·457	·016	·404
27	·0164	·416	·014	·360
28	·0148	·375	·012	·321
29	·0136	·345	·011	·285
30	·0124	·314	·010	·254

FOOT POUNDS TO KILOGRAMETRES

	0	1	2	3	4	5	6	7	8	9	
—		0·138	0·227	0·415	0·553	0·691	0·830	0·968	1·106	1·244	—
10	1·383	1·521	1·659	1·797	1·936	2·074	2·212	2·350	2·489	2·627	10
20	2·765	2·903	3·042	3·180	3·318	3·456	3·595	3·733	3·871	4·009	20
30	4·148	4·286	4·424	4·562	4·701	4·839	4·977	5·116	5·254	5·392	30
40	5·530	5·668	5·807	5·945	6·083	6·221	6·360	6·498	6·636	6·774	40
50	6·913	7·051	7·189	7·328	7·466	7·604	7·742	7·881	8·019	8·157	50
60	8·295	8·434	3·572	8·710	8·848	8·987	9·125	9·263	9·401	9·540	60
70	9·678	9·816	9·954	10·093	10·231	10·369	10·507	10·646	10·784	10·922	70
80	11·060	11·199	11·337	11·475	11·613	11·752	11·890	12·028	12·166	12·305	80
90	12·443	12·581	12·719	12·858	12·996	13·134	13·272	13·411	13·549	13·687	90

MILES TO KILOMETRES

	0	1	2	3	4	5	6	7	8	9	
—		1·609	3·219	4·828	6·437	8·047	9·656	11·265	12·875	14·484	—
10	16·093	17·703	19·312	20·922	22·531	24·140	25·750	27·359	28·968	30·578	10
20	32·187	33·796	35·406	37·015	38·624	40·234	41·843	43·452	45·062	46·671	20
30	48·280	49·890	51·499	53·108	54·718	56·327	57·936	59·546	61·155	62·765	30
40	64·374	65·983	67·593	69·202	70·811	72·421	74·030	75·639	77·249	78·858	40
50	80·467	82·077	83·686	85·295	86·905	88·514	90·123	91·733	93·342	94·951	50
60	96·561	98·170	99·780	101·389	102·998	104·608	106·217	107·826	109·436	111·045	60
70	112·654	114·264	115·873	117·482	119·092	120·701	122·310	123·920	125·529	127·138	70
80	128·748	130·357	131·967	133·576	135·185	136·795	138·404	140·013	141·623	143·232	80
90	144·841	146·451	148·060	149·669	151·279	152·888	154·497	156·107	157·716	159·325	90

POUNDS TO KILOGRAMS

	0	1	2	3	4	5	6	7	8	9	
—		0·454	0·907	1·361	1·814	2·268	2·722	3·175	3·629	4·082	—
10	4·536	4·990	5·443	5·987	6·350	6·804	7·257	7·711	8·165	8·618	10
20	9·072	9·525	9·079	10·433	10·886	11·340	11·793	12·247	12·701	13·154	20
30	13·608	14·061	14·515	14·968	15·422	15·876	16·329	16·783	17·237	17·690	30
40	18·144	18·597	19·051	19·504	19·953	20·412	20·865	21·319	21·772	22·226	40
50	22·680	23·133	23·587	24·040	24·494	24·948	25·401	25·855	26·308	26·762	50
60	27·216	27·669	28·123	28·576	29·030	29·484	29·937	30·391	30·844	31·298	60
70	31·751	32·205	32·659	33·112	33·566	34·019	34·473	34·927	35·380	35·834	70
80	36·287	36·741	37·195	37·648	38·102	38·855	39·009	39·463	39·916	40·370	80
90	40·823	41·277	41·731	42·184	42·638	43·091	43·545	43·998	44·452	44·906	90

MILES PER GALLON (IMPERIAL) TO LITRES PER 100 KILOMETRES

10	28·25	15	18·83	20	14·12	25	11·30	30	9·42	35	8·07	40	7·06	50	5·65	60	4·71	70	4·04
10½	26·90	15½	18·22	20½	13·78	25½	11·08	30½	9·26	35½	7·96	41	6·89	51	5·54	61	4·63	71	3·98
11	25·68	16	17·66	21	13·45	26	10·87	31	9·11	36	7·85	42	6·73	52	5·43	62	4·55	72	3·92
11½	24·56	16½	17·12	21½	13·14	26½	10·66	31½	8·97	36½	7·74	43	6·57	53	5·33	63	4·48	73	3·87
12	23·54	17	16·61	22	12·84	27	10·46	32	8·83	37	7·63	44	6·42	54	5·23	64	4·41	74	3·82
12½	22·60	17½	16·14	22½	12·55	27½	10·27	32½	8·69	37½	7·53	45	6·28	55	5·13	65	4·35	75	3·77
13	21·73	18	15·69	23	12·28	28	10·09	33	8·56	38	7·43	46	6·14	56	5·04	66	4·28	76	3·72
13½	20·92	18½	15·27	23½	12·02	28½	9·91	33½	8·43	38½	7·34	47	6·01	57	4·96	67	4·22	77	3·67
14	20·18	19	14·87	24	11·77	29	9·74	34	8·31	39	7·24	48	5·89	58	4·87	68	4·16	78	3·62
14½	19·48	19½	14·49	24½	11·53	29½	9·58	34½	8·19	39½	7·15	49	5·77	59	4·79	69	4·10	79	3·57

CONVERSION TABLES

PINTS TO LITRES

	0	1	2	3	4	5	6	7	8
—	—	·568	1·136	1·705	2·273	2·841	3·841	3·978	4·546
¼	·142	·710	1·279	1·846	2·415	2·983	3·552	4·120	4·688
½	·284	·852	1·420	1·989	2·557	3·125	3·125	4·262	4·830
¾	·426	·994	1·563	2·131	2·699	3·267	3·836	4·404	4·972

GALLONS (IMPERIAL) TO LITRES

	0	1	2	3	4	5	6	7	8	9	
—	—	4·546	9·092	13·638	18·184	22·730	27·276	31·822	36·368	40·914	—
10	45·460	50·005	54·551	59·097	63·643	63·189	72·735	77·281	81·827	86·373	10
20	90·919	95·465	100·011	104·557	109·103	113·649	118·195	122·741	127·287	131·833	20
30	136·379	140·924	145·470	150·016	154·562	159·108	163·645	168·200	172·746	177·292	30
40	181·838	186·384	190·930	195·476	200·022	204·568	209·114	213·660	218·206	222·752	40
50	227·298	231·843	236·389	240·935	245·481	250·027	254·473	259·119	263·605	268·211	50
60	272·757	277·303	281·849	286·395	290·941	295·487	300·033	304·579	309·125	313·671	60
70	318·217	322·762	327·308	331·854	336·400	340·946	245·492	350·038	354·584	359·130	70
80	363·676	368·222	372·768	377·314	381·860	386·406	390·952	395·498	400·044	404·590	80
90	409·136	413·681	418·227	422·773	427·319	431·865	436·411	440·957	445·503	450·049	90

POUNDS PER SQUARE INCH TO KILOGRAMS PER SQUARE CENTIMETRE

	0	1	2	3	4	5	6	7	8	9	
—	—	0·070	0·141	0·211	0·281	0·352	0·422	0·492	0·562	0·633	—
10	0·703	0·773	0·844	0·914	0·984	1·055	1·125	1·195	1·266	1·336	10
20	1·406	1·476	1·547	1·617	1·687	1·758	1·828	1·898	1·969	2·039	20
30	2·109	2·179	2·250	2·320	2·390	2·461	2·531	2·601	2·672	2·742	30
40	2·812	2·883	2·953	3·023	3·093	3·164	3·234	3·304	3·375	3·445	40
50	3·515	3·586	3·656	3·726	3·797	3·867	3·937	4·007	4·078	4·148	50
60	4·218	4·289	4·359	4·429	4·500	4·570	4·640	4·711	4·781	4·851	60
70	4·921	4·992	5·062	5·132	5·203	5·273	5·343	5·414	5·484	5·554	70
80	5·624	5·695	5·765	5·835	5·906	5·976	6·046	6·117	6·187	6·257	80
90	6·328	6·398	6·468	6·538	6·609	6·679	6·749	6·820	6·890	6·960	90

U.N.E.F. SCREW THREADS

Dia.	No. of thds.	Core dia.	Tap drill	Dia.	No. of thds.	Core dia.	Tap drill
1/4 in.	32	·2162 in.	5·60 mm.	1 in.	20	·9459 in.	61/64 in.
5/16 in.	32	·2787 in.	7·20 mm.	1-1/16 in.	18	1·0024 in.	1·010 in.
3/8 in.	32	·3412 in.	11/32 ins	1-1/8 in.	18	1·0649 in.	1·072 ins.
7/16 in.	28	·3988 in.	10·20 mm.	1-3/16 in.	18	1·1274 in.	1·135 in.
1/2 in.	28	·4613 in.	11·80 mm.	1-1/4 in.	18	1·1899 in.	1·196 in.
9/16 in.	24	·5174 in.	13·30 mm.	1-5/16 in.	18	1·2524 in.	32·00 mm.
5/8 in.	24	·5799 in.	14·75 mm.	1-3/8 in.	18	1·3149 in.	33·50 mm.
11/16 in.	24	·6424 in.	·6480 in.	1-7/16 in.	18	1·3774 in.	1·385 ins.
3/4 in.	20	·6959 in.	45/64 in.	1-1/2 in.	18	1·4399 in.	1·447 in.
13/16 in.	20	·7584 in.	49/64 in.	1-9/16 in.	18	1·4948 in.	1-1/2 in.
7/8 in.	20	·8209 in.	53/64 in.	1-5/8 in.	18	1·5649 in.	1·572 in.
15/16 in.	20	·8834 in.	57/64 in.	1-11/16 in.	18	1·6274 in.	41·50 mm.

B.A. SCREW THREADS

No.	Dia. of bolt	Thds. per inch	Dia. tap drill	Core dia.
0	·2362	25·4	·1960	·1890
1	·2087	28·2	·1770	·1661
2	·1850	31·4	·1520	·1468
3	·1614	34·8	·1360	·1269
4	·1417	38·5	·1160	·1106
5	·1260	43·0	·1040	·0981
6	·1102	47·9	·0935	·0852
7	·0984	52·9	·0810	·0738
8	·0866	59·1	·0730	·0663
9	·0748	65·1	·0635	·0564
10	·0669	72·6	·0550	·0504
11	·0591	81·9	·0465	·0445
12	·0511	90·9	·0400	·0378
13	·0472	102·0	·0360	·0352
14	·0394	109·9	·0292	·0280
15	·0354	120·5	·0260	·0250
16	·0311	133·3	·0225	·0220

CONVERSION TABLES

B.S.W. SCREW THREADS

Dia. of bolt (inch)	Threads per inch	Dia. tap drill (inch)	Core dia.
1/4	20	·1968	·1860
5/16	18	1/4	·2412
3/8	16	5/16	·2950
7/16	14	23/64	·3460
1/2	12	13/32	·3933
9/16	12	15/32	·4558
5/8	11	17/32	·5086
11/16	11	37/64	·5711
3/4	10	41/64	·6219
13/16	10	45/64	·6844
7/8	9	3/4	·7327
15/16	9	13/16	·7952
1	8	55/64	·8399

B.S.F. SCREW THREADS

Dia. of bolt (inch)	Threads per inch	Dia. tap drill (inch)	Core dia.
7/32	28	·1770	·1731
1/4	26	·2055	·2007
9/32	26	·238	·2320
5/16	22	·261	·2543
3/8	20	·316	·3110
7/16	13	3/8	·3664
1/2	16	27/64	·4200
9/16	16	·492	·4825
5/8	14	35/64	·5335
11/16	14	39/64	·5960
3/4	12	21/32	·6433
13/16	12	23/32	·7058
7/8	11	25/32	·7586
1	10	57/64	·8719
1-1/8	9	1	·9827
1-1/4	9	1-1/8	1·1077
1-3/8	8	1-15/64	1·2149
1-1/2	8	1·358	1·3399
1-5/8	8	1-31/64	1·4649

U.N.C. SCREW THREADS

Dia.	No. of thds.	Core dia.	Tap drill
1/4 in.	20	·1959 in.	5·20 mm.
5/16 in.	18	·2524 in.	6·60 mm.
3/8 in.	16	·3073 in.	8·00 mm.
7/16 in.	14	·3602 in.	9·40 mm.
1/2 in.	13	·4167 in.	10·80 mm.
9/16 in.	12	·4723 in.	12·20 mm.
5/8 in.	11	·5266 in.	13·50 mm.
3/4 in.	10	·6417 in.	16·50 mm.
7/8 in.	9	·7547 in.	49/64 in.
1 in.	8	·8647 in.	22·25 mm.
1-1/8 in.	7	·9704 in.	63/64 in.
1-1/4 in.	7	1·0954 in.	1-7/64 in.
1-3/8 in.	6	1·1946 in.	1-13/64 in.
1-1/2 in.	6	1·3196 in.	1-21/64 in.
1-3/4 in.	5	1·5335 in.	1-35/64 in.
2 in.	4-1/2	1·7594 in.	1-25/32 in.

U.N.F. SCREW THREADS

Dia.	No. of thds.	Core dia.	Tap drill
1/4 in.	28	·2113 in.	5·50 mm.
5/16 in.	24	·2674 in.	6·90 mm.
3/8 in.	24	·3299 in.	8·50 mm.
7/16 in.	20	·3834 in.	9·90 mm.
1/2 in.	20	·4459 in.	11·50 mm.
9/16 in.	18	·5024 in.	12·90 mm.
5/8 in.	18	·5649 in.	14·50 mm.
3/4 in.	16	·6823 in.	11/16 in.
7/8 in.	14	·7977 in.	0·804 in.
1 in.	12	·9098 in.	23·25 mm.
1-1/8 in.	12	1·0348 in.	26·50 mm.
1-1/4 in.	12	1·1598 in.	29·50 mm.
1-3/8 in.	12	1·2848 in.	1·290 in.
1-1/2 in.	12	1·4098 in.	36·00 mm.

VELOCEPRESS MANUALS – MOTORCYCLE BY MAKE

AJS 1932-1948 SINGLES & TWINS 250cc THRU 1000cc (BOOK OF)
AJS 1945-1960 SINGLES 350cc & 500cc MODELS 16 & 18 (BOOK OF)
AJS 1955-1965 SINGLES 350cc & 500cc (BOOK OF)
AJS 1957-1966 FACTORY WSM - ALL SINGLES & TWINS
ARIEL UP TO 1932 (BOOK OF)
ARIEL 1932-1939 PREWAR MODELS (BOOK OF)
ARIEL 1933-1951 (WORKSHOP MANUAL)
ARIEL 1939-1960 4 STROKE SINGLES (BOOK OF)
ARIEL 1958-1964 LEADER & ARROW FACTORY WSM & PARTS LIST
ARIEL 1958-1964 LEADER & ARROW (BOOK OF)
BMW R26 R27 (1956-1967) FACTORY WORKSHOP MANUAL
BMW R50 R50S R60 R69S (1955-1969) FACTORY WORKSHOP MANUAL
BRIDGESTONE 90 SERIES FACTORY WSM & PARTS CATALOGUE
BRIDGESTONE 175 SERIES FACTORY WSM & PARTS CATALOGUE
BRIDGESTONE 350 SERIES FACTORY WSM & PARTS CATALOGUES
BSA SERVICE SHEETS MASTER CATALOGUE ALL MODELS 1945-1967
BSA BANTAM D1 TO D7 1948-1966 FACTORY SERVICE SHEETS MANUAL
BSA BANTAM ALL MODELS FROM 1948 ONWARDS (BOOK OF)
BSA BANTAM D14 FACTORY SERVICE MANUAL
BSA DANDY FACTORY WORKSHOP MANUAL (COMPILATION)
BSA SINGLES & V-TWINS UP TO 1926 inc. 1927 SUPPLEMENT (BOOK OF)
BSA SINGLES & V-TWINS UP TO 1930 (BOOK OF)
BSA SINGLES & V-TWINS UP TO 1935 (BOOK OF)
BSA SINGLES & V-TWINS 1936-1939 (BOOK OF)
BSA C10, C11 & C12 1945-1958 FACTORY SERVICE SHEETS MANUAL
BSA OHV & SV SINGLES 250-600cc 1945-1959 (BOOK OF)
BSA C15 & B40 1958-1967 FACTORY SERVICE SHEETS MANUAL
BSA OHV & SV SINGLES 250cc (ONLY) 1954-1970 (BOOK OF)
BSA B31, B32, B33 & B34 1945-60 FACTORY SERVICE SHEETS MANUAL
BSA OHV SINGLES 350 & 500cc 1955-1967 (BOOK OF)
BSA M20, M21 & M33 1945-1963 FACTORY SERVICE SHEETS MANUAL
BSA TWINS A7 & A10 1948-1962 FACTORY SERVICE SHEETS MANUAL
BSA TWINS A7 & A10 1948-1962 (BOOK OF)
BSA TWINS A50 & A65 1962-1965 FACTORY WORKSHOP MANUAL
BSA TWINS A50 & A65 1962-1969 (SECOND BOOK OF)
DOUGLAS 1929-1939 PREWAR ALL MODELS (BOOK OF)
DOUGLAS 1948-1957 POSTWAR ALL MODELS FACTORY SHOP MANUAL
DUCATI 160cc, 250cc & 350cc OHC MODELS FACTORY SHOP MANUAL
HONDA 50cc ALL MODELS UP TO 1970 INC MONKEY & TRAIL (BOOK OF)
HONDA 90cc ALL MODELS UP TO 1966 (BOOK OF)
HONDA TWINS & SINGLES 50cc THRU 305cc 1960-1966 (BOOK OF)
HONDA TWINS ALL MODELS 125cc THRU 450cc UP TO 1968 (BOOK OF)
HONDA C100 50cc SUPER CUB O.H.V. 1959-1962 FACTORY WSM
HONDA C110 50cc SPORT CUB O.H.C. 1960-1962 FACTORY WSM
HONDA 50-65-70-90cc O.H.C. SINGLES 1959-1983 FACTORY WSM
HONDA 100-125cc SINGLES CB/CD/CL/SL/TL 1970-1984 FACTORY WSM
HONDA 125-150cc TWINS C/CS/CA 1959-1966 FACTORY WSM
HONDA 125-160-175-200cc TWINS 1965-1978 WORKSHOP MANUAL
HONDA 250-305cc TWINS C/CS/CB 1961-1968 FACTORY WSM
HOHDA 250-350cc TWINS CB/CL/SL 1968-1973 FACTORY WSM
HONDA 250-360cc TWINS CB/CL/CJ 1974-1977 FACTORY WSM
HONDA 350F & 400F 4-CYLINDER 1972-1977 FACTORY WSM
HONDA 450cc TWINS CB/CL 1965-1974 K0 TO K7 WORKSHOP MANUAL
HONDA 500cc & 550cc 4-CYL 1971-1978 FACTORY WORKSHOP MANUAL
HONDA 750cc SHOC 4-CYL 1969-1978 K0~K8 WORKSHOP MANUAL
INDIAN PONYBIKE, BOY RACER & PAPOOSE ILL PARTS LIST & SALES LIT
J.A.P. ENGINES 1927-1952 & MOTORCYCLES 1934-1952 (BOOK OF)
MATCHLESS 1931-1939 ALL MODELS 250cc THRU 990cc (BOOK OF)
MATCHLESS 1945-1956 350 & 500cc SINGLES (BOOK OF)
MATCHLESS 1955-1966 350 & 500cc SINGLES (BOOK OF)
MATCHLESS 1957-1966 FACTORY WSM - ALL SINGLES & TWINS
NEW IMPERIAL ALL SV & OHV FROM 1935 ONWARDS (BOOK OF)
NORTON 1932-1939 PREWAR MODELS (BOOK OF)
NORTON 1932-1947 (BOOK OF)
NORTON 1938-1956 (BOOK OF)
NORTON 1945-1963 MODELS 16H, Big4, ES2, 19 & 50 WSM'S & PARTS
NORTON 1955-1963 MODELS 19, 50 & ES2 (BOOK OF)
NORTON 1948-1970 DOMINATOR TWINS FACTORY WSM'S & PARTS
NORTON 1955-1965 DOMINATOR TWINS (BOOK OF)
NORTON 1960-1970 TWIN CYLINDER FACTORY WORKSHOP MANUAL
NORTON 1970-1975 COMMANDO 850 & 750cc FACTORY WSM
NORTON 1975-1978 MK 3 COMMANDO 850 cc FACTORY WSM
PANTHER 1932-1958 LIGHTWEIGHT MODELS 250 & 350cc (BOOK OF)
PANTHER 1938-1966 HEAVYWEIGHT MODELS 600 & 650cc (BOOK OF)
RALEIGH MOTORCYCLES 1919-1933 (BOOK OF)
ROYAL ENFIELD 1934-1946 SINGLES & V TWINS (BOOK OF)
ROYAL ENFIELD 1937-1953 SINGLES & V TWINS (BOOK OF)
ROYAL ENFIELD 1946-1962 SINGLES (BOOK OF)
ROYAL ENFIELD 1948-1963 500cc TWINS FACTORY WORKSHOP MANUAL
ROYAL ENFIELD 1952-1963 700cc TWINS FACTORY WORKSHOP MANUAL
ROYAL ENFIELD 1956-1966 250cc CRUSADER & 350cc NEW BULLET WSM
ROYAL ENFIELD 1958-1966 250cc & 350cc SINGLES (SECOND BOOK OF)
ROYAL ENFIELD 1962-1970 INTERCEPTOR WSM'S & PARTS (Compilation)
RUDGE 1933-1939 (BOOK OF)
SACHS 1968-1975 100cc & 125cc ENGINES WSM & M/CYCLE PARTS LIST
SUNBEAM 1928-1939 (BOOK OF)
SUNBEAM 1946-1957 S7 & S8 (BOOK OF)
SUZUKI 50cc & 80cc UP TO 1966 (BOOK OF)
SUZUKI T10 1963-1967 FACTORY WORKSHOP MANUAL
SUZUKI T20 & T200 1965-1969 FACTORY WORKSHOP MANUAL
SUZUKI TWINS 1962 ONWARDS 125-500cc WORKSHOP MANUAL
TRIUMPH 1935-1949 SINGLES & TWINS (BOOK OF)
TRIUMPH 1937-1961 SINGLES SV & OHV 250cc-600cc + TERRIER & CUB
TRIUMPH 1945-1955 PRE-UNIT 350cc, 500cc & 650cc TWINS WSM No.11
TRIUMPH 1945-1959 TWINS (BOOK OF)
TRIUMPH 1956-1969 TWINS (BOOK OF)
TRIUMPH 1956-1962 PRE-UNIT 500cc & 650cc TWINS WSM No.17
TRIUMPH 1957-1963 UNIT CONSTRUCTION 350-500cc WSM No.4
TRIUMPH 1963-1974 UNIT CONSTRUCTION 350-500cc FACTORY WSM
TRIUMPH 1963-1970 UNIT CONSTRUCTION 650cc FACTORY WSM
TRIUMPH 1968-1974 TRIDENT T150 & T150V FACTORY WSM
TRIUMPH 1971-1973 650cc OIL-IN-FRAME FACTORY WSM
TRIUMPH 1973-1978 750cc BONNEVILLE & TIGER FACTORY WSM
TRIUMPH 1979-1983 750cc T140, TR7 & TR65 FACTORY WSM
VELOCETTE 1925-1970 ALL SINGLES & TWINS (BOOK OF)
VELOCETTE 1933-1952 MOV-MAC-MSS RIGID FRAME FACTORY WSM
VELOCETTE 1954-1971 MSS-VENOM-THRUXTON-VIPER FACTORY WSM
VILLIERS ENGINE UP TO 1959 INC. 3 WHEELERS (BOOK OF)
VILLIERS ENGINE UP TO 1969 (BOOK OF)
VINCENT 1935-1955 (WORKSHOP MANUAL)
YAMAHA 1961-1967 YA5 & YA6 (WORKSHOP MANUAL & ILL PARTS LIST)
YAMAHA 1971-1972 JT1& JT2 (WORKSHOP MANUAL & ILL PARTS LIST)

VELOCEPRESS TECHNICAL BOOKS – MOTORCYCLE

1930'S BRITISH MOTORCYCLE CARBS & ELEC COMPONENTS (BOOK OF)
1930'S BRITISH MOTORCYCLE ENGINES (OVERHAUL & MAINTENANCE)
1930'S BRITISH MOTORCYCLE GEARBOXES & CLUTCHES (BOOK OF)
CATALOG OF BRITISH MOTORCYCLES (1951 MODELS)
LUCAS ELECTRONICS BRITISH M/CYCLES REPAIR & PARTS (1950-1977)
MOTORCYCLE ENGINEERING (P.E. Irving)
MOTORCYCLE ROAD TESTS 1949-1953 (Motor Cycle Magazine UK)
SPEED AND HOW TO OBTAIN IT (Motor Cycle Magazine UK)
TUNING FOR SPEED (P.E. Irving)
WIPAC (COMBO) MANUAL NUMBER 3 + M/CYCLE & SCOOTER MANUAL

VELOCEPRESS MANUALS – SCOOTERS BY MAKE

BSA SUNBEAM SCOOTER WORKSHOP MANUAL 1959-1965
BSA SUNBEAM SCOOTER 1959-1965 (BOOK OF)
LAMBRETTA 1947-1957 ALL 125 & 150cc MODELS (BOOK OF)
LAMBRETTA 1957-1970 LI & TV MODELS (SECOND BOOK OF)
NSU PRIMA 1956-1964 ALL MODELS (BOOK OF)
TRIUMPH TIGRESS SCOOTER WORKSHOP MANUAL 1959-1965
TRIUMPH TIGRESS SCOOTER (BOOK OF)
VESPA 1951-1961 (BOOK OF)
VESPA 1955-1963 125 & 150cc & GS MODELS (SECOND BOOK OF)
VESPA 1955-1968 GS & SS (BOOK OF)
VESPA 1963-1972 90, 125 & 150cc (THIRD BOOK OF)

VELOCEPRESS MANUALS – MOPEDS & MOTORIZED BICYCLES

CYCLEMOTOR (BOOK OF)
NSU QUICKLY 1953-1963 ALL MODELS (BOOK OF)
PUCH MAXI N & S MAINTENANCE & REPAIR (3 MANUAL COMPILATION)
RALEIGH MOPEDS 1960-1969 (BOOK OF)

VELOCEPRESS MANUALS - THREE WHEELER'S

BOND MINICAR THREE WHEELER 1948-1967 (BOOK OF)
BMW ISETTA FACTORY WORKSHOP MANUAL
BSA THREE WHEELER (BOOK OF)
RELIANT REGAL THREE WHEELER 1952-1973 (BOOK OF)
VINTAGE MORGAN THREE WHEELER (BOOK OF)

VELOCEPRESS MANUALS – AUTOMOBILE BY MAKE

ALFA ROMEO GIULIA WORKSHOP MANUAL 1300 TO 2000cc 1962-1975
ALFA ROMEO GIULIA TECH MANUAL CARBURETED CARS FROM 1962
ALFA ROMEO GIULIA TECH MANUAL FUEL INJECTED CARS FROM 1969
ALFA ROMEO GIULIETTA & GIULIA 750 & 101 SERIES 1955-1965 WSM
AUSTIN-HEALEY SPRITE & MG MIDGET WORKSHOP MANUAL 1958-1971
BMW 600 LIMOUSINE FACTORY WORKSHOP MANUAL
BMW 600 LIMOUSINE OWNERS HAND BOOK & SERVICE MANUAL
BMW 2000 & 2002 1966-1976 WORKSHOP MANUAL
CORVAIR 1960-1969 WORKSHOP MANUAL
CORVETTE V8 1955-1962 WORKSHOP MANUAL
FERRARI HANDBOOK ROAD & RACE CARS (SERVICE/SPECS) 1948-1958
FERRARI 250/GT SERVICE & MAINTENANCE MANUAL 1956-1965
FIAT 500 FACTORY WORKSHOP MANUAL 1957-1973
FIAT 600, 600D & MULTIPLA FACTORY WORKSHOP MANUAL 1955-1969
JAGUAR E-TYPE 3.8 & 4.2 SERIES 1 & 2 WORKSHOP MANUAL
JAGUAR MK 7, 8, 9 & XK120, 140, 150 WORKSHOP MANUAL 1948-1961
METROPOLITAN FACTORY WORKSHOP MANUAL
MGA & MGB OWNERS HANDBOOK & WORKSHOP MANUAL
MG MIDGET TC, TD, TF & TF1500 WORKSHOP MANUAL
PORSCHE 356 1948-1965 WORKSHOP MANUAL
PORSCHE 911 2.0, 2.2, 2.4 LITRE 1964-1973 WORKSHOP MANUAL
PORSCHE 911 2.7, 3.0, 3.2 LITRE 1973-1989 WORKSHOP MANUAL
PORSCHE 912 WORKSHOP MANUAL
PORSCHE 914/4 & 914/6 1.7, 1.8, 2.0 LITRE 1970-1976 WSM
TRIUMPH TR2, TR3, TR4 1953-1965 WORKSHOP MANUAL
VOLKSWAGEN TRANSPORTER, TRUCKS & WAGONS 1950-1979 WSM
VOLVO 1944-1968 ALL MODELS WORKSHOP MANUAL

VELOCEPRESS TECHNICAL BOOKS - AUTOMOBILE

HOW TO BUILD A FIBERGLASS CAR
HOW TO BUILD A RACING CAR
HOW TO RESTORE THE MODEL 'A' FORD
MASERATI OWNER'S HANDBOOK
PERFORMANCE TUNING THE SUNBEAM TIGER
SOUPING THE VOLKSWAGEN
SOLEX CARBURETORS (EMPHASIS ON UK & EU AUTOMOBILES)
SU CARBURETORS (EMPHASIS ON UK AUTOMOBILES)
WEBER CARBURETORS (EMPHASIS ON ALFA & FIAT)

VELOCEPRESS BOOKS & GUIDES - AUTOMOBILE

COMPLETE CATALOG OF JAPANESE MOTOR VEHICLES
FERRARI 308 SERIES BUYER'S AND OWNER'S GUIDE
FERRARI BROCHURES AND SALES LITERATURE 1968-1989
FERRARI SERIAL NUMBERS PART I - ODD NUMBERS TO 21399
FERRARI SERIAL NUMBERS PART II - EVEN NUMBERS TO 1050
HENRY'S FABULOUS MODEL "A" FORD
MASERATI BROCHURES AND SALES LITERATURE

VELOCEPRESS BOOKS – RACING

CARRERA PANAMERICANA - MEXICAN ROAD RACE (BOOK OF)
DIALED IN - THE JAN OPPERMAN STORY
VEDA ORR'S NEW REVISED HOT ROD PICTORIAL

www.VelocePress.com